The Spirit of Canada

Chicken Soup for the Soul: The Spirit of Canada
101 Stories of Love and Gratitude
Amy Newmark & Janet Matthews

Published by Chicken Soup for the Soul, LLC www.chickensoup.com
Copyright ©2017 by Chicken Soup for the Soul, LLC. All Rights Reserved.

The publisher gratefully acknowledges the many publishers and individuals who granted Chicken Soup for the Soul permission to reprint the cited material.

Front cover photo of barn courtesy of iStockphoto.com/capturedessence (©capturedessence), photo of Canadian flag courtesy of iStockphoto.com/MiroNovak (©MiroNovak)
Back cover photo courtesy of iStockphoto.com/jimfeng (©jimfeng)
Interior photos in collage: Polar bear courtesy of iStockphoto.com/JackF (©JackF), canoe courtesy of iStockphoto.com/Veni (©Veni), Toronto courtesy of iStockphoto.com/JavenLin (©JavenLin)
Interior photo of Amy Newmark courtesy of Susan Morrow at SwickPix
Interior photo of Janet Matthews courtesy of Brock Weir

Cover and Interior by Daniel Zaccari

Distributed to the booktrade by Simon & Schuster. SAN: 200-2442

Publisher's Cataloging-In-Publication Data
(Prepared by The Donohue Group, Inc.)

Names: Newmark, Amy, compiler. | Matthews, Janet, 1951- compiler.
Title: Chicken soup for the soul : the spirit of Canada : 101 stories of
    love and gratitude / [compiled by] Amy Newmark [and] Janet Matthews.
Other Titles: Spirit of Canada : 101 stories of love and gratitude
Description: [Cos Cob, Connecticut] : Chicken Soup for the Soul, LLC
    [2017]
Identifiers: LCCN 2017937595 | ISBN 978-1-61159-968-8 (print) | ISBN
    978-1-61159-268-9 (ebook)
Subjects: LCSH: National characteristics, Canadian--Literary collections.
    | National characteristics, Canadian--Anecdotes. | Canada--Literary
    collections. | Canada--Anecdotes. | Canadians--Literary collections. |
    Canadians--Anecdotes. | LCGFT: Anecdotes.
Classification: LCC F1021.2 .C45 2017 (print) | LCC F1021.2 (ebook) | DDC
    971/.073--dc23

PRINTED IN THE UNITED STATES OF AMERICA
on acid∞free paper

25 24 23 22 21 20 19 18 17   01 02 03 04 05 06 07 08 09 10 11

The Spirit of Canada

101 Stories of
Love and Gratitude

Amy Newmark
Janet Matthews

Chicken Soup for the Soul, LLC
Cos Cob, CT

Changing the world one story at a time®
www.chickensoup.com

Table of Contents

❸

~A Nation of Helping Hands~

❹

~Honouring Those Who Served~

❺

~We're All in This Together~

❻

~Into the Wild~

❼

~Rising to the Occasion~

8

~Living a Dream~

9

~Our Canadian Heroes~

10

~Grateful to Be Canadian~

⓫

~How the World Views Canada~

Introduction

This special year of 2017 is Canada's sesquicentennial! Now that's a big word — and a challenge for most of us to even say, let alone spell. But it means that this year Canada turns 150 years old. On July 1st we celebrate 150 years of Confederation and, in keeping with this celebratory theme, I'm honoured and excited to have been asked to co-author this special edition, *Chicken Soup for the Soul: The Spirit of Canada*. In this collection you will find 101 wonderful stories that celebrate who we are as Canadians, and here at Chicken Soup for the Soul it is our contribution to **Canada 150.**

We began with no idea what people might write that would reflect their feelings about "The Spirit of Canada." But after a few months of reading stories I felt a unique consciousness beginning to form around the project as a whole. I'm a musician, and as I sat alone at my desk working with the stories, organizing them into chapters, I started to feel like I was working inside a symphony — fine tuning the themes, organizing the movements. I could almost hear the music — a distinct sound that began to emanate from the collection and touched me deeply.

The stories in this book are as diverse as the people who make up this magnificent country. Yet regardless of the topic or where the author comes from, the golden thread that runs through them all is the love and the gratitude that Canadians have for this country. For the freedom and those who have fought for it, the abundance, the many opportunities, the richness of the land, our modern cities, our ancient wilderness, the harsh beauty of our far north, the simple civility and kindness Canadians are known for, how we are regarded in other parts of the world, and the welcome we give to newcomers.

As Canadians, we've never been known for being noisily patriotic. It's just not our way. But perhaps that has been subtly changing in the last decade or so, and that change seems to be reflected in many of these stories, particularly when it comes to our national anthem. Today, as we sing "O Canada" it is no longer by rote as many of us did in school, but with a new kind of emotion and a deep gratitude.

When it comes to our beloved song "O Canada," Lesley Marcovich wrote what is for me the ultimate story about our anthem — and what it really means. Lesley came with her family from South Africa many years ago, and her passion for her chosen country truly touches my heart. In her story, "This Village Called Canada," she takes us to a school gymnasium where an audience has assembled for the school's spring concert. They begin by singing "O Canada," and with each line of the song she invites us into a deeper understanding of the words and what they mean to us right here, right now. Using flashbacks to the challenges of her old life in South Africa, she takes us on a journey of such deep insight and appreciation that it brings me to tears each time I read it.

You can see this new passion for Canada most obviously on Canada Day, when all generations of Canadians come together in a joyous sea of red and white to celebrate with festivities and fireworks and proudly sing. In Chapter 2 you will find stories about the different ways Canadians celebrate Canada Day in different parts of the country. In her story, "Canada Day North of Terrace," author DG Peterson shares the time she headed north out of Vancouver with her son in a big rig to deliver a huge generator to power Canada Day celebrations in the remote northern community of Gingolx. Her breathtaking story of Canada Day with the First Nations shows so clearly how diverse we truly are in our experiences, in our communities, and how we celebrate across this great land. During the formal festivities, when she heard a muffled sound coming from the direction of the mountains, she stared in stunned disbelief at what she saw emerge from around a bend in the road. I won't spoil that one for you — you just have to read it and let your spine tingle the way mine did when I first read it.

One of the biggest displays in recent years of our love for Canada happened during the 2010 Vancouver Olympics. During those sixteen days, in downtown Vancouver that joyous mob of red and white was a daily occurrence. In Chapter 5 Gerri Nicholas shares her own story, "The 2010 Winter Olympics," which included viewing the gold medal hockey game from a café on Robson Street and watching Sidney "Sid the Kid" Crosby score his gold medal goal. She was there to witness and participate in the unbridled joy that erupted and consumed the fans. It was a great day for Canada — and she shares it all with us.

When it comes to Sidney Crosby, I think Darryl Pottie tells us the ultimate Sid the Kid story. Darryl and his family had recently moved to Enfield, Nova Scotia, not far from Sidney Crosby's home in Cole Harbour. Neighbours had reported that Sid would sometimes travel the area during the summer while at home. Darryl had admired this gifted hockey player and followed his career for years. Excited by the possibilities, he got creative and made a big sign that he put out by the road inviting Sid to come and sign his jersey. One day while at work he received an e-mail from his wife with a photo attached. When Darryl finally figured out what the photo meant he started yelling out loud, "HE'S IN MY HOUSE, HE'S IN MY HOUSE!" Darryl was more than happy to share the full story of that exciting day when one of our Canadian hockey heroes made a fan's dream come true. You can read Darryl's story, "Sid, Please Sign My Jersey," in Chapter 9.

Speaking of having a dream come true, in Chapter 8, I was particularly inspired by Lorette Smith's story, "The Ice Pond of My Dreams." As a young girl Lorette had been a passionate ice skater and she particularly loved skating outdoors on frozen ponds. In fact, she had a dream to travel and skate on the most beautiful frozen rivers and ice ponds in the world. She grew up, got married and became the mother of five, and her dreams of travelling and skating on faraway frozen ponds was all but forgotten. Many years later her son was transferred to work in Ottawa and invited her to visit. And so it happened that at age eighty, Lorette found herself lacing up her old skates and heading out to skate the full length of the Rideau Canal — and then back. And then she did it again. If you have a dream that somehow you've let go of, I invite you to read Lorette's passionate story of a dream finally realized — and be inspired to go make your own dream happen.

This past year brought several huge events into the minds and hearts of all Canadians. The first was the Syrian refugee crisis. The news stories brought the plight of modern day refugees into sharp relief as around the world people struggled to come to grips with how to respond. Canada is unique in this regard — as we have a program that allows individual citizens and organizations like churches to sponsor refugees. Money must be raised, but it also means that when refugees arrive they are guided and helped to get on their feet, and their sponsors coach and mentor them into their new lives in Canada.

In Chapter 1 Rahaf Bi tells her personal story of leaving war-torn Syria. She was prepared to try the dangerous boat escape that was causing so much loss of life, when her Canadian cousin dissuaded her, and offered instead to sponsor her. Rahaf's dramatic escape from Syria and eventual arrival and welcome at her new home in Kelowna, British Columbia entitled "My Canadian Dream" is sure to touch you. And, told in Rahaf's own voice, it's the first story in the book.

Anne Phillips of Uxbridge, Ontario is part of a church congregation that along with a group of other churches sponsored five Syrian refugee families. Each church was responsible for one aspect of helping a family settle in and feel welcomed in Canada. Anne shares her own experience of meeting their family, helping them with some simple furniture for their new home, and how life changing it was for her and for many others to realize these were ordinary people who, just like them, had families and dreams for their children to live safely and freely. But unlike them, their lives had been ripped apart by a dreadful war. "Our Syrian Family" is also in Chapter 1, and I hope it makes you as proud to be Canadian as it does me.

The other recent event that filled our hearts was the huge fire in Fort McMurray; it devastated and changed the lives of so many people, and Canadians everywhere immediately stepped up to help. There are several stories in this book that open dramatic windows into that event, but in Chapter 7, "Perspective by Fire" from firefighter Anthony Hoffman is unique. Anthony grew up in Fort McMurray and when his parents retired and moved away, he rented out his own condo and moved back into his family home to renovate it. On the morning of the fire he takes you with him through the emotional roller coaster of fighting the fire while, from the roof of the hospital, he watches his city burn. From this dramatic vista, looking in one direction he can see that his condo has burned. When he looks in the other direction he realizes that his family home has also been destroyed. Knowing he has just lost everything, he must dig deep and, in the midst of his own personal pain, somehow find the strength to keep going, to keep doing his job and fighting the fire so that others will not suffer the same loss. The new perspective he finds from this experience is life changing — and we think it will touch you as much as it touched us.

The moving stories in Chapter 4 honour Canadians who have served. In her story, "A Bloom of Friendship," author Anne Renaud connects a modern day event in Ottawa — the Canadian Tulip Festival — with its origins at the end of World War II. Anne recounts her uncle's story of being in Holland with Canadian troops during the Liberation of The Netherlands. But it was only after he returned from the 1995 anniversary celebrations that he finally shared his story with her. She learned then that the Dutch have never forgotten the pivotal role Canadians played in their liberation from the Nazis and how, during the war, Canada provided safe haven for their Royal Family. In 1945 their gratitude was expressed by a gift of 100,000 tulip bulbs from the Dutch Monarchy, the genesis of the Canadian Tulip Festival. But what most Canadians don't realize is that 20,000 tulip bulbs still arrive in Canada every year — a gift of thanks that will continue in perpetuity. Anne's efforts to make sure this story is remembered by future genera-tions of Canadian children — as it is by all Dutch children — include writing a book by the same name as this short story. We think her story beautifully exemplifies in every way our theme — The Spirit of Canada.

On a lighter note, in Chapter 6 we've gathered together some great stories about how Canadians love the wilderness: the camping, the canoeing, the wildlife — and Canada's far north. Then in Chapter 7, about "rising to the occasion," John Silver from Orillia, Ontario tells us a classic Canadian tale of six friends, three canoes, some white water, a case of beer and a roll of duct tape. I don't want to spoil the fun for you but when the canoe gets damaged going down the rapids, the ingenuity required to keep it afloat delighted me. The image of the newly customized "Canadian Canoe" atop their roof carrier on the way home attracted the amused attention of passing motorists, and inspired many hours of retelling this fun tale over coffee at Tim Hortons. We hope you enjoy John's story, "All You Need Is Duct Tape and Beer," because here too you will find The Spirit of Canada.

And finally in Chapter 11, in her story, "A Trip to Remember," Isolde Ryan tells us about a motorcycle trip she took with her husband and other soldiers from the Canadian Armed Forces base in Germany. On this trip the motorcycle club was coming down from the Swiss Alps and rode into a small Italian village. There they encountered people who were so grateful to see these Canadians they laid out a spread of food and drink for them in the village square. It seemed that back in the 1970s an enormous earthquake had devastated their village, and Canadians were the first to arrive with help. The grateful villagers finally saw their chance to thank Canadians, and this astonished group were the lucky recipients. Isolde's lovely story highlights the help and generosity that Canadians are known for around the world, and how they are welcomed everywhere.

These days, whether we were born here, or whether we chose this country, most Canadians are very aware of how fortunate we are to be Canadian. The love we feel for this country, the gratitude I hear expressed by so many people everywhere I go — are never far from the surface any more. Yes, we feel proud — especially when Canada does something that makes us proud. Like being a role model for the world in how to help desperate refugees. Or responding quickly to a crisis in our own country by helping our fire-devastated Alberta neighbours. But more than proud, I find people are grateful. And the 101 stories in this book truly express that. Because the one theme that weaves its way through this book is the passionate love that all Canadians have for this land that offers so much. We hope these stories will inspire you, touch your heart and make you smile. Perhaps you will be reminded of your own stories of what Canada means to you, and why we truly are the most fortunate people in the world. After all, we are Canadians!

~Janet Matthews
Aurora, Ontario

Chapter 1

The Spirit of Canada

Welcome Home

In a world divided by differences of colour, race, language, religion, and ideology, the Canadian experience stands out as a message of hope. My prayer is that you will continue to offer this message to mankind.
~Her Majesty Queen Elizabeth II

My Canadian Dream

*Canada is my home because: it works, however
imperfectly and reluctantly; it has a social
conscience which can be stirred to howl; it
is utterly beautiful from sea to sea.*
~June Callwood

When people say "follow your dreams," they should add that they don't always come true, or that a lot of terrible things may happen before your dream comes true. My own dream began many years before the horrible civil war that now grips Syria. In 2001, when I was sixteen, my cousin came to Syria to work and learn Arabic. All I knew was she was twenty-three, she lived in Canada, and two decades earlier my mother had visited Toronto when she was a baby.

We had an instant connection. My cousin had such a kind, warm smile, and was so excited to hear about our lives. She encouraged me to practice my English as long as I would teach her Arabic! When I told her that my dream was to go to Canada, her response was warm and honest. "Canada is a wonderful place, but you're lucky to be surrounded by family in Syria. Still, I hope your dream will come true one day."

The years passed. I graduated high school and earned my university degree in applied chemistry. I found good jobs, lived at home with my family, and enjoyed time with friends. Life was good. Life was safe and comfortable. And then the war started.

There are so many terrible things about war. We all know this.

But when you face the horror firsthand, war becomes despicable. This war began to steal everything from me. It took the lives of my friends and co-workers. War was destroying the lives of an entire generation of children. I began losing my desire to live. I had had enough.

In 2015, I decided to do what thousands of others had done. I contacted a human smuggler to get me on a rubber dinghy to Greece. Yes, I was prepared to risk my life to get out of the living hell that my country had become. Some friends had recently made the journey. They survived, and reported that it wasn't that bad.

My plans were all but set when my cousin in Canada posted a powerful image on Facebook — a cartoon depicting Syrian refugees who had drowned in the sea trying to get out — with blurbs of their dreams: "My dream is to live and be a better person." Or "My dream is to live in peace." These were my dreams too — but the punch line in the image was its title: "Even dreams can sink." In that moment, I realized I could easily die on this journey.

I wrote a comment on my cousin's post. It would be the first time she and I had been in contact since the war started. I wrote: *No matter how dangerous this journey across the sea, I will emigrate because our life here has become an unbearable hell.*

That was the best way I could describe it in English. And it was true. Within minutes a private message popped into my Facebook inbox from my cousin. She wrote: *Salam alaikum Rahaf, keefik? InshAllah you are ok. I am sorry we haven't kept in touch for a long time…*

After a few message exchanges, my cousin begged me to not embark on this perilous journey. The images of death were streaming on the news every day. Alan Kurdi, the young Syrian boy who drowned making the same journey, was fresh in everyone's mind. Many say the image of his small, lifeless body on the beach in Turkey changed the course of the Syrian refugee crisis. My cousin then explained that Canada was on the verge of accepting thousands of Syrians. That there was hope. She was going to help. That my dream could actually come true.

I didn't know what to say. I loved my cousin, but I didn't quite believe her. How could she get me from this dangerous death zone to the safety of Canada? She explained that private Canadian citizens, churches and other organizations were sponsoring refugees to come to Canada. Canada was truly a special place, she explained. No other country in the world had the same program.

Because I worked for the government it was illegal for me to leave the country. When I left my home in Damascus I had to do it with extreme caution. When I said goodbye to my parents, brother and sisters, we had to act as though it was a short-term journey. We all knew it would be years before we saw each other again.

My journey was long and truly terrifying. With a group of others I travelled by land on buses and on foot, through sixteen checkpoints—each manned by a different armed group. Some men were kind and helpful, but most were aggressive and war-torn, filled with hate—and they filled us with terror.

The two days it took to travel north to the Turkish border were filled with fear and death. We saw war. But we survived.

I finally made it to the Turkish border and travelled to Istanbul. I had never travelled outside of Syria, let alone travelled alone. I was lucky though. One of my cousins had left Syria a few weeks before and was living in Istanbul with her thirteen-year-old daughter. I would live with them in their apartment until the paperwork my cousin was working on in Canada was complete.

Six months later I found myself on a plane flying to Vancouver. My dream was coming true.

The day I arrived in Kelowna, British Columbia was nothing short of magical. I was exhausted, but I was finally home. I can't quite explain why I felt like I was "home"—it was simply a feeling. I can barely remember the short flight from Vancouver to the Okanagan Valley; I do recall looking out the window and being completely enchanted by the lake and the surrounding mountains.

As we approached Kelowna, I gazed down at the city and wondered where I would live. It was spring, so everything was green, and the sun was just barely peeking behind the clouds after a rainstorm. So many emotions were running through my head. I was worried, I was excited, and I couldn't believe I would soon finally see my cousin in Canada!

I rushed down the long hallway and my heavy bags felt like

nothing; all I wanted was to get there. Finally, I saw them — familiar faces. I saw my cousin, with that same warm smile I knew so well. With her was her delightful sixteen-month-old daughter who I had grown to love through photos and videos. Her husband was there, too, with his mother, and a member of the local church that had helped make this happen.

We hugged, we cried, and we laughed. I had made it!

When we walked out into the parking lot, the setting was surreal. There's nothing quite like the smell after a fresh rain in the spring — especially when you've spent the last five years smelling war.

I was in Canada! And only in Canada, just moments after arriving in my new home, would I be greeted by a rainbow. My cousin laughed, with tears in her eyes, and said, "Look, Rahaf! Canada is happy you are here too!"

Dreams do come true!

~Rahaf Bi
Kelowna, British Columbia

Best Surprise Ever!

Canada was built around a very simple premise. A
promise that you can work hard and succeed and build
a future for yourselves and your kids, and that future
for your kids would be better than the one you had.
~Prime Minister Justin Trudeau

"I have a great idea," said Mom. My sister Keira and I looked at each other, wondering what we were in for.

"What if," she said, with a long pause for dramatic effect, "we set up Nancy's apartment while she's away?"

Nancy, our nanny had returned to the Philippines to get her children and bring them back with her to Canada. She was on the final leg of a ten-year journey. When her children were only one and five years old, she had left them to find work because there was no work in the Philippines.

Through friends she heard that Canada was the land of opportunity. But, to be granted admission to the live-in caregiver program she first had to gain experience as a caregiver in Hong Kong. Working in Hong Kong was like boot camp. Conditions were harsh. She slept in the stock room of a family's apartment and was at their beck and call almost twenty-four hours a day.

I remember the day we picked her up at the airport. We had a winter coat ready to help welcome her to Canada. Once here, she immersed herself in starting a new life. She was a great addition to our family. She joined a church, a choir, and took driving lessons. She called home to the Philippines once a week and sent money to her mother and sister, who were caring for her kids.

Two years after arriving she was allowed to apply for Canadian permanent resident's status. It took five years to get it, and we celebrated with cake the night the letter finally came. Nancy would finally be able to bring her children to live with her in her new country.

As luck would have it, an apartment became available in our neighbourhood right before she left. She quickly secured it and prepared to leave for two months.

"Could you do me a big favour?" Nancy asked Mom as she was leaving. "I've ordered some mattresses so we have something to sleep on when we arrive. Do you think you could let the delivery man into the apartment?"

"No problem," said Mom.

What Mom didn't say was that she'd already begun hatching a plan to completely furnish the whole place.

"Hey Mom, I hate to burst your bubble," I said, "but how are we possibly going to furnish an entire apartment?"

"Well, we have some extra stuff in the attic," she replied. "Maybe we can help our neighbours and Nancy at the same time. The neighbors can purge their extras, and we can piece together a great home for Nancy. Let's send an out an e-mail and see." So the e-mail went to about seventy neighbours:

> *After ten years of working day and night, Nancy has finally gone home to bring back her children. Let's surprise her by turning her empty apartment into a proper home! If you have any "extras" after doing your spring-cleaning, let me know.*

Mom shared more of Nancy's story, and made suggestions for useful donations — really just about everything!

"I'm in! How can I help?" shouted Keltie, as we walked past her house on our way to school the next morning.

"Me too," chimed in Lisa from further up the street, as she jumped in her car to head to work. "I had tears in my eyes reading your e-mail," she told us. "We're so incredibly lucky to have been born in Canada... and have this abundance all around us! I want to help!"

That night at dinner, Mom, as usual, asked about the highlights of our day. But I could tell she couldn't wait to tell us something, too. Finally, we relieved her of her misery and asked about her day.

"Well," she said with a grin, "I got a few replies to our e-mail... and by a few I mean dozens! We have chairs, couches, dressers, tables, quilts, and TVs! We might even have more donations than we can use!"

That entire week the e-mails and texts kept flooding in. Shawn wanted to help with the set-up. A chair and loveseat from Susi, a coffee table from Beth, a kitchen table from Kim, and a dresser from Shannon. A barbeque from Kate and a TV from Lori. Deanna the gardener offered to make flower and herb pots for Nancy's front porch. Rita the principal offered to help Nancy navigate the school system and set up desks with school supplies for the kids. Sarah who works at East Side Mario's provided a gift certificate for a celebration dinner! Jennifer baked some goodies for Nancy's freezer! The list went on and on! Everyone pitched in.

The landlord, Meghan, was in on the surprise as well. She let our little team in with clipboards, measuring tapes and graph paper to plan everything.

Unbeknownst to Nancy, her empty apartment was slowly filling with love. Nancy had served others her entire life, and now a team of mothers and kids was looking after her. We all knew the bravery, sacrifice and perseverance that Nancy had demonstrated. Her hope, faith and a strong work ethic were impressive and we wanted to do this kind thing for her, to give her a break for once.

Set-up weekend arrived. We loaded our van with our own donations, and then we made a trip around the "hood" to pick up the remaining items. We had so much fun setting up! It was amazing how everything fit perfectly to make a beautiful home. Finally we were done, and we were so excited! Nancy and her children were arriving the next day. We made a "Welcome Home!" sign, baked some cookies and went to bed with huge grins.

The next day, when Nancy and her children arrived at their new home, we were there too. It was absolutely the best surprise ever, better than Christmas! Nancy held onto the door for support while her confused look slowly turned into a beaming smile as Mom explained what the neighbours had done.

"Thank you," she managed to whisper.

I've heard adults talk about their "bucket list." Things they want to do or have before they die. Well I think that bucket list should include things you want to do *for others* before you die. This experience was better than anything I've seen on any bucket list!

Mom told Nancy how the whole neighbourhood had pitched in. She explained that Nancy had inspired them all, and it was her turn to be looked after for a change.

Nancy flopped down on her new bed. With tears in her eyes she explained that on the flight over she had felt exhausted. She had wondered how she was going to create a home for her kids. But now, she said, "I feel like I never need to sleep! I want to march down the street shouting 'THANK YOU!' to everyone! Wow, I really feel like *I'm*... no, *we*... are part of this community now."

And indeed they are. That's what it's like here in Canada. We welcome, embrace and appreciate diversity, and we are all better for it!

~Brooke and Keira Elliott, ages 14 and 9
Aurora, Ontario

Fort McMurray Strong

If you want to know, really know, what it means to be
a true neighbour, ready to help in hard times, go
to Alberta. It's the prairie code, and in our
best times — it's the Canadian code too.
Every citizen — is your neighbour.
~Rex Murphy, The National, *May 7, 2016*

The northern city of Fort McMurray was my home for twenty-two years. During those years I made many wonderful friends from all over Canada. But this community is really an island surrounded by boreal forest. And everyone who lives there knows there's always a danger of fire.

In May of 2016 I was visiting friends in Victoria when the wildfire started. Fort McMurray was suddenly plunged into a state of emergency. My friend Lynn was working as a teacher's aide and, at lunchtime on May 3rd her downtown school was clear. But an hour later the wind had shifted and she could see the angry red and orange balls of fire and heavy smoke as the monster fire rolled down Abasand Hill. Somewhere up that hill was her two-and-a-half-year-old grandson, Jedrik, at the nanny's where her daughter Alyssa had dropped him earlier. The boy had breathing challenges, and after trying unsuccessfully to reach the nanny, Lynn quickly decided to leave school to find out what was happening. Moments later came the official order to evacuate the entire city.

Jedrik's mother Alyssa was at work across the river near their family home in Thickwood. A prior arrangement had established the home of Lynn's ex-husband Terry as the family's emergency meeting place. Before heading there, Alyssa raced home to pick up her fiancé Sean and her brother Nick. After quickly grabbing a few essentials, and their two cats, they all jumped in Alyssa's vehicle and headed across the river to their father's.

It took Lynn almost forty minutes to drive the few block's to Terry's. The roads were chaotic, as some people were trying to leave town while others tried to return home. Just as she arrived there was an explosion in Abasand as the fire hit a gas station. Surely lives would be lost from this.

There was still no word about Jedrik. The rest of the family arrived and continued trying to reach the nanny. As the smoke grew heavier, all they could do was go inside and pray. Finally, the nanny called. "I have to make a run for it!" she said, and then the phone went dead. This cryptic message was unclear, as they knew she'd be trying to make it down Abasand Hill — on a road where traffic was gridlocked and fire spewed on either side. It seemed a miracle when not long after she burst in the door and handed the frightened child to his mother. "A cop knocked on my window, shouting, 'if you want to get out of here, you have to get out of the car and run!'" she explained. She left quickly to try to find her own people.

Now that they were reunited, the five adults, two cats and the toddler piled into Alyssa's vehicle. Highway 63 south was completely blocked so everyone was directed to head to the camps north of the oil sands. But when they arrived the camps were full. By this time the hardworking firefighters had managed to re-open the southbound highway. Heading back to Fort Mac they picked up Lynn's van and split into two vehicles. With a bit more space they now headed south on the slow moving highway, with the fire running along both sides of them in the ditches.

"At Anzac we pulled over for the night," Lynn said. "We couldn't go any further. A twenty-five minute trip had taken us two and a half hours. The next morning we joined the long line to the gas station, and waited over two hours to fill up."

With no usable phones they relied on radio broadcasters to guide them to their next stop, which was Lac La Biche, about two hours away. The entire community of 25,000 had been preparing for the evacuees. Beds had been set up in an arena, but when Lynn's family arrived they found that one family had actually vacated their home so they could move in. People were soon knocking at their door with clothes, food, toiletries and toys for little Jedrik. They were fed and welcomed, and they were safe. After the stress of the past two days, they were truly overwhelmed by the kindness and welcome they received.

After a few days of catching their breath they decided to go further south. They all knew people in Edmonton and when they called to ask if there might be a spare bed, again they were welcomed.

I was already back in Edmonton when they arrived, so I was the one who opened the door at the home of our mutual friends. Lynn was smiling, but it was clear that the past few days had taken their toll. I could have donated through the Red Cross, but it felt so good — and much more personal — to hand her a small envelope containing a gift card.

As events continued to unfold in Fort McMurray, Canadians quickly rose to the challenge. Across Alberta and parts of British Columbia people opened their hearts and homes. A woman I knew invited a displaced couple to move into her empty condo; others offered their basement suites, an empty bedroom, or a place to park an RV. Companies sent new clothes and shoes. In Manitoba and Ontario kids set up lemonade stands, while ad hoc sports meets popped up all across the country — all to raise money. People turned to the Internet to find help or information, or to offer anything from shelter to diapers. As the donations poured in, the Canadian Red Cross began handing out money cards to families, many of which had lost everything.

I volunteered at one of the centers where people with notes from the Red Cross dropped by to pick up some basics. Even when the shelves began running low people were thrilled with the simplest things — a pair of shoes in the right size, the last small can of shaving cream, a blanket or a pillow. It was truly an emotional time. That week an army of firefighters from South Africa landed in Fort Mac to join our own "Boots on the Ground" to help fight the Beast. They came because they felt they owed a debt of gratitude to Canada, which had supported them as they fought to end apartheid over twenty years before. This was their way of paying us back.

As people kept arriving the news was grim. Whole sections of the city had been destroyed. However, due to the relentless dedication of all those firefighters, other sections were saved. As the fire was brought under control, people slowly started to return — some to their homes, and others to whatever was provided for them.

The people of Fort McMurray came together to thank Canadians for doing what we are known for around the world — demonstrating kindness and compassion during what has been designated as the worst natural disaster in Canadian history. Everyone who helped made a difference. And despite the enormity of the disaster, not one person died in that fire.

~Paula L. Gillis
Edmonton, Alberta

Just in Time

*Resettlement is an important part of how Canada can
contribute to help those who have fled the violence in
Syria. We join Canadians from across the country
in welcoming Syrian refugees here.*
~CARE Canada

"Almost every day I hear about another friend dying, and I am grateful to be alive," said Khatchig. "I love to share the stories from my life."

"Tell us then, how did you get here?" I asked. I was with my friend Lara at Tim Hortons that afternoon, and she had just introduced me to this twenty-something Armenian fellow from Syria. I was immediately curious about him. Although I was born in Lebanon, I am also Armenian and, if we had not moved to Canada when I was a child, all that has happened to him could so easily have happened to me.

"I was happy with my family in Syria," he began. "Then one day our home was just not safe anymore. At work I saw a Muslim co-worker beaten to within an inch of his life. Blood — so much blood was oozing from his woolen hat. They beat me too, but the attackers took out all of their rage on my co-worker. I thanked God I escaped further beating," he said before finally taking a breath.

"So home was not safe, work was not safe, and then came the bombing at school. I was taking a final exam in my first year of university. Three walls of the room were made of floor-to-ceiling glass.

I chose to sit away from the glass and so did two of my friends. At first the professor told us to ignore what sounded like a jet flying too close to our building. By the time we realized it was a bomb, the glass walls were shattered to pieces. More blood. I could only help the two friends — two girls — I was with. Being the guy I had to protect them from bomb fragments. I yelled at them to run, and we started running." Khatchig recalled, almost like he was out of breath.

"What happened then?" asked Lara.

"All I remember is yelling at them to keep running. Finally we made it across the field to safety. I thanked God again that day. And I realized that my life in Syria was gone. I had no safe home to live, no safe place to work, and I could not go back to school."

"And then you came here?" queried Lara.

"Not yet," said Khatchig. "We had to leave immediately, so my family went to Lebanon. We were planning to stay there when my dad's friend told us we should come to Canada. I don't know how, but he managed to convince my dad. And when my dad says we go, we go!"

Both Lara and I nodded. This we know about. Our dads were the same.

"I'm the youngest of four," Khatchig continued, "and my oldest sister was pregnant. We didn't want to leave her, but she would not put her baby at risk. My dad didn't want us to suffer any more. We thought Canada could give us a better future so, with my parents and two other sisters, we came to Canada. We were now refugees. We landed first in Montreal and then we were told there was room for us to go to Toronto."

He paused. "When we arrived in Toronto we were taken to a hotel. We were there only one night when we learned about a place called Silas Hill, which is a transitional home for refugees run by The People's Church. That's where I eventually met Lara," he said, smiling at her. "We were so happy at Silas Hill that both my dad and I stopped smoking for two weeks! It was so cold outside, and we could not smoke inside. Being still so new, we did not know where to find anything to buy. We were so thankful that these wonderful people were bringing our whole family food to eat. We could not ask for cigarettes, too."

"We were only the second family to live at Silas Hill," explained Khatchig. "We quickly felt like it was our home. When new bedroom furniture arrived for the house we assembled it, and it felt good to contribute and give back. I still go back there to help."

"People from Silas Hill helped us find a place to live. There are a lot of Armenians in our neighbourhood, and they made us feel at home too. Church people showed us how to use the subway, and others from the Armenian community showed us where to shop for things we needed. And I was able to get a job within one month."

Shaking his head, he continued. "I still don't believe all of this has happened, but the most incredible part of it all is what happened with my father. Just two months after we arrived, Dad began complaining of having pain all over his body. But being my dad, he would not go to a doctor."

Lara and I nodded again. Same dads.

"So our pharmacist called a doctor. The doctor saw my dad and forced him to get cardiac testing for his heart. It turned out that three out of four of his arteries were 100% blocked. 100%! We all became very scared. My dad needed surgery, and he was very frightened. No one in my family had ever had surgery." Still shaken, Khatchig continued.

"Preparing for the worst, Dad called my sister over Skype to say goodbye. She felt so helpless so far away in Syria. We are right here with him in Toronto, and we felt helpless. We could do nothing except agree to this surgery. Even now I can see my dad on the stretcher saying goodbye to me. When they wheeled him away I wanted to cry, but I could not let my mom and sisters see this.

"We waited so long for the news. It seemed like forever. No matter what I have been through so far, the worst time was that wait. And then, almost as if out of thin air, the doctor appeared and told us the surgery had been successful!" Khatchig stops, his eyes damp, and we breathe a sigh of relief with him.

"Dad was in the hospital for five days before being sent home to recover. And you know what? There is no way he would have survived in Syria or Lebanon. No way. And not only did he survive, but because we came as refugees we did not have to pay for anything. I don't know how all that happened, but it did. We thank God, for this — and we thank God for Canada — every day!"

Both Lara and I nodded — we thank God for Canada, too. With a spring in his step as he swung open the door of Tim Hortons to head to work, he said, "Canada kept my dad alive. *Getseh Kanadan!* Long live Canada!"

~A. A. Adourian
Toronto, Ontario

Our Syrian Family

*This is not a federal project, this is not even
a government project, this is a national
project that will involve all Canadians.*
~John McCallum, Minister of Immigration

efore the world was shocked by the image of three-year-old Alan Kurdi, whose body washed up on a beach in Turkey after his family attempted to flee war-torn Syria; before Justin Trudeau promised during his campaign that his new government would welcome 25,000 Syrian refugees into Canada by the new year; and before Prime Minister Justin Trudeau greeted the first planeload of refugees at Pearson International Airport in Toronto, our church had already put the wheels in motion to sponsor a Syrian refugee family.

Our church is in the Presbytery of Pickering Ontario, part of The Presbyterian Church in Canada. An Arabic-speaking community within this presbytery had reached out to the mission committee asking if they would consider sponsoring a refugee family. A number of families in the community had Syrian family and friends who were living in refugee camps in Lebanon.

We would need to raise $27,600 to sponsor one family of five. The churches in our presbytery began to strategize fundraising initiatives. One small congregation raised their goal in a matter of weeks and decided to raise more; a large congregation quickly raised over

$100,000 in cash and pledges. Other churches also raised significant amounts and, when it was all tallied, we had enough to sponsor five families, not just one!

The congregations were divided into small groups, and each group was assigned one family. Our congregation in Uxbridge, along with four others, was responsible for one family of five people. We had no idea when they would arrive, but planning began immediately. We needed to find them a place to live and furnish it with donations.

Each of the five congregations was assigned a room in the apartment to furnish. We got the kitchen. A list of the items needed was posted in our church hall. Not only did we get everything we needed but everything was brand-new! A local newspaper and a cable TV station did features on our sponsorship program, and this prompted more calls and offers of support from the local community.

Our family arrived first — on December 31, 2015. We had found them an apartment in Scarborough so they would be close to the Arabic-speaking community. A few weeks later my husband and I went to visit. We were probably all a bit nervous, but our anxieties quickly dissipated. They were such gracious hosts, and so thankful for all they had received. We, on the other hand, were very humbled by the whole experience, and by their very openness and graciousness. As we were about to leave, the mother hesitantly inquired if it would be possible to get an old table or some kind of storage unit for the kitchen, somewhere to keep the food for a family of five. When we looked at the kitchen I could see how inadequate it was, and immediately promised we would work something out.

I called some other church members and we began looking. But nothing really showed up, so one member suggested we ask his friend who was a cabinetmaker to build what was needed. On a snowy morning that friend came with us as we drove to Scarborough to take exact measurements for the cupboard. Once again, we were the beneficiaries of this family's warm hospitality. It turned out the father and our friend had been in the same line of work so, in spite of some language issues, they were able to communicate while he measured the space for the cabinet.

Once outside we asked him for his thoughts. "Well, originally I was opposed to our church getting involved in this," he said. "But after meeting these lovely people, I am happy to do anything for them. You just have to ask."

For me, this was a very emotional moment. I realized then we only had to introduce this family to our congregation, and even those who had been less supportive would realize that this was a family like any other family. They were not just a statistic, but real people who had been dealt a horrific hand based on where they were born.

And the help kept coming. A pantry was donated and the cabinet-maker made some minor repairs to it. Another person made his truck available to move the new furniture into the apartment. The cabinet cost a bit more than we intended, but additional funds were quickly donated. When we delivered and installed the cabinet and pantry, the mother had tears in her eyes.

In May of 2016 our congregation hosted a Mother's Day break-fast and we invited our Syrian family to join us. My husband and I picked them up early and brought them north to Uxbridge. It was so heart-warming to see how the people responded and made them feel welcome. Later the family came to our house for lunch, and it was good to just sit and enjoy conversation. That day we learned what if feels like to leave your family, your home, and your country. A few things were said about the war in Syria, but they didn't really want to talk about it, and we respected that.

By Christmas it was hard to believe that our family had been here a year already. They are all doing well, and already think of themselves as Canadians. There have been many emotions throughout this journey, but I am so glad to have been part of this amazing experience. I am also terribly proud to be a Canadian. When others reacted only with fear, Canada opened its doors in this humanitarian crisis. We have welcomed refugees in previous crises, and I believe Canadians will continue to respond positively in the future. Our wonderful country is so much greater because we have stretched out our arms—and made our new residents welcome.

~Anne Phillips
Uxbridge, Ontario

Plane People

You never really know your friends from
your enemies until the ice breaks.
~Inuit Proverb

We were flying high above the North Atlantic on September 11, 2001 en route from Frankfurt, Germany to Atlanta, Georgia. Our captain, Michael Sweeney, announced that we had a slight mechanical problem and would be putting down in Gander, Newfoundland to take a look. He also told us we would have to dump 30,000 pounds of fuel since we were too heavy to land at Gander.

My friend Jo Hopkins, who was sitting beside me, said, "Well, I guess that means we'll miss our connection in Atlanta." Jo was travelling home to Florida and I to Ohio. Little did we know that it would be many days before we would make our connections.

Once we landed, Captain Sweeney apologized for the "ruse" and told us the real reason we'd had to land; planes had hit the Twin Towers in New York City, the Pentagon in Washington, D.C., and something had happened in Pennsylvania, too. We had to remain on board the plane, and throughout the time we sat there Captain Sweeney monitored the BBC and kept us apprised of whatever information he was able to glean.

Ultimately, we learned there were many planes destined for American airspace that had been diverted to Gander, and thousands of passengers sat waiting in addition to the 218 of us on board Delta

Flight 15. Finally, after twenty-eight and a half hours, we saw long lines of yellow school buses approaching. Emotions ran high as we disembarked and boarded the buses that took us to the terminal where we cleared customs and security. Once we were cleared we re-boarded the buses and were transported to many small towns and villages surrounding Gander. Much later I learned that bus drivers had actually been on strike, but had walked off picket lines to help the "The Plane People," as we were called.

Four planeloads of passengers were taken to the tiny town of Lewisporte. There we were greeted with open arms by warm, wonderful, funny people who truly cared what had happened in the United States. Throughout the hours we sat waiting, I had not allowed myself to give in to fear or panic. I just knew we'd be okay.

As we entered Lewisporte, we saw flags flying at half-staff everywhere — the Canadian flag, the Newfoundland flag, and my own Stars and Stripes! That's when I started crying. I thought to myself, *these people are truly remarkable*. The second thing that brought me to my knees was when I stepped off the school bus and saw where I had been assigned — the Lewisporte Lions Centre.

Many years ago when I began school, the only way I could see was to hold things close to the tip of my nose. The school nurse sent a note home indicating that I needed an eye exam and glasses, but our large family simply had no money for that. So, the nurse arranged with a local Lions Club to pay for that exam and glasses. For nearly sixty years I had been eternally grateful to those anonymous Lions. Now, there I was — standing in front of the Lewisporte Lions Centre. I couldn't stop the tears from streaming down my face as I blurted out to Jo, "The Lions are still taking care of me!"

Although Captain Sweeney had told us details of the terrorist attacks, it was more than thirty hours later that what he described became real, as we stood silently watching the horror on tiny TV screens wherever we had been assigned. Housed in churches, schools and service clubs, we slept in pews, on school gymnasium mats and in chairs. We were fed wonderful food, and local students played with and read to the "plane children." Fishermen took many passengers on their boats, while others invited us to their homes for showers and a quiet place to unwind.

For security reasons we were not permitted to take our checked bags off the plane. That was a serious problem — especially for many passengers who had packed their prescription medications in their checked luggage. No problem — Mayor Bill Hooper and his wife Thelma took those passengers to the local doctor who checked them out and wrote new prescriptions for the local pharmacists to fill. All this was done at no charge! It was amazing!

Three days later we received word that we could leave and continue our flight home. As we began our emotional departure, many of us attempted to leave funds to help defray some of the expenses for the million-and-one things the people of the Lewisporte area had done for us. But no one would take our money. They simply smiled and said we would have done the same for them.

Once we "Plane People" re-boarded our plane on Friday, September 14th, we talked among ourselves and decided we had to do something. But how do you do something for someone who doesn't want you to, and yet you know you *have* to. How do you do that and not offend their dignity?

We came up with the idea of establishing an endowed scholarship fund that would benefit graduates of Lewisporte Collegiate. We wanted those kind, gentle Newfoundlanders to know that we would *never* forget what they had done for us.

Thanks to wonderful publicity provided by the media, the scholarship continues to grow. People from all corners of the world have joined the passengers and crew of Delta Flight 15 to ensure that the Lewisporte Area Flight 15 Scholarship will continue for years to come — certainly long after we "Plane People" have left this earth.

~Shirley Brooks-Jones
Dublin, Ohio, USA

Author's Note: As of May 2017 there have been 256 recipients of the Lewisporte Area Flight 15 Scholarship.

Welcome to Canada

Kindness is like snow — it beautifies
everything it covers.
~Kahlil Gibran

A number of years ago I worked at a reception centre for newly arrived refugees. The initial stage of the project involved conducting focus groups. Over several weeks, I met individuals and families who had often arrived with nothing more than their hope for a better life for their children and/or themselves. Their experiences, their courage and strength, and their hopes for their future in Canada made a lasting impression on me. It was an honour to meet them. They were no different from current refugees; only the family names change, and sometimes the countries they fled.

"Tell me about your journey before coming to Canada," I would begin. After a moment of silence, slowly and quietly the focus session would begin — first with one person, and soon others joining in.

"We are from Afghanistan. I was a dentist... we had a good life... but my father spoke out against them, then just disappeared one day. Things began to change for us... my brother and his family went to Pakistan... my wife would not leave the house because she feared they would accuse her of some wrongdoing. I knew it was only a matter of time before they came for us."

Every so often their speaking voices were so soft the words floated in the air around the room, barely heard. "We are Colombian... I can still hear the machine guns firing as I carried my daughter… we ran down our village road… my daughter screaming… I thought she screamed because she was so frightened, but that wasn't the reason—a bullet had hit her leg."

Other times those who related their own stories spoke with such depths of anguish their words seemed like emotional projectiles that hurtled through the air, compelling others in the room who wanted to remain silent—who did not want to reopen past memories—to speak.

"They arrived around mid-morning. My mother and I ran into the woods. Others did the same but they came after us… killed some… took others back to the village. By late afternoon, the stillness in the air told us what we already knew. We hid in the woods until the next morning. We were afraid they might still be in the village, afraid that if we did go back they would return and find us. We feared what we would find when we did return, and we feared knowing we would have to return to find supplies, because the few of us who had survived knew we had no other choice but to leave. We found the bodies of my father and brother… We walked for days to get to the refugee camp in Kenya… A year later I buried my mother. I have no family, so I have come alone to Canada. My life is here now."

Usually, when I asked my second question—tell me about your expectations for your life in Canada—the answer varied very little from group to group. Their hope for the future was that they could build a better life—for first their children, and then for themselves.

"I want my child to be safe. I want him to be able to play outside and not worry about being shot." "We want our children to get good educations so they can have a better life." "I just want my children to be able to walk down the street, without me worrying about whether they will return."

They made me feel proud to be Canadian when they said these things. I came to realize that all the things I value and love about my country are the same things that newcomers also see, want and value about this wonderful country. Truly, it is a privilege to live here.

Occasionally I am asked the question, "Were you born in Canada?" I had never particularly reflected on my family's past. But from the very first time I had to answer this question, I suddenly recognized the similarity between their journey, and my own family's journey to Canada.

"Yes, I was born in Canada." I began, "My family was of German / English descent, and had originally settled in the United States. When the States were fighting for their independence from England, my family, like other families who remained loyal to England, feared for their safety. They fled to Canada, part of a group called United Empire Loyalists. So, my family's journey was much like yours; they came as refugees."

The mandate of the reception centre was to assist refugees with initial settlement services, as well as provide them temporary on-site accommodation. Arrivals and departures could occur on any day or evening of the week.

I only observed the arrival of a new group once. I had stayed late to complete some work. It was after seven o'clock when they arrived. Our staff had prepared a light supper for those who would like something to eat; rooms were ready for those who wanted to go straight to bed.

I sat in the front office and looked at the group arriving. Men, women, and children quietly stood in the entrance hallway. They looked tired and anxious. Some parents gently stroked their child's shoulders; others bent down to speak quiet words that only their child could hear. Other parents, whose children clung to their sides, wrapped a loving arm around them. Actions that offered assurance to their children, and perhaps even themselves, that everything would be okay. Once they were gathered, a staff member greeted them, first in English, and then again in their own language, with words that pushed them a little further from their previous lives, and brought them one more step closer to their new future;

"Hello; welcome to Canada and to your home for the next few days."

The following week I was back at the reception centre. That same front hall which the week before had been filled with subdued anticipation was now alive with the hum of comfortable conversations. I recognized two women from the previous week sitting and chatting on a sofa, in the same hallway where only a week before they had stood quietly, tired and apprehensive. They smiled as I passed them, and I smiled in return. I headed toward the dining room for my focus session. Three young boys came charging down the hallway. They ran past me, then came back, and stood in front of me, wearing big smiles. I could think of nothing else to do other than return the smile. Then, only silence as they stared at me. I was about to say "Hi" when the one boy carefully said, "Hel-lo."

"Hello."

"Hel-lo," repeated the other two boys.

"Hello."

The first boy stepped closer toward me. "How-are-you?"

"I'm fine, thank you. How are you?"

The three of them looked at each other, than back at me.

"I-am-fine," they all said at the same time.

Then, just before turning and running off again — all three of them chorused, "Wel-come — to — Can-na-da."

That day I was delighted to answer back, "Thank you, and I welcome you to Canada also."

~Wendy D. Poole
Markham, Ontario

Christmas in Canada

Never worry about numbers. Help one person at a
time, and always start with the person nearest you.
~Mother Teresa

Brian paced the floor as he prayed that they would be able to get out of their country unscathed. Even with the proper papers, many men who tried to leave were thrown in the army. Families were torn apart. Lives were shattered.

It was late November and Brian was waiting for his new employee, Alex, to arrive from Ukraine with his family. Brian had first gotten to know Alex when he hired a few students from Ukraine for his previous business. As he described him, Alex was "a computer nerd" just like him, and now that Brian was starting a new business he could use Alex's help again. Now Alex was married, with a six-year-old daughter, and Brian had undertaken to move the whole family to Canada permanently.

Our family had already gone through our cupboards, looking for those extra items we could donate to the young couple's new home. Who needs two electric mixers? And why did I need to keep that extra coffeemaker I had stashed away?

When the plane landed, Brian welcomed Alex with a warm handshake and a sigh of relief. He met his wife Marina, a tiny pretty lady, and their beautiful daughter Julia. Her eyes filled with wonder as she looked around the bustling airport, and she shyly hid behind her mommy's skirt.

They came with two suitcases. That was it. All their other belongings were left behind. It must have been so bittersweet for them, leaving their families and almost everything they owned to come to Canada for freedom and opportunity.

Brian set them up in a hotel for two days and helped them shop for food and other essentials. It didn't take us long to set up house for this war-torn family. Brian and his wife Shannon rented Alex and Marina a neat and clean tiny bungalow on the south side of town.

Alex gasped as Brian opened the door to their new home. Marina burst into tears, and Julia ran from room to room, delighted.

"How many people live with us?" Alex asked, as his eyes grew larger and larger with every room that they explored.

"What do you mean?" Brian asked, not understanding the question.

"At home we live in one room, in a tenement, with lots of other families," Alex explained.

"Who does that lovely green grass outside belong to? Can Julia go outside to play?" Alex couldn't believe his good fortune. He held his head in his hands and wept.

It didn't take them long to bring Julia to Colasanti's, a giant greenhouse filled with plants and video games, bumper cars, jumpy castles and loads of entertainment for young and old alike. They walked along the riverfront enjoying the sculptures and Julia ran and danced in the park near their house.

"Canada so good to us, "Alex stated in his broken English. "We celebrate Christmas on December 25th like real Canadians. In the Ukraine, Christmas is celebrated on January 6th."

"They must join us," I exclaimed, already planning Julia's Christmas stocking.

"Mom do you have any idea how overwhelming all twenty-six of us are?" Brian asked. "We are so noisy. There are so many gifts and twelve children will be running around screaming their heads off and chasing one another from room to room. They are probably going to come in one door and run wailing out the other!"

"I thought that they wanted to experience a real Canadian Christmas!" I countered.

"But what about Secret Santa for the adults?" Brian asked.

"Ed and I will choose their names and surprise them. And please let me have the joy of buying precious little girly items for Julia!"

At 2:00 p.m. on Christmas Day the doorbell rang and the children and their parents started spilling into the house.

Meat pies, bread stuffing, mashed potatoes and gravy, sweet potatoes, cinnamon honey squash, corn, honey-laced carrots, shrimp rings, salsa, veggies, homemade buns, and cabbage rolls covered the counters and extra table. And the smells of honey roasted ham and succulent golden turkey were the crowning glory.

Alex, Marina and Julia brought a bottle of wine and some homemade fruit-filled buns, sharing their own special Christmas treats.

Even though she spoke little English, Julia was soon running around the house with our granddaughter Maya. She soon found herself sitting in a circle with the twelve other children as they opened their gifts. Julia was so excited. The very first present she opened was Ana's beautiful blue dress from the movie *Frozen*. She tried it on immediately and twirled and spun as we all applauded.

She then opened a doll, coloured pencils, crayons, pencil cases, books of all kinds, hair clips, lip gloss, fairy wings, an Ariel nightlight and a stocking filled with goodies. Julia squealed with joy as she displayed a Barbie, an Olaf and a princess T-shirt from her never-ending magic bag.

When the grownups played Secret Santa, Alex and Marina were astonished as we called their name and they got to open their special gifts.

First came their Santa stockings filled with a mug for each of them, tea towels, Canada socks, Canada hats and boxes of chocolates. Alex got a Nike Canada sports hoodie and Marina got a sweater, with matching hat and gloves.

As the parents gathered up their sleepy children and hauled all their loot to their cars, my husband Ed and I assessed the damage to the house. Leftovers, wrapping paper, tinsel and messy floors were our souvenirs of the grand celebration that had taken place. We hugged one another tightly, appreciating our time together, our affluence, and our family.

As Alex, Marina and Julia put their arms around me to say good night, I asked them, "Are you alright? Are you happy?"

They crossed their arms in front of their hearts and whispered, "Canada beautiful. Here we safe!"

~Barbara Bondy-Pare
Amherstburg, Ontario

Living Abroad in Canada

"Having adventures comes naturally to some people,"
said Anne serenely. "You just have a gift
for them, or you haven't."
~Lucy Maud Montgomery, Anne of Avonlea

As I stepped off the plane the cold reality of my decision hit me as hard as the −26-degree Celsius temperature. The plane had landed in a barren treeless landscape; the only sign of life was the smoke rising from roofs and the small crowd of people huddled at the window inside the terminal. In my shiny new parka, I shuffled off the plane not sure who would be inside to meet me. For the millionth time I wondered, *what had I done?*

Soon after graduation my friends had started to leave for faraway countries to teach English as a second language. The adventures they were having sounded like so much fun, learning to live in a place where they didn't speak the language and trying new cuisine. My friend Nadia had moved to Japan, and told me stories of how she would be stopped on the street by people who wanted to touch her long, strawberry blond hair. "It's kind of creepy to have strangers touching my hair," she once told me, "but I'm starting to get used to it." I wanted those adventures too, but I was afraid to leave the safety net of my province, my family and my country. Prince Edward Island was safe, Canada was safe, and outside my bubble was a big scary world.

In early May of 2004 I had it all: a great job in human resources with the government, a fiancé who would be graduating from law school, and plans for the future. But by the end of May it had all changed. While watching the evening news I heard that my job would be cut from the budget, and a couple weeks later I heard the words, "Jennifer, I think we should break up."

Just like that I had no job and no fiancé. The closeness of family and friends suddenly became suffocating. Maybe it was finally time for me to face my fears and go abroad like my friends.

Searching online, I found and applied for a job as a Human Resources Officer with the Government of Nunavut. It was still in Canada, but I had to look at a map to find where it was. After an interview in August they offered me the job. I'd be looking after all the nurses on Baffin Island. I had one semester to go to earn my master's degree so I said, "No thanks, I don't finish my last paper until November 10th." The recruiter then called me on that very day and offered me the job again. This time I accepted. *Wow! What had I done?*

In January of 2005 I packed up my possessions and boarded a plane headed for a small, remote northern community on Baffin Island approximately thirty kilometres south of the Arctic Circle. We landed in a tiny hamlet called Pangnirtung, population 1,500: 96% Inuit, 4% other. Here, I was definitely part of the other 4%. For the first time in my life I was a visible minority, and also in the minority of English-as-a-first-language speakers.

When I entered the terminal, everyone seemed to know one another as shouts of "hello" and "welcome back!" echoed all around me. I was quickly approached by a trio of women, and the shorter one, with a big smile said, "*Ullaakkut.* Good morning. You must be Jennifer. We are so happy to meet you." I immediately felt my decision to move north had been the right one.

Her name was Mona, and very quickly she became just like one of my gal pals from Southern Canada. She loved her Internet, her music, her husband and child. She loved getting her hair done and hanging out with friends. But she could also shoot a gun, run a snow machine and gut a seal. Mona was a huge help to me in settling into life in Pangnirtung, and she was there when I started my new job.

During coffee breaks I would listen to my colleagues speak to each other in Inuktitut. They would talk about their families, tell stories or talk about hunting and camping out on the land. "Why are you laughing?" Mona would ask me. "Do you know what she is talking about?"

"No, but I know it is a funny story," I would reply.

Most of the time I had no idea what they were talking about, so Mona would often interpret for me. After a few months of listening and watching it suddenly didn't matter that I didn't know the words. I knew by the actions and facial expressions what the story was about. Laughter is contagious, and laugh we did. I remember so fondly the coffee breaks I enjoyed while working in Pang, the laughter ringing through the building as everyone shared a bite to eat and a story.

Mona introduced me to radio Bingo, a favourite activity in the small community. It was a time to connect with friends around the kitchen table, while listening to the Bingo caller over the radio. Of course it was all in Inuktitut and the only part I could understand was "B-9." One night I hosted Bingo at my home for Mona, her son Wayne and her cousin Rita. "Did you make your yummy dip?" she asked as she tossed her coat on the chair and made herself at home. Wayne lay on the floor in the living room and coloured, while the ladies sat in the kitchen sharing stories and food while listening with one ear to the radio so as not to miss a number and lose out on the jackpot. I never won at radio Bingo, but I made friendships that will last a lifetime around those tables, friendships that did not feel a language barrier.

After three years, I left Nunavut and returned to life in the South. My friend Mona still lives in Pangnirtung. It is her home. She has two boys now and a husband who loves her very much. We are still in touch thanks to social media, and a few months ago she helped me put a fur ruff on my winter coat via e-mail. I may never have the opportunity to return to Nunavut again, but the experiences I had there will never leave me.

Northern Canada is one of the last places I ever thought I would find myself living. What I experienced while living there was nothing short of amazing. The Northern Lights put on spectacular shows almost nightly and, in the summer, I was mesmerized by the sun's inability to set. I hiked to the Arctic Circle, saw and ate polar bear, whale blubber, and raw caribou. I camped out under the midnight sun, made snow angels on a frozen fjord at –35 degree Celsius and, as one friend put it, "How many of your friends can say they helped build an igloo?" I experienced the same types of adventures my friends who travelled abroad had: I learned how to communicate with non-English speakers, walked the streets in towns where I couldn't read the street signs, and ate foods I had never heard of before. I had my travel abroad adventure, but in my own country, my home, Canada.

"*Qujannamiik* — Thank you."

~Jennifer Caseley
Sexsmith, Alberta

This Village Called Canada

I liken Canada to a garden… a garden into which
have been transplanted the hardiest and brightest
flowers from many lands, each retaining in its new
environment the best of the qualities for which
it was loved and prized in its native land.
~Former Prime Minister John G. Diefenbaker

The music begins. On stage a few of the JKs bumble about. Others snap to attention. In the audience families and friends lift their chins and sit up straighter. We are crammed into this school gym on a misty spring night, and we all know this song, the song of our nation.

Why do we flock to Canada, to this curious, comfortable "village"? I know why I did.

For a village to flourish its people must band together in the name of solidarity, shelter and strength, through life's sleepy seas and brutal storms. And when I lived in South Africa, that wasn't happening.

In high school during the 1970s I belonged to The New Progressive Club. There were underground rooms. Whispers. "One voice for social justice." Shhh. "One voice for all South Africans."

Back then, my boyfriend (who I later married) and I fantasized about a progressive country called Canada. Handsome Mounties, white-capped mountains and ice blue lakes, matching mittens and scarves, and quiet, mild-mannered people and creatures, all scratching out a living in the endless landscape.

Our home and native land

Our voices meet in harmony. Stresses are soothed. Moods uplifted. In the front row a teacher leans across to wipe a running nose. Everyone in the village should feel at home, rooted, knowing they belong.

In 1987 South Africa, the ground rumbled under protest marchers, bombs blew us apart, and my husband was called up for yet another military stint. His orders were to conduct night raids on the very people he loved and worked with during the day.

It was time. We stuffed our lives into four suitcases, and with our children's hands clutched firmly, we headed to the airport. As the plane soared into the sky, leaving our tear-stained relatives below, I knew I wasn't leaving home. Rather, I was going home. Home to the safety of the globe's great village.

True patriot love in all thy sons command

Our sound wave lifts the room. We are all rock stars! Villagers must see themselves in everyone else, doing all things in the name of ONE.

When one Canadian falls, another rises to help. When a grade-two teacher was frazzled in the classroom I volunteered for half the year. When a family member was diagnosed with Asperger's the public school system took him under its wing. When the community needed help, I volunteered in hospice care.

We command love from Canada, which in turn, commands love back. Canada is the center hole of the cosmic wheel, which spins through eternity in a never-ending cycle of give, take… and give.

With glowing hearts we see thee rise

A small boy in a Senators hockey shirt, arms outstretched, voice strong, pirouettes on stage. A village strives for more than just survival. It strives for honour.

A few years after we immigrated to Canada my cousin and her family left Africa's Karoo desert, and arrived in Barrie, Ontario five days before Christmas. "I'm home now too, kuzzie," she grinned through saucer-size snowflakes.

Today her family flourishes. And beware anyone who would complain about our weather, our people; anything about this land called Canada. My kuzzie will have you know there is no finer place on earth. She may even wag her finger at you and tell you to go back to where you came from. For her, if you are in her "home" you'd better mind your manners!

The True North strong and free

Our pitch fans the fiery flame of patriotism. A baby in a stroller shakes a sunflower rattle. A person's true north is their spiritual enlightenment. And in a healthy village one is free, and encouraged, to reach it.

And so it was in Canada where I began my "enlightenment" journey. After a friend and two family members were murdered back in South Africa, I turned to writing. I practiced ghostwriting, I created bereavement workshops, I became a writing coach. Here, at "home," we have the back-up and brain space to re-join our soul's journey.

From far and wide O Canada, we stand on guard for thee

Our song has wings now, carrying our artistry, our wit, our bravery. An old man, hand on walker, dabs his eyes. A great village is sought after by those who yearn to hold their heads high.

Several years ago a family fled Zimbabwe at gunpoint and arrived in Ontario. I asked all our Canadian friends to bring plant cuttings to our Canada Day barbeque, which we presented to the family.

The following day, from sunrise to sunset, the refugees planted. For compassion, they planted a peony, in the deepest coral. For grace, a lavender, in royal purple; for gratitude, a snowball hydrangea; and more… much, much more.

Like their garden, these newcomers have taken root, nurtured their lives, as well as other refugees' lives, as they continue to embellish this exquisite tapestry we call home.

God keep our land glorious and free

Our cadence is a perfect pulse. The principal beams behind the podium. The skyline is the face of the village.

Canada's skyline reveals its glory: mountains and mosques, steeples and superstructures, cliffs and construction cranes, towers and temples, forests and factories, barns and bluffs, and lighthouses attending our wide horizons.

But our true beauty is our people, who pick peace over war, who are quietly courageous, who are placidly proud, and who will fight fiercely for the good of all mankind.

Like Canada's trees that withstand the great north wind, we bow to the seasons. Spring ignites hope. Summer, joy. Fall, gratitude. And winter — as we gaze upon nature's bare bones — introspection.

O Canada, we stand on guard for thee

Along the back wall a row of teenagers belt out the finale. Villagers — young, adult, frail, strong — come together in rituals.

At my kitchen table there are always debates, as platters are passed and spoons scoop up seconds. Loud debates! Two generations can't always agree, but we all vote during elections and we all wear the Maple Leaf proudly. And none of us has ever gotten a finger wag from the auntie in Barrie.

O Canada, we stand on guard for thee

The anthem's spirit lingers in the gym, a perfect "om," encompassing all languages, cultures, and history. I know why I came home to this village called Canada.

Canada is the globe's true north. It beckons us all to return home, in our cloaks, in our sandals, in our flower garlands. Century after century. Against the piercing blue sky our flag waves red for *prana*, the life-giving force, and white for purity.

People don't come to Canada; souls return to Canada. To gather and grow.

The cameras start rolling. The spring concert begins. And life blossoms forth as it is meant to. In glory. In freedom. And in love. We invite the world to join in our song.

~Lesley Marcovich
Newmarket, Ontario

Chapter 2

The Spirit of Canada

Canada Day

We have it all. We have great diversity of people, we have a wonderful land, and we have great possibilities. So all those things combined there's nowhere else I'd rather be.
~Bob Rae

A Centennial Project

Life is either a daring adventure or nothing.
~Helen Keller

It was 1967 and Canada was turning 100. Our teachers had encouraged us to develop a "Centennial Project" to help mark Canada's 100th birthday, but I had left that to the kids who had better grades.

Summer came along, and my friend Neil suggested we ride our bicycles eighty miles from Saskatoon to Lake Diefenbaker for the official opening of the Gardiner Dam. He called this adventure a "Centennial Project," thus turning an irresponsible lark into a noble pursuit. It took a bit of convincing to get parental permission but, after promising to be careful and make a collect call home from every town we went through, the answer was "yes."

Neil was thirteen and I was twelve. Today, the idea of allowing two boys to head off on their bikes for a two-day trip along one of Saskatchewan's busiest highways would be unheard of. But back then it was just an idea that took a little selling.

We set off for our big adventure. I had a borrowed three-speed bicycle, five dollars in my pocket, a one-quart canteen, and a cotton sleeping bag lashed to a rattrap carrier. A few hours into our trip, our adrenaline kicked in as our bikes accelerated down the mile-long hill at the end of newly constructed, man-made Blackstrap Lake. We held on for dear life as we careened faster on two wheels than we ever thought possible. It was a lot less fun when we had to climb up the other side of the valley. We learned the simple truth of the prairies: "what goes down must come up!"

Hours later we were in the middle of nowhere. Our water was gone, I had a flat front tire, and we were trudging under the enormous prairie sky. The highway stretched on forever in front of us. We had been walking for what seemed like an eternity when a huge yellow Department of Highways truck pulled up.

"You boys need a ride?"

"Yes we do," we replied, and seconds later two big workers threw our bikes up into the dump box and we were off: five people squished onto a bench seat designed for three. We told the men our story and they thought it quite amusing. Ten minutes later we were off-loaded at the Kenaston Garage, where I was able to get my tire fixed for fifty cents. Just that quickly we were back on the road!

The sun filled the western sky as we approached the little community of Hawarden. Night was coming and we cycled the town looking for a place to sleep under the stars. What a great adventure! The schoolyard looked promising as it offered a caragana hedge to tuck under. Hopefully the night would be clear, as we had no tarp or rain gear.

Hungry, we entered the hotel café and began to tell the proprietor about our Centennial Project. She seemed quite taken with us. Then she asked, "Where are you boys planning on sleeping tonight?"

"We aren't sure," we replied. "Maybe the school playground?"

This response triggered an immediate, "Oh no you won't. You boys are coming home with me and staying at my house!"

Her tone of voice left no room for argument, so that night we found ourselves sweating in the heat of the unventilated attic of her three-story home. After all, how can you say no to someone who gives you dinner and doesn't charge you? The schoolyard might have afforded us a better sleep, but in the morning she fed us bacon and eggs and sent us on our way with best wishes for the successful completion of our project.

Now that we had discovered the power of telling our Centennial Project story, we wondered if it would work again at the next town.

It was a half-mile detour to find out, but we had a hunch it might be worth the effort. We found a little café attached to a garage, and there we told our story to the morning coffee crowd. In response, the proprietor asked if we would like free milkshakes! It was magic, successfully trading our story for a stainless steel container full of cold chocolate milkshake on a hot day!

Thrilled with our good fortune, we pedaled back to the highway and into a headwind that used up those free calories pretty quickly. Late that afternoon we arrived at Gardiner Dam. Speeches were made and the floodgates of the spillway opened to the delight of the crowd. It was a dusty, thrilling scene and a great experience. CKKR Radio from Rosetown was covering the event and, when the announcer learned of our venture, he asked if he could interview us.

"How did you boys get here today?" he asked. And we told our story again, this time for all the invisible listening audience to hear. A two-day Centennial Project completed! At a cost of only fifty cents!

My partner and I are thinking of doing the trip again to celebrate Canada's 150th. If we do we'll likely take better bikes and a tire repair kit. Imagine a country where two ill-prepared, underequipped and inexperienced kids could leap into an adventure and succeed largely due to the kindness, care and generosity of strangers. People offered help, food, accommodations, chocolate milkshakes and a chance at fame on the radio… and why? Because this is Canada!

~Wayne Boldt
Caron, Saskatchewan

The Ultimate Playlist

*A great nation cannot be made, cannot be discovered
and then coldly laid together, like pieces in a picture
puzzle. No! Canada is a theme. It is a tune, and
it must be sung together.*
~Emily Murphy

It's July 1, 2006 and the weather forecast says there is a possibility of rain, but my husband, two kids and I are determined to spend the afternoon and evening in downtown Ottawa. It's not a quest for the claustrophobic; our land is vast and our population spread wide, but on this day, thousands of us flock to the capital for sweet beaver tails and savoury poutine.

It's not the first Canada Day we've driven in from our Ottawa suburb, but it will be the first year we've stayed for the evening concert. I heard on the radio that a very special guitar will be played throughout the performances, and I want to be there.

The guitar is made from sixty-four pieces of our Canadian history and heritage, items such as decking from the Bluenose II, metal from Maurice "Rocket" Richard's Stanley Cup ring, a piece of Nancy Greene's ski, and reclaimed wood from the building where Louis Riel went to school. The instrument was built by Nova Scotian guitar craftsman George Rizsanyi, at the request of Canadian writer and broadcaster Jowi Taylor, who wanted to create a symbol of national unity that represented every province and territory. Named "The Six String Nation" the guitar will be played publicly for the first time tonight.

My husband tosses four fold-up camp chairs into the back of the minivan, while I make sure we have all the other essentials: sunscreen, snacks, water bottles, maple leaf shaped hats, and Canadian flag "tattoos." Thirty-five minutes later we blend into the river of red and white filling the streets of the downtown core. We inch our way to Major Hill Park where there are activities, shows… and ice cream carts.

The rain starts later in the afternoon but, inspired by countless others, we duck into a pharmacy and buy supersized garbage bags that we turn into raincoats. By evening the rain has stopped and we head to the Hill to stake out our spot for the concert. The grass is wet but we have our camp chairs. We offer our extra garbage bags to those around us who don't have chairs, so they can sit more comfortably on the wet lawn.

The concert begins and we are introduced to The Six String Nation guitar as it's handed first to singer-songwriter Stephen Fearing. The thousands of us who have come to the Hill this warm July evening are quiet as the first rich ripples of music come through the giant speakers. There are hoots and whoops of appreciation. Stephen Fearing is playing his song "The Longest Road," but with each strum of the guitar we are also listening to Paul Henderson's hockey stick, Pierre Trudeau's canoe paddle, a 300-year-old golden spruce, ancient rock, and wood from a sideboard belonging to Sir John A. Macdonald, Canada's first Prime Minister. Not one of the sixty-four pieces in the guitar is musical on its own: but together they fill the night sky with incredible sound.

It made me think of the pieces of Canada I've collected myself over the years: a piece of pinkish rock from the Canadian Shield; sand from a beach near Barry's Bay; a napkin from a trip across Canada by rail; an acorn from the grounds of Stephen Leacock's home in Orillia; two keys — one to my childhood home in Montreal and the other from my first apartment in Victoria; and many concert ticket stubs from the Montreal Forum. Some pieces of Canada live in my memories: my wedding in Quebec City, watching waves crash in Peggy's Cove, and my first view of Lake Louise.

The Six String Nation guitar is passed throughout the evening to other artists and performers. When musician Colin James plays "Into the Mystic," it sounds like sunlight bouncing on water. The lyrics "we were born before the wind…" wash over the thousands of us gently waving little paper Canadian flags.

Canada is often referred to as a mosaic, but I've never really liked that image because a mosaic is usually made of broken pieces and Canadians are strong. That night, as each musician brought forth something different but equally lovely from a guitar made of history, culture and the land itself, I saw Canada as a beautiful instrument that we all play.

We are not pieces of a mosaic. We are folk songs, symphonies, rock, and opera. We are pop, classical, hip-hop, R&B and jazz. I look around at the thousands of people waving Canadian flags and imagine that, just like me, they have all collected their own bits and pieces and memories of this country: the notes to their personal songs. Tonight I see Canada as a beautiful acoustic guitar, and Canadians themselves as the ultimate playlist.

~Kim Reynolds
Orleans, Ontario

Canada Day in the Governor's Canoe

There is nothing — absolutely nothing — half so much
worth doing as simply messing about in boats.
~Kenneth Grahame, The Wind in the Willows

It was a sunny July 1st — Canada Day. I locked my car and began walking west along Queen's Quay through the throngs of people toward the Harbourfront Canoe and Kayak Centre. I was looking forward to an adventure on the water.

"Hey Peter — I'm here," I announced when I arrived. Handing me a costume, Peter said, "Here Jan, put this on. You'll be the famous artist Frances Anne Hopkins." Others were already dressed as voyageurs, with hats or bright bandanas on their heads. Most wore a loose shirt and a *ceinture fléchée* — the traditional French Canadian colourful sash — tied around the waist. A young boy wearing a formal blue coat with tails and white top hat was the Governor himself! Intrigued, I pulled on my costume, complete with a hat, and voilà — I was ready for the adventure.

Once we were all dressed Peter gathered us together. He wore his own favourite voyageur costume as the "Gouvernail" — the back paddler in charge of steering the big canoe. In addition to his loose shirt and red scarf, he wore a brown felt hat with a buckle and multi-coloured feathers — including a red ostrich plume, and a clay pipe tucked into the hatband. He was quite a sight! From a cabinet he began distributing matching wooden paddles with red blades. "Okay everyone," he said, "grab a lifejacket from the rack and follow me."

He led us down to the dock where his big thirty-four-foot "Governor's Canoe" was tied up. Decorated as it would have been in the 17th century, it boasted a high rounded bow and measured six feet across the centre beam. Fully loaded it carried about twenty-two people — sixteen safely in Toronto Harbour. From his post at the stern Peter would steer his historic craft, tell stories and get people singing, and he was really good at it!

That day there were fourteen of us and, as an experienced paddler, I landed an outside seat. Another strong paddler was chosen to be the "Avant" up front, and Peter gave him a bowler hat with feathers. Once we were all aboard he ran through some basic safety and paddling instructions and taught us the "voyageur salute."

In unison we all banged our paddles (with vigour) three times on the gunwales, raised them in the air and shouted "Hey!" This was repeated three times. With that under our belts, we pulled away from the dock.

In the safety of the slip it took a few minutes for us to find our paddling rhythm, but soon we got up some speed and, with a reveille blast from the Gouvernail's bugle, we executed our first voyageur salute and headed out into Toronto Harbour. Our goal was the wharf at the east end where the boats participating in the night's Parade of Lights were all gathering. Being the only craft powered by muscle we gave ourselves plenty of time, but with fourteen paddlers and the wind at our back it didn't take long. As usual, Toronto's inner harbour was alive with colourful watercraft: sailboats of all shapes and sizes, motorboats, yachts, ferries heading to and from the Toronto Islands, canoes, kay-aks, police boats, tugboats, you name it, it was out there — including Toronto's famous red and white fireboat, the William Lyon Mackenzie. We watched as other boats decorated with Canadian flags and strung with lights lined up for the parade. They were all motoring along and laughing at us with our paddles. "We'll show them!" we declared, and executed a vigorous voyageur salute.

Boats continued arriving until finally the Parade Marshall sounded the signal to begin. One by one we pulled away from the wharf and began heading back west toward the centre of Harbourfront for the sail past. Every boat displayed a banner for a chosen charity sponsor. Community Centre 55 — a Toronto charity that helps families in need — was ours. Using old rope, Peter had tied a large banner displaying their name onto the side of the canoe.

In addition to the bow and stern nautical lights required to operate in the harbour, Peter hung an old candle lantern beside the historic Hudson's Bay Company Ensign flag flying off the stern. There was no way to power anything else. With a formal bugle blast to announce our departure, we were off.

The setting sun was now a blaze of colour lighting up the Toronto skyline. Paddling straight into it — along with the wind — we had to really dig in. To keep us going, Peter led us in singing traditional canoeing songs — like "Land of the Silver Birch", and everyone's favourite — Stan Rogers' "Northwest Passage." Then we sang — to the tune of "Jingle Bells" — "Paddling hard, paddling strong, paddling all the way…!" Enjoying the good-natured comments from passing boats, we somehow managed to keep our place in line.

Finally we approached the centre of Harbourfront where throngs of people stood enjoying the parade of boats. Peter announced our arrival with appropriate reveille blasts on his bugle. "And here comes the Governor's Canoe — paddled by a group of Voyageurs!" we heard over the loudspeakers. "Stroke! Stroke! Stroke!" the waiting watchers shouted with appreciative laughter. After executing our loudest Voyageur salute yet we broke into a rousing rendition of "O Canada", and the enthusiastic flag-waving crowd joined in. With grins on our faces we completed our "paddle past" and I thought to myself, *what a great way to spend Canada Day!*

But we weren't done yet. After a quick stop at home base we headed back out — this time straight through the western gap and out into Lake Ontario. It was time for the annual fireworks display at Ontario Place, and there was no better place to view it than from the water.

By now the wind had died, and once through the gap we settled in one spot to wait for full dark. It was truly memorable, sitting in a traditional Canadian canoe on a warm summer night, surrounded by hundreds of other boats — everyone celebrating Canada's birthday and enjoying the fireworks and music. After the last explosion had lit the night sky we turned the canoe around and, along with hundreds of others, headed back through the western gap. All those motorized craft had the water running like a river and we barely had to paddle!

Back at the dock we turned in our gear. After thanking Peter for the best Canada Day ever, I started walking along Queens Quay toward my car. Not yet ready for it to be over, I cut back down to the water. I love walking along the waterfront on a summer night with the throngs of happy people, waterside cafés, sounds of laughter, music from the outdoor stage and the many party boats. It was not the first time in my life that I reflected on how lucky I am to live in this wonderful city — in this amazing country — the best country in the world. With a full heart I took one last look as I turned toward the street, knowing this was a Canada Day I would never forget.

~Janet Matthews
Aurora, Ontario

Many Shovels

*Every successful individual knows that his or her
achievement depends on a community of
persons working together.*
~Paul Ryan

The morning of June 30, 2014 was warm and fine. We sat on the cottage dock, relaxing on Muskoka-style lawn chairs with our dear friends from Oakville, Gwyneth and Todd. Our kids were playing on a giant white paddle-board in the lake.

As the children screamed in delight and swam, we adults joked about middle age, discussing our desires to eat more fibre and reduce belly fat, but only *after* this Canada Day long weekend! We were all equally guilty of eating too many s'mores roasted to perfection over the crackling campfire, and devouring bacon and fried eggs for breakfast.

"We'll start behaving later; absolutely no dieting today," I said. "There are still runny butter tarts on the kitchen counter."

Everyone chuckled. The mood was light.

Then black clouds rolled in over the calm blue lake and blocked out the sun.

"Looks like rain," announced my husband, Ian. "Let's head up the hill before it starts to pour."

The kids reluctantly pulled the paddleboard to shore and we hiked up the trail to the cottage that my parents built in 1969. I set out a tray of watermelon slices, cheese and crackers on the knotty pine table. We nibbled. We giggled. We poured ourselves cold drinks.

The wind picked up. The tall pine trees surrounding the cottage swayed. White caps formed on the lake. Thunder boomed and echoed through the rolling Haliburton Highlands hills. We were glad to be indoors and cozy.

I welcomed the pounding drops of water as the rain began. A good downpour meant keeping the forest damp and fire burning bans away. Yay for more campfires!

"Do you think the rain will last long?" asked Gwyneth.

"Nah. I bet this storm will pass quickly," I said. "The weather up north can change fast, but that's Canada for you."

Gwyneth smiled. "Good, I'm glad." She looked around and noticed the men were no longer inside. "Where did you put our husbands?"

I grinned. "I gave them a honey do list. They went out to check if the vans' windows are up and the bunky door is closed."

"They're going to get soaked!"

"Better them than us!"

We both chuckled.

"Boy, it's really coming down, eh?" said Gwyneth.

"Sure is," I said.

I took a seat in a reclining chair and glanced out the A-frame's giant glass windows. The raindrops bounced off the lake. And bounced. And bounced.

Gwyneth sat beside me in a comfy chair. We put our feet up on stools and rested. We flipped through magazines and chatted while the kids relaxed on the bedroom's bunk beds, swapping stories of their own. Shortly afterward, the guys came inside, damp but not wet enough to need a change of clothes.

The rain kept pounding. Minutes passed and it didn't let up.

Ian decided to poke his nose outside again. He stepped onto the cottage's small covered porch. A moment later, he called me to join him.

"Come out here, Patricia," he said.

"No, I'm good in here, honey," I said. I felt sleepy in my chair. I was enjoying my downtime and the sound of the rain on the roof.

"Come, please," he said. "NOW!"

I recognized the anxious tone in his voice; it meant trouble.

When I stepped outside, I couldn't believe the scene before me. Water poured down our driveway, and our neighbours' lane, turning both into gushing rivers that filled our yards with water and gravel. The culverts designed to carry water away were full and overflowing. Water coursed everywhere, tearing its own path as small streams formed and took over the properties.

Ten minutes later, our yard was filled with water like a toddler's wading pool. Our friend, Todd, joined us outdoors while Gwyneth kept the kids safe and dry inside. Our cottage neighbours, Katherine and Dave, came out and joined us in our yard.

Katherine hugged me hard. "I am so, so sorry."

"Me, too." I hugged her back and stifled my tears.

We watched our cottage yard wash away. The water tore away the grass and gardens. It carved out a jagged, deep ditch along one side of the building, exposing the pier footings that my dad, now gone, had poured forty-five years ago when he and my mom built our cottage.

Ian stepped forward. "We need to get all the cars to the main road before the driveways wash completely away. I'll get shovels." He disappeared below the cottage.

Soon, every adult had a shovel in hand, including Katherine's sister and her husband who arrived from their family cottage across the lake to help us, along with their guests. Katherine and Dave's lane was cut so deeply that it was impassable. We worked to fill holes in the dirt so we could push all of our vehicles one by one up our driveway.

The rain kept coming. Our side stairs were torn away from the cottage. The municipal road at the top of our driveway washed out. We were covered in mud, soaked to our cores and cold. But we were standing together, leaning on the shovels in our hands.

"Are you okay?" Ian asked me once the last vehicle made it to the road.

I choked up. "I will be."

"Good," he said and kissed my cheek.

Gwyneth called to us from the kitchen window, "Come in now. Dinner is ready!"

I smiled. My girlfriend did her part to help, too, by cooking a hot meal and taking care of us.

Ian and I walked through water to the door.

"I get it now," I said.

Ian lifted a furry eyebrow. "Get what?"

"Why my dad kept so many shovels under the cottage. How he and my mom, with my uncle and aunt's help, managed to build this sweet cottage. We really pulled together today."

The rain stopped. We ate delicious chicken and then played board games together. We listened to water rushing down the ditch to the lake, as it did all night long. The lake rose so high that our floating dock was level with the rest of the dock, and the water turned brown from mud washing in. Nobody swam. The bakery in Haliburton Village taped a handwritten sign on its door: "Closed due to flood." Many local properties, businesses and roads were damaged.

The next morning we woke to the sounds of beeping dump trucks and construction workers repairing the road at the top of the driveway. The kids ran out to the yard and kicked a soccer ball over piles of mud and driveway gravel, laughing and running like nothing had happened. Gwyneth and Todd poured us strong coffee.

I stepped outside. Ian followed. The air smelled peaty. The place was a mess.

"We'll fix this, Patricia," he said. "We're Canadian. We're tough."

I felt a bit overwhelmed. "Ya?"

"Yes. Call your mom now. Wish her a happy Canada Day. Tell her about the damage. Tell her we'll get it fixed for her and our family. We can do this!"

And I'm proud to say that we did.

~Patricia Miller
Bradford, Ontario

Canada Day
North of Terrace

My people's memory reaches into
the beginning of all things.
~Chief Dan George

ravel crunched under the wheels of the big rig as we stopped at the side of the Yellowhead Highway. Three men stood waiting beside two other trucks parked in a clearing just off the road. My son, Brett, jumped from the cab of the F550 he was driving and hurried over to speak with them.

We had left Vancouver, British Columbia on June 29, 2004, travelling north 1,500 kilometres to be in Terrace the next day. Brett was hauling a 1,200-pound generator on a trailer behind a flat-deck. It would provide all the power for the July 1st Canada Day celebration. One of the men waved some papers in the air. I heard exclamations of disbelief. Concern darkened Brett's face as he climbed back into the truck. "We're not setting up in Terrace," he said.

"Why not?" I asked.

"Because we're going to Gingolx — 170 kilometres that way." He pointed north. "We've got to be set up for tomorrow, and it's almost 6 p.m. now."

"Is that possible?" I queried.

"Guess we're going to find out." The truck rumbled back into motion.

Brett had worked at the local television station in Terrace and knew the area well. Gingolx (pronounced Gingoluk) is one of the four Nisga'a First Nation villages northwest of Terrace.

One of British Columbia's jewels, Terrace's geographic beauty is world-renowned. So many German tourists visit the town that the street signs are in English and German. I'd looked forward to staying there and wanted to visit a store Brett had mentioned where handmade First Nations' goods were sold. I was disappointed, but we had to get going.

Our little convoy whisked through Terrace, then set off up the Nisga'a Highway. We traversed the Memorial Lava Beds, an eerie landscape where lava flowed for miles after a 16th century eruption. Now well into Nisga'a territory, we passed two enormous totems, hand carved and majestic, flanking a little bridge over the Nass River.

Soon we began to descend the mountainside on the brand new highway extension. Down, down, down we rolled, all the way to the mouth of the Nass, to the ancient village of Gingolx.

I had always lived in "Super, Natural British Columbia," as it's advertised, but had never experienced the exquisite beauty of Gingolx. It mesmerized me. Dwarfed on three sides by mountains green with forest, this tiny place, with a population of 250, faced the Nass River, with more mountains beyond. I inhaled air so pristine I wondered if it was pure oxygen. Stillness enveloped us, broken only by the quiet voices of villagers and birdsong. Isolated for millennia in wilderness, Gingolx is truly unique.

Tired and hungry after having set up most of the equipment, we gobbled burgers and fries in the general store that also housed a soda fountain and a few booths. Ready to bed down, I asked Gerry, the proprietor, where we could rent some rooms.

"None available," he said.

After a day's journey nearing a 1,000 kilometres, plus the equipment set-up time, his answer came as a shock. Had I misheard him?

"Did you say *none*?" I asked.

"Yep. The B&B's reserved for the celebrities. And it's full."

Several of Gerry's children were watching now. They had been in the store, taking in the flurry of activity.

"Any chance we could sleep in the cab?" I asked Brett. Before he could answer, Gerry interjected.

"No, no! This is my responsibility." He studied us, pondered a minute. His extended arm swept toward the café's booths.

"My children will sleep here."

The children looked horrified. He turned to us.

"You will sleep at my house, in their beds."

We were astonished. Filled with guilt, but having no alternative, we gratefully accepted his generous offer.

The next morning, refreshed and relaxed, Brett and his workmates put the finishing touches to the sound and lighting equipment on a stage in the centre of the village. One hundred-fifty benches, staggered in rows before it, stood ready. A banner of welcome read: "Strangers are only friends we haven't met yet." The festivities were to celebrate the monumental completion of the highway extension, allowing the first ever road access to Gingolx.

As I sat on one of the benches, I gradually became aware of a muffled sound coming from the direction of the mountains. I gaped in stunned disbelief as a procession of a hundred or more First Nations people, walking five abreast, some hidden behind symbolic masks, emerged from around a bend in the road, chanting to the beat of their drums. Their capes in scarlet or black, called button blankets, bore intricate designs outlined with scores of white buttons. Embroidered depictions of the wolf, killer whale, raven or eagle accented the designs. Deep white fringes on some capes swept just above the ground and swung in time to the beat. The senses of power, dignity and intimidation were overwhelming. I felt I'd entered a time warp, and a thrill ran through me as I marvelled at this ancient tradition few outsiders had ever witnessed.

The procession stopped in front of the stage. Speeches were made, the individual villages and dignitaries were recognized, and the visitors were welcomed. Dancers twirled in their capes. They wore headdresses of fur, or hats carved or woven of cedar. Handmade moccasins and mukluks of leather and fur completed their regalia.

Everyone crowded the benches, applauding and cheering.

The village thronged with visitors. We roamed about, taking in the natural beauty of Gingolx. It spoke of an earlier time, when nature was not just respected but revered. First Nations people consider the hummingbird a symbol of beauty, intelligence and love. Countless numbers of the tiny birds zipped past our ears, perhaps symbolic of the love the Nisga'a have for their land.

As the "Seafood Capital of the Nass," Gingolx holds an annual "Crabfest." Soft-shell crabs cooked in huge pots. "Burnt" salmon, which wasn't burnt but cooked to perfection on stakes beside a huge campfire, was a true delicacy. Baked potatoes and corn on the cob accompanied each delicious item. Tantalizing aromas filled the air, but you had to act fast — they sold out in no time.

Bald eagles provided entertainment, clucking and chirping as they eyed the fish from perches high in the evergreens lining the riverbank. First Nations' handcrafts and clothing filled the community centre across from the stage, where I felt lucky to purchase a beautiful embroidered vest.

Friday and Saturday the stage filled with performers. The long-awaited celebrities, Tom Jackson from *North of 60* and Buffy Sainte-Marie, performed on Saturday evening, Canada Day, to a joyous crowd.

Sunday morning the crew finished packing the equipment for the long journey home. We bid fond farewells to our gracious host and his children, grateful for their kindness. We had received an exceptional gift in being allowed to visit such an extraordinary place, surpassed only by the genuine friendship of its people. We were honoured and proud, as Canadians, to have been included with Canada's first people, in a celebration of a part of Canada entirely new to us, yet older than the country itself.

~DG Peterson
Vancouver, British Columbia

A Birthday Cake for Canada

Every birthday, every celebration ends with
something sweet, a cake, and people remember.
It's all about the memories.
~Buddy Valastro

"We're celebrating another birthday this year," Mom announced one gloomy day while we sat indoors watching the rain fall.

"Whose birthday?" my sister asked.

"Canada's," replied Mom.

"Whose?" Sonya repeated, as we followed Mom into the kitchen and gathered around the freshly baked chocolate cake she had made.

In 1963, my mom had immigrated to Canada from England and settled in the Toronto suburb of Scarborough, where she immersed herself into the Canadian way of life, learning its customs and how to cope with its changing seasons. Ten years later, Mom, now a proud Canadian citizen, had married my father and had given birth to my brother, sister and me. Having no other family in Canada and wanting us to appreciate our Canadian heritage, she began looking for ways to teach us about Canada.

During our early years, when money was tight, Mom kept our lessons simple but fun. Regardless of the season, the great outdoors was our classroom. When the weather allowed, we examined plants and insects, watched wildlife, and explored the endless trails surrounding our home. As we got older, Mom got more creative. This year, she was trying something new, and now we gathered around the big rectangular sheet cake she had baked for Canada Day.

"This is silly," said my brother when Mom confirmed we were indeed making a birthday cake for Canada. But when she positioned several bowls of icing on the table, along with an assortment of photographs of Canadian symbols and landmarks, Michael quickly changed his tune.

"I like this one," said Sonya, grabbing an aerial shot of the Great Lakes. Michael chose an image of a beaver gnawing on a tree, and I chose the Canadian flag, something familiar and, for a child my age, oddly comforting. Mom selected a few of the remaining photos, and then chatted away about the importance of each while she mixed food colouring into the bowls.

When we were done icing our cake, a magnificent design emerged. The fact that my Canadian flag was pink, Sonya's Great Lakes had trees growing inside of them, and Michael's beaver looked more like a buck toothed dog chewing on a bone made no difference to us. We were proud of our creation, and so was Mom.

Several years later, while watching the Canada Day parade unfold on television, I turned to Mom and said, "Why did you stop baking those birthday cakes?"

Mom answered with a sad but serious expression. "You all grew up and didn't want to waste time icing a cake with your mom." Her words shook me. I was shocked. Did she really not know how special those Canada Day celebrations were?

That evening, I sat at our kitchen table and ran a finger along the wood grain, reminiscing about the many birthday cakes we had made for Canada when we were kids. Each cake was different, but one ingredient was the same: Mom. It was her patience and encouraging remarks that helped us move past our insecurities and learn to work harmoniously with each other.

The very next day I left a gift bag on the kitchen table for Mom with a card that read: *Inside this bag is a box of Betty Crocker cake mix, just like the ones you used to bake for Canada's birthday. Let's practice decorating!*

And practice we did! Two days after Canada Day, with Mom's first grandchild propped up in her highchair and all of us seated around the kitchen table, we returned to our childhood tradition. As we began to ice our cake, Mom said, "Did I ever tell you the story about Diefenbaker? In England, he was known as Mr. Canada..."

That day, Mom placed three candles on our cake. "For yesterday, today and tomorrow," she said. Happy birthday, Canada!

~Lisa Reynolds
Ajax, Ontario

The Spirit of Canada

Chapter 3

A Nation of Helping Hands

*There are no limits to the majestic future which
lies before the mighty expanse of Canada
with its virile, aspiring, cultured, and
generous-hearted people.*
~Sir Winston Churchill

The Wedding Dress

*Because that's what kindness is. It's not doing
something for someone else because
they can't, but because you can.*
~Andrew Iskander

When we added up the costs, we discovered the wedding we were planning would cost over $20,000. Our plan included flying home to Cape Breton Island from Fort McMurray and inviting about 200 people. But the price tag ruled it out. After tossing around a few options, we decided to get married in Toronto and keep it small — only twenty people. I found the Rectory Café on Ward Island, and booked our wedding for Saturday May 7, 2016. I also found a great Toronto-based photographer named Alex Neary.

A year before, I'd seen a wedding dress I loved at a store in Fort McMurray. They ordered one in my size and it arrived just in time to take it to the dressmaker for alterations before our May 4th flight. I was so excited!

When fire broke out in Fort McMurray on May 1st I wasn't concerned. But on May 3rd the fire escalated and the evacuations began.

My dressmaker was up Abasand Hill where the fire was really concentrated. Around 2:00 I called to see if she might be able to grab my dress as she evacuated. "Élise, I'm so sorry," she said. "I'm not even home, and I won't be able to get there." I realized, then, my beautiful dress was gone.

Our flight was the next day, but the road south to the airport was already closed, fire was raging everywhere, and we were pretty much trapped. My fiancé, Brandon, was an hour south in Anzac on the other side of the fire. It was time to go, so I packed up our four animals, picked up Brandon's cousin's girlfriend and their little boy, and we all crammed into my SUV. Like everyone else, we could only go north to the camps.

Four hours later, we heard the road to the south had been re-opened. So we headed back down to meet Brandon in Anzac. The Fort Mac airport was closed, so we debated the whole night whether to even bother with the wedding. Brandon's mother convinced us to go ahead with it, so we headed farther south to Edmonton. The traffic was awful and we missed the evening flight, but we managed to catch a flight to Toronto the next morning.

By now, Canadians everywhere were rallying to help those evacuating from Fort McMurray. My friend Alana in Halifax, and my Toronto photographer, Alex, both asked how they could help. "I don't have a wedding dress," I said. "If you know anyone with a dress I could borrow, that would be awesome." They both jumped right on it with social media, and within an hour there were offers pouring in! Overwhelmed with this outpouring of generosity, I had no idea what to do.

Then Alex forwarded me an e-mail from a bridal boutique in Toronto. "If you would like to come in and pick out a dress there will be no fee. You can take whichever one you want."

I was totally blown away. "Okay," I responded to Alex, "I think this is the best option. I can look at a few dresses and choose one. This is my wedding day, and I still want to feel good in my dress." So Alex set it up.

After checking in at the Toronto hotel, I went with my mother and Alex to the bridal shop. We were greeted by the shop manager, who was absolutely lovely. She told me to pick any dress I wanted. I was overwhelmed by her generosity.

The first dress I tried was lovely, but looking in the mirror, I started crying. "I can't wear this dress," I said. "It reminds me too much of the dress I'm supposed to be wearing, and how much I loved it."

I finally narrowed it down to two dresses, but I couldn't decide between them. That's when the manager said, "You're going to take both." She pointed to one of them — a beautiful lace dress with spaghetti straps — and said, "You're going to wear this dress to be married in." She pointed to the other one — a champagne satin dress — "and you're going to wear this one to the reception, so you'll just have to find time to change."

I felt like a celebrity. I mean, who gets to wear two dresses on their wedding day? And while the lace dress I wore for the ceremony was a loaner, they actually gave me the other dress to keep. I had everything else I needed with me, including two pair of shoes that went perfectly with the dresses, and some little blue flowers for my hair.

The next day Brandon and I were married on Ward Island in a lovely spring garden overlooking Lake Ontario. There were twenty-two of us altogether, including our families. My dress was perfect, and the 3:00 p.m. ceremony went off without a hitch. Everybody had a great time, and we danced the night away.

I had been worrying about the firefighters back home. A number of them were clients of my massage business. Two days before the wedding my firefighter clients had texted that my house was safe. I certainly appreciated knowing, but responded, "I'm glad you are safe. Please don't worry about my home, just stay safe."

I still cry thinking about those kind firefighters. I knew how hard they were working and how devastating the fire was, so I sent messages all day Friday and Saturday to help keep their morale up. On my wedding day, I got calls from two firefighters, with congratulations and best wishes. "Why are you calling?" I asked. "You must be exhausted." But the day before the wedding they kept seeing the story of my dress in the news, and said it was great to have something positive to think about.

The whole experience changed me. I don't make a big deal out of small things now. Like many people here, I'm purging my possessions. Things are just stuff, after all. That fire gave me a new perspective on what is really important in life — things like friendship, people helping each other, and strangers who are so kind they will give you a wedding dress.

~Élise Phillippo
Fort McMurray, Alberta

18

Still Good

*I slept and I dreamed that life is all joy. I woke
and I saw that life is all service. I served
and I saw that service is joy.*
~Kahlil Gibran

I grew up near Roncesvales and Dundas Street West in Toronto, close to High Park. My dad, Howard, walked a fair bit around our neighbourhood and knew most of our neighbours. He always stopped to say hello and share a joke. Dad also carried lots of change in his pocket for those who asked, and he would often buy lunch for those who told him they were hungry.

One year, as the weather got colder, Dad dug his warm grey coat out of his closet and noticed the sleeves and the collar were starting to fray. Having grown up during the Depression, he was not one to throw anything out, certainly not if it was "still good." Dad knew it could be mended, so he asked Zenny, my stepmom to buy him some fabric. After giving it some thought, Dad decided something fuzzy would make a good trim. Zenny bought him a piece of black faux fur. It was a bit thicker than he anticipated, yet he painstakingly sewed it on to all the edges of his old wool coat — the sleeves, the collar, and even along the bottom edge, so it would all match. I think Zenny may have helped him with some of the sewing.

The old grey coat — now trimmed in black faux fur — suited him and he wore it proudly. Then, one cold evening, a man my father affectionately called "Old Joe" pushed his shopping cart past our house, loaded with all his possessions. He was wearing tattered boots with the soles flapping as he walked in the snow. Dad was just arriving home from work, and I heard him call out, "Wait, Joe, wait — I have some boots for you."

While he looked for his extra boots, he asked Zenny if she would pack a warm dinner for Joe, because he had refused to come inside.

Then Dad asked me to get some of his socks. "The blue ones, Michelle," he said, because in the morning he often confused them with the black ones, and would end up at work wearing one of each. He put the socks in a plastic bag, took the food that Zenny had packed, and went back outside. I went with him.

And then it happened… I really shouldn't have been surprised when Dad took off his warm wool coat and handed it to Old Joe, too.

As we re-entered the house, I was full of admiration for my dad, although I didn't tell him. All I managed to say was, "What are you going to wear tomorrow?" Dad put his arm around me and replied, "I have that nice blue jacket that Zenny got me from Tilleys." Then he gathered up some of his paperback books and put them in an old briefcase with some pens and paper and a few subway tokens. He was already preparing his next gift for Joe.

Every time I saw Old Joe after that, wearing that grey coat with black faux fur trim, my heart would fill with warmth.

My father died many years later, but I would still see Old Joe pass by when I went to visit Zenny. He was still wearing my father's coat, and that always made me smile. It brought back such fond warm memories of my dad, and who he was as a person, and how he lived his life.

Then, one chilly winter evening I was leaving Zenny's house and keeping an eye out for Joe as usual. Well, more for the coat, really. It had been a while since I'd seen Joe, so I was happy when I saw that old grey coat coming down the street. Filled with sudden warmth, and tears, I strained to see Joe's face, not really expecting him to look up. Suddenly he did!

But it wasn't Old Joe's face that looked back at me. I smiled, realizing that my dad's old coat had once again found new life, in a new owner. I was overcome with emotion as I thought about how happy Dad would be to know, that even after all these years, his old coat was "still good."

~Michelle Dinnick
Alliston, Ontario

19

Twelve Days of Kindness

If compassion was the motivating factor behind
all of our decisions, would our world not be
a completely different place?
~Sheryl Crow

Twinkling Christmas lights on our Charlie Brown Christmas tree reflected off the shiny ornaments, throwing flashes of light on the wall. Outside a few snowflakes drifted down as the grey Sunday afternoon sky darkened. My mood was as dark as the sky. Although it was less than two weeks before Christmas, I found it difficult to be in a festive mood. We had immigrated to Canada from south of the border, and holidays were difficult for us because we missed our family in Minnesota.

Our family was also going through a very difficult year, with major health issues, a serious work-related problem for my husband, and trouble with our rebellious teenage son. I made a half-hearted effort to put up a few decorations around the house, but my heart just wasn't in it.

"Mom, I wish we could spend Christmas with Grandpa and Grandma in Minnesota," said my fifteen-year old daughter, Rachel. She was sitting on the floor, wrapping a small gift for one of her friends.

A wave of homesickness swept over me. How could I encourage my daughter when I was also struggling? "I know you'd like to spend Christmas in Minnesota, Rachel. So would I." I looked up from the notes I was writing on my printed Christmas letters. "But Minnesota is 2,000 kilometres from Calgary. You remember how hard it was to drive in that snowstorm two years ago? And then the temperature dropped to –30 on the way back?"

"I remember," she sighed. "Tim and I almost froze our feet when the heater didn't work well." She shivered just thinking of it.

We had concluded driving to Minnesota for Christmas was simply too risky and buying airline tickets for four people was totally out of the question. No one was coming over for Christmas either; I just didn't have the energy to invite anyone. We would be spending Christmas alone.

I was startled when the doorbell rang. It was dark outside, and we weren't expecting anyone. Rachel went to open the door, and then said, "Mom, there's a box on the doorstep — with presents… and nobody is out here!"

Who could have left it? It was indeed a mystery. The box contained numerous packages wrapped in bright Christmas paper. Each had a typewritten tag: Open Dec. 14, Open Dec.15. There were a total of twelve — the "Twelve Days of Christmas."

It was December 14th, and the tag for that day was attached to a turkey still wrapped in the plastic from the store — so we wouldn't miss the fact that it needed to be put into the freezer immediately, and not get placed under the tree by mistake! The tag read:

Our LOVE is given anonymously, so enjoy fun with your family, but don't tell anyone please.

I put the turkey in the freezer and the rest of the gifts under the tree. After that, we gathered each day as a family to open one more gift. Each one had a clever little note. We would try to guess what each package contained. It became a game for us. Even our son joined us on occasion. As the days passed we discovered potatoes, sweet potatoes, a package of marshmallows, cranberries, packages of gelatine, pickles, olives, cans of green beans, corn, mints, ginger ale and nuts.

All together the packages made a complete Christmas dinner for four people. As we opened each package, we realized an unknown

Canadian friend was thinking of us, loving us, wishing us a wonderful Christmas — someone who wished to remain anonymous.

We opened the 12th package on December 25th. But it turned out we didn't need to use our packages of food on Christmas Day because a family from work kindly invited us over for Christmas dinner. We wouldn't be spending Christmas alone after all! Instead we used those food packages for our New Year's Day dinner. We felt so blessed, and were so thankful to be loved!

Now, two decades later, that difficult year is a distant memory. We never found out who gave us the anonymous Christmas gift. At first I wanted to know, but later it became unimportant. I'm thankful for the Canadian spirit of kindness and generosity that came at a time we desperately needed to know we were not alone after all.

~Janet Seever
Calgary, Alberta

20

Night on Grouse Mountain

Carry out a random act of kindness, with no
expectation of reward, safe in the knowledge that
one day someone might do the same for you.
~Princess Diana

I t was my last night in Vancouver. It was a beautiful summer day in late June and I'd been staying with friends in North Vancouver. With the evening to myself, I knew exactly what I wanted to do. The previous year I'd spent three months living in the Kitsilano neighbourhood of Vancouver, recovering from a broken heart. Vancouver had provided me with the sea and mountain air that enabled my healing to begin. I had walked on the autumn beaches and the seawall, climbed the mountain trails, and fully explored this beautiful city.

Over the past week I had revisited many of those places. On my last night I wanted to take the cable car up Grouse Mountain to enjoy the spectacular view of Vancouver and English Bay, and watch the sunset from the peak.

I learned there was a bus that ran every half hour to the base of the cable car. It was getting late, so I shoved some cash in my pocket and headed out. I found a bus stop, but when thirty minutes had passed with no bus I started walking. I reached the next stop, and still no bus. I kept walking until finally an hour had passed, and I realized it would soon be too late to enjoy the sunset. Eventually I reached a point where the road began to climb the mountain. Here, on the darkening street, standing at the last bus stop, I gave up on my plan. I was very disappointed and also hungry. Spotting a convenience store across the road I dashed across and bought a snack.

As I left the store, lo and behold along came a bus. I raced across the road and up the steps, the door closed and off we went. There was no one else on the bus, so I sat down behind the driver and we began to chat. I spoke about my frustration waiting so long for the bus and the driver, whose name was Bill, was mystified and very apologetic. As we chatted, the whole experience began to take on a surreal quality as we carried on up the mountain road. By now I realized I probably didn't have enough money to complete my pilgrimage — I'd spent it on the snack. When I asked Bill how much the cable car cost, he confirmed my fear — I was now about three dollars short. I figured I would simply keep going, and return back down with the bus.

When we arrived at the parking lot Bill told me the transfer he'd given me would get me back on the bus when I was ready to go back down. It was then I told him I'd have to return now with him; I no longer had enough money for the cable car.

"How much are you short?" he asked. "Three dollars?"

When I nodded yes, he reached into his pocket and handed me three dollars. "Here, take it. My treat. I'm not attached to it; it's only money." He brushed aside my mild protests and confusion, and insisted.

I found myself stunned by these events. The entire experience seemed to be outside of life, like a page with a single paragraph that's been highlighted with a yellow marker. I gratefully accepted the money from this total stranger and, with some confusion, descended the bus.

"I'd come up with you if I could," he called, "but I gotta take this bus back after the next car comes down." I waved to him and hurried to the cable car.

As the ascent began, the bus quickly disappeared from view. Once at the top, I found a place to perch just as the sun began to set. As I sat there at the top of Grouse Mountain, enjoying the spectacular view and the sun setting over English Bay, eating my snack, I thought about the special gift I had just received. I knew Bill, from his point of view, had only given me three bucks. But from my point of view, he'd given me my night on Grouse Mountain. I was full of awe.

I wondered what it all meant. Did I now owe him something? Or had I somehow earned this gift and it had come out of my own "good" karmic bank account? Upon reflection I decided it was both. I was sure I needed to somehow repay this gift, but I was also pretty sure I would never see this kind soul again. Right there I vowed to watch for an opportunity to pay forward this gift to someone else in need.

Later, as I descended the mountain in the cable car, my heart was full of gratitude for my last night in my favourite city. At the parking lot I hurried aboard the waiting bus with the faint hope that I might find Bill. But it was a stranger to whom I handed the transfer, and the last leg of my evening's adventure passed in silence.

***

Back home in Toronto the memory of the experience remained with me. Then, a few months later, the opportunity I'd been watching for occurred.

I was at Sears to buy some vacuum cleaner bags. In front of me in the checkout line was an elderly woman buying a pink nightgown. The clerk rang up her purchase and asked her for fourteen dollars. The woman slowly dug out her money, and began to count out her bills. Then she began with shaking hands to count out quarters and dimes, then the nickels, and finally the pennies. I watched with dismay when she ran out at thirteen dollars.

"How much was that again dear?" she asked.

"Fourteen dollars," the girl replied, "you owe me another dollar."

The poor woman, embarrassed and defeated, was about to give up when I reached into my wallet and handed a dollar to the clerk saying, "Here's a dollar. Is that all you need?"

"Sure that's fine," she responded. She finished the sale, put the nightgown in a bag and handed it to the woman.

The woman was overcome with the experience, and I knew just

how she felt. To me it was only a dollar, but as far as she was concerned, I'd given her the new nightgown she needed. I felt warm and fuzzy inside. Maybe that's how Bill had felt back there in his bus at the foot of Grouse Mountain.

Looking at me, she said, "Oh, thank you dear! You are so kind! God will bless you for this!"

I took her hand and looked into her aging eyes. Somehow, I managed to say, "He already has. Believe me, He already has."

As I walked to my car I danced a little dance of happiness, filled with gratitude for the joy of giving I had experienced. I thanked the universe for this special experience, and the opportunity to give back. And I thanked Bill for his generous heart.

~Janet Matthews
Aurora, Ontario

Because of Bob

*You give but little when you give of your possessions. It
is when you give of yourself that you truly give.*
~Kahlil Gibran

I stared into the empty coffee cup as if the answers to all my
problems were written on the bottom. But it was as empty as
my life seemed to be that night. As busy as I was with work and
other activities, I felt something was missing. Something had to
change. It was time to immerse myself in life and connect with other
human beings in a way where I could make a difference. I made a
decision right then to find a way to volunteer.

I connected with the Children's Wish Foundation of Canada, a non-
profit organization that grants wishes to children with life-threatening
illnesses. They were glad to have me.

The morning of my first "tour of duty" dawned bright and warm — a
perfect day for the picnic, aka "Wishnic," at the Toronto park to which
I'd been assigned.

I found a cold drink to beat the heat and began strolling the
grounds, while keeping an eye out for a group described to me only as
"The Characters." My job, I'd been told, would be to "look after" them.

It was the raucous laughter that first caught my attention. I turned
to see a small band of what appeared to be very jovial garbage collectors traipsing toward me. They joked and jostled, and each carried a
lumpy green garbage bag slung over one shoulder.

"Hi, I'm Bob," said one. "We need a place to change."

"Of course — over here," I said, escorting them to a private area. I watched, fascinated, as before my eyes they transformed into instantly recognizable cartoon characters. There were red plush tongues, big goofy gloves, oversized pearls and giant shoes.

Once they were dressed, they filed into the picnic area, where they were greeted with squeals of laughter from the enthralled children. The kids swarmed all over them, hugging, kissing, giggling and squeezing. A surge of unexpected emotion swept over me, and suddenly I wanted to be more than just an observer.

I approached Bob and said, "I notice there's a full bag left in the change area. Are you missing someone?"

"As a matter of fact, we are," he answered with a twinkle in his eye. "Help yourself and come join the fun."

Before I knew it I was Simon the Chipmunk, complete with furry horn-rimmed glasses. The children charged me on sight. They climbed onto me and hung on like little koalas. I was laughing right along with them, enjoying their joy. When finally they'd had enough of Simon, I had a moment to actually breathe. Sweat trickled down my face and my hair was plastered to my head, but my heart was full.

And then I spotted him. Across the park, a child sat quietly in his wheelchair, away from the crowd. I lumbered over and knelt awkwardly beside him. When he smiled and did his best to hug me, the discomfort I felt instantly evaporated. He raised his hand and gently pressed it to my furry face as he gazed deeply into my eyes. At that moment his limitations fell away and he was just another child enjoying a picnic — a child wise in the ways of getting the most from each moment.

I was captivated by his gaze and stilled by the pressure of his small hand. I forced my eyes to stay dry, even while my heart ached. All the trappings of success couldn't match this. I had connected with this child, and in doing so had become one again myself. The moment became etched in my memory.

The memorable day ended, and somehow many months passed before I was to have another such moment. The voice over the phone said, "You probably don't remember me, but my name is Bob and I had the costumes at the Wishnic."

"Not remember you? How could I forget you?" I exclaimed. "It was one of the best days of my life!"

Bob had called to invite me to a reunion of the characters, which I learned were known as the SAPS. Using Bob's last name, the initials stood for "Savuluk's All Purpose Sillies." I was touched that he considered me and I immediately accepted.

"Thanks so much for coming, Leslie," said Bob when I arrived. "By the way, I have something for you," he continued, handing me an 8 x 10 photo of the SAPS at the Wishnic. "Oh, and this too," he said, placing a video in my other hand. Then he dug into his jacket pocket and produced three tiny toy chipmunks. "Can't forget these," he grinned. "Now go enjoy the party."

By the end of the evening, I was in the SAPS once more, this time as a very famous bouncing tiger. Thrilled to be part of this eccentric group again, I decided to learn more about them and, in particular, more about Bob.

We met in a coffee shop and during our conversation he offered me a glimpse into his life. When I asked him where the costumes came from, he responded modestly, "Oh, I make them. I pick up all sorts of odds and ends — inner tubes, hoops, liquid latex, that kind of thing. I find the clothes at Goodwill. It takes about fifty hours to complete one costume, and then there's repair and maintenance work as well. It's become pretty involved, but it didn't start that way. The costumes were originally meant for Halloween, but then my friends and I decided we could put them to better use. So we contacted some local charities, and that's how the SAPS were born."

I was moved by the quiet conviction of this seemingly ordinary man who did extraordinary things. When I asked about the rest of his life, he said simply, "I work for the city, cleaning streets and doing snow removal. But most of my spare time is taken up with SAPS. But when his smile faded and he looked thoughtful, I asked if anything was wrong.

"You know Leslie, it's probably silly, but sometimes I worry about who will take over when I'm not around. I even made a tape of myself making a costume, complete with step-by-step instructions." Not sure how to respond, I just nodded my head. I couldn't imagine who could fill this man's giant shoes.

Our coffee was long cold, but I asked one more question. "Why do you do it?"

"Because humour heals," he answered promptly. "When we put on those costumes, we become kids again. And if our hugging and dancing and goofing around can make the kids forget their pain and suffering even for one moment, well, then..." I had my answer.

I was a proud member of SAPS for over ten years and whenever I "donned the fur" I felt like I was really doing something that mattered. Bob did eventually retire, and sadly, nobody took over for him. He did, however, have a grand farewell party and I am now the proud owner of one Tigger costume! I often think of all the joy those hand-made characters brought to countless children and their families. It's partly because of the people who actually wore the costumes and I guess I can claim a little of the credit as well. But mostly, it was because of Bob.

~Leslie Lorette
Toronto, Ontario

22

Shipwreck

All things bright and beautiful, All creatures great
and small, All things wise and wonderful,
The Lord God made them all.
~Cecil Frances Alexander, Hymns for Little Children

It was late afternoon when our canoe slipped from the mouth of the Gibson River into the silvery sparkle of the lake and headed for home. My husband and I had spent the sunny June morning checking the numerous beaver lodges, dams, and bank dens that crisscrossed the length of the meandering Gibson River. The many obstacles made the river challenging to navigate for boaters, leaving an unspoiled natural environment — perfect for the kind of quiet observations so pertinent to Ron's research.

My field biologist husband was gathering information on the beaver population for a book he was writing. Earlier, when I was packing his lunch Ron had said, "Why don't you come with me and try out your new camera? I'll do the bulk of the paddling and you can be the lookout."

"Great idea," I responded. "I'll pack some extra water and trail rations."

The sun was still shining but the air was cold and blustery. Unwelcome wind gusts buffeted our canoe as we headed out of the river and onto the lake. "Pick up your paddle," called Ron, "the wind is getting stronger!" I grabbed my paddle, dropped to my knees in the front of the canoe, and dug in.

Partway across the lake I noticed a small movement in the water about seventy-five feet ahead. Waving my right arm and pointing I called out, "There's something in the water!"

Intrigued, we paddled harder, while Ron steered to bring us up to the object on the left. The thrashing remained more or less in the same spot, so in just a few strokes we were about ten feet away.

It appeared to be a small animal struggling in the water. We were still at least half a mile from shore, so how it had come to be in that situation was certainly puzzling.

One more stroke and Ron shipped his paddle and waited, hand ready, as we approached the struggling creature.

"Steady the canoe," he called. Unlike Ron, I was not a seasoned paddler, but I feathered my paddle as best I could to keep us balanced while he reached into the water. It was a chipmunk! How did it get there? Then, just as Ron reached forward to grasp it, the little creature began to sink, small silvery bubbles escaping from its open mouth.

"Oh no!" I cried, as I held my breath and said a prayer.

In desperation Ron leaned forward and plunged his hand and arm into the nippy water, almost upsetting us in the process. But he managed to grab the descending little body and bring it to the surface. It was quickly apparent that the chipmunk was hypothermic, and had stopped breathing.

Without hesitation, my hero husband began to gently massage the chippie's swollen belly until she disgorged about a tablespoon of water. He patted her back softly, but still she lay belly down on his hand without movement. So he opened the small mouth, fastened his lips to it and, breathing gently, began mouth-to-mouth resuscitation. Six tries failed to revive the little fur ball.

"Try again," I pleaded. This time the chipmunk uttered a little gasp, moved her legs and turned on her side, vomiting up more water. Then, she sat up in his hand. We both breathed a sigh of happy relief.

Shipwreck, as we christened her, was cold and shivering. Ron unbuttoned his shirt and popped the half drowned furry bundle inside, next to his left side so she could feel the warmth of his body and hear his heartbeat. Then we paddled vigorously toward home.

"I'll beach the canoe, and you pull it up as far as you can," he instructed. So while I dragged the canoe up onto the beach, he dashed up the steep embankment toward the house. Before going in I headed to the shed and grabbed the old birdcage and some wool rags to make a cozy nest.

When I entered the living room Ron was stoking the coals in the fireplace and adding kindling. I removed Shipwreck gently from inside his shirt, wrapped her in the wool rags, and placed her carefully in the birdcage.

Once the fire was crackling and warming up the room we set the cage on the hearth, and waited for her to revive. I made coffee while Ron exchanged his wet shirt for a dry one. Ten minutes passed, and then fifteen. We sipped the hot brew in silence, waiting anxiously for movement in the birdcage. Finally, twenty minutes later, the little chipmunk began to move. When Ron took her out of the cage, she sat placidly on his open hand while he carefully examined her.

"Look at this, Sharon," he said. "She has fresh talon marks on her right hip." Thankfully, these were the only injuries on her body. The mystery was solved. Shipwreck had been caught by a hawk. After grabbing her, the bird must have lifted her high in the air and headed across the lake with his squirming prize. Somehow the chipmunk had managed to wriggle free, and had fallen, likely from quite a height, into the water. We had no idea how long she'd been swimming, but it was clear she would have drowned if we'd not rescued her from the cold water of Gibson Lake.

By supper time that day Shipwreck appeared fully recovered. We had several feeding stations around our home, and there were plenty of places where a chipmunk could shelter. After leaving an extra stash of sunflower seeds and peanuts on the back step, we released Shipwreck outside the back door.

Early the next morning I noticed, through the window, that Shipwreck was staying close to the house. She must have spent the night in the rock and earthen wall at the back of our home, for there she sat staring at the window.

"Ron, come quick," I called. "Shipwreck is waiting outside the door for handouts." My husband always carried a pocket full of peanuts and sunflower seeds in his work pants. He stepped outside, preparing to throw some food to the chippie, but she leaped off the wall and scurried toward him. As soon as she reached his boots she scooted up his pant leg, selected the biggest peanut in his open hand, raced back to the row of pink granite, and disappeared between two boulders. From that day on Shipwreck lived in the rock wall, imposing a peanut toll every time anyone stepped out the back door.

She was a young chipmunk, but old enough to present us with a litter of two fluffy babies the following spring. Like their mother, her impish offspring soon learned how to demand a peanut and manipulate the humans that doted on them.

Although they healed, the talon scars on her side were always visible.

I'll never forget Shipwreck, nor her incredible story and how she touched my life.

~Sharon Lawrence
Minden, Ontario

23

The Red Phone

*Caring is a reflex. Someone slips, your arm goes
out. A car is in the ditch, you join the others
and push... You live, you help.*
~Ram Dass

Back in the 1980s I was a telephone repairman in Burnaby, British Columbia. I mostly did install and telephone repair work, and over the thirty-four years of my service with the telephone company I dealt with thousands of customers. One story stands out for me, however, and still makes me smile.

It was early September, shortly after Labour Day, when one afternoon I drove up to a small 1950s style rancher on the east side of Burnaby. The homeowner, a little old lady, answered the doorbell and let me in. The problem with the telephone, she explained, was that it was very noisy, for both incoming and outgoing calls. The telephone set was red, a deep dark red like you used to see in old spy movies — you know — for the "hot line" between the White House and the Kremlin. It was in beautiful condition for an old rotary phone — indeed it looked like new.

In addition to the red phone, just about everything else in the living room was red, black or white. It looked like it had been decorated in the 1950s or 1960s and nothing had been changed in all those years. The phone fit right in with the décor and had likely been chosen for its very redness!

"Hmm, I haven't seen one of these in years," I told the lady. "They are very hard to get parts for…" I opened up the old phone, hoping for a quick fix, but it was not to be. The handset cord had an intermittent open and that was causing the crackle on the line. Shrugging my shoulders, I said, "I'll see what I have in the back of the truck." On the way out to the truck I mentally ran through my stock. I didn't think I even had a rotary phone, let alone a red handset cord. Sure enough all I had was a sad-looking beige rotary. I brought it in to show her and said, "I could pull the cord off of this set and install it on yours, but that would look really dumb." And she agreed. But then she said, "The beige phone is okay."

I could see she was really sad to see her old red phone go. So I went ahead and installed the beige phone for her, and it looked totally out of place. I handed the old phone to her and said, "You keep this old set in a safe place, and if I can find the parts to fix it I will return — but no promises." She understood, and thanked me.

Returning to the office that night I asked around if anyone had an old red rotary wall phone that was any good for parts, but no one had. Then I put a notice up on the office board and at the Phonemart Store looking for parts.

Weeks went by with no luck. But then in late October I got a call from one of the guys. He had just recovered a red rotary with a good handset cord. Fortunately I had kept the woman's address clipped to my sun visor.

Off I went the next day, and then a few days later, and then a couple of weeks after that, but she was never home. I was starting to think that something had happened to her, or maybe she had moved, so I pretty much forgot about the whole thing.

As it would happen, that year it was my turn to work Christmas Eve and Christmas Day. Christmas Eve found me working in her neighbourhood, and when I passed her house I saw the lights on. I could see friends and family gathered in her front room around a gaily-lit Christmas tree. I parked the truck and hurried up the front steps with the red phone held behind my back. When the little old lady answered the door, she didn't recognize me. So I pulled the red telephone set out to show her, and said "Merry Christmas!"

Well, she started to cry. One of her son's quickly came to her side asking, "What's wrong, Mum?" "Nothing" she said. "This wonderful young man has come to fix my red phone."

So with her friends and family looking on, I tore both sets apart on the coffee table and built one good phone out of two old ones. After more cookies, coffee and cake than I could possibly handle, I made my way back out to the company truck with her family cheering and wishing me a "Very Merry Christmas." And you know what? Even though I had to work, it was!

~N. Newell
Duncan, British Columbia

An Inukshuk to Guide Me Home

No act of kindness, no matter how
small, is ever wasted.
~Aesop

Kurt walked into my office. "We'll be meeting in the board-room at eleven o'clock."

"Why the boardroom?" I asked nervously.

"It will be fine," he replied, as he smiled and left.

Oh no, I thought, *what's going on?* It was my last week of work at the school division, as I was returning home to the United States. I was a union member, and usually the group just bought a cake and said their goodbyes in the break room. I figured today there would be an American flag cake, and a casual send-off back to my home country. But Kurt wasn't a union member, he was a director. *Oh geez, not the boardroom.* My mind began racing. *What on earth was going on?*

Being a timid person, I was shaking at the thought of what was coming. It had been a rocky road coming to Canada. Just one sentence out of my mouth and heads would turn. People would ask "What part of the south are you from?" or "Where is Indiana anyway?"

I tried very hard to fit into my new life in Canada. As the years passed it became clear that in Canada I had found some of the kindest, friendliest and most generous people I had ever met. In the end, they came to realize that all Americans were not as they had imagined. I was truly blessed.

Now the time had come to say goodbye to my Canadian job. Still anxious, I gathered up my courage and walked into the boardroom of the school division. I couldn't believe my eyes. The room was filled with union members and administration and board members, and the screen was set up for a presentation. I was escorted to a table that was covered with gifts and cards. There was a Canadian flag cake.

I couldn't even speak. They began the presentation with a warm Canadian send-off to this American girl. It was clearly not what I was expecting. As I read the cards, tears filled my eyes. I realized I had been accepted. I was loved by these wonderful people, and it was overwhelming.

I thanked everyone and told them I would love to give a speech but I was afraid I would cry — just as the tears began to roll down my cheeks. Everyone laughed and clapped. I laughed at myself. Then, just when I thought it was over and I could walk out before breaking down completely, the hostess said, "And now we have a special guest to present you with a gift." *There's more?* I thought to myself.

The doors to the boardroom had been closed during this time and, as she sat me in a chair, the doors slowly opened. Through the boardroom doors walked a fully dressed and decorated Canadian Mountie carrying a large present. I became totally choked up and was simply in awe. Then my friend gave a beautiful speech about me and how much I was loved. The Mountie handed me the gift and that's when I broke down, overcome with emotion. I opened the package and inside was an Inukshuk. My friend then told the story of the Inukshuk, and what it represented: "The Inukshuk will always guide you home," she said.

I could not have been more honoured or felt more valued than I did by these wonderful Canadian people. Years have passed, and I have long since returned to the United States. Though by birth I am an American, I will always have a little Canadian in my heart. And in my yard, pointing north, is my Inukshuk, telling me I have another home outside the boundaries of my land.

~Lacy Gray
Clarksville, Indiana, USA

Chapter 4

The Spirit of Canada

Honouring Those Who Served

We honour those who have given their lives
serving Canadians and helping people
of other nations.
~Author Unknown

On the Highway of Heroes

We are planting 117,000 trees along this 170 km
stretch of highway — one tree to honour each of
Canada's war dead since Confederation.
A living, breathing memorial.
~A Tree for Every Hero — Highway of Heroes Tribute

I went and stood on a bridge one night. I was part of a crowd, yet I was alone, listening. All of us were watching the ebb and flow of traffic from a Highway 401 overpass, facing east toward Kingston. The sky was beautiful, the blue turning to pink and gold as day faded to evening, but no one was interested in the sunset. We were there for a reason, to recognize our fallen soldiers.

The 172-kilometre stretch of the 401 Highway in Ontario, from Canadian Forces Base Trenton to Toronto, has officially been renamed the Highway of Heroes in remembrance of the heroes who served our country. In their long and final journey home, the bodies of soldiers killed in the line of duty are brought to CFB Trenton and then transferred to the coroner's office in Toronto. Each and every one of these soldiers, killed in Afghanistan since Canada's mission began there in 2002, has travelled along that same route, along that same highway.

For those of us who live along that route, along that highway, this has created a unique opportunity. It's an opportunity to show our support for the troops, and to pay our respects to the soldiers who have lost their lives in service to their country. It is an opportunity but also a responsibility; it feels like those of us who live in this small portion of Ontario are standing for all Canadians, from all corners of the country.

Residents, police officials and firefighters gather on 401 overpasses along the route, as the motorcades carrying the bodies of the soldiers killed in Afghanistan pass by.

I don't know how long we stood waiting that day but suddenly I could sense a change in the mood of the crowd. Conversation faded to silence as the highway seemed somehow to empty. All I could see was a long line of headlights led by Ontario Provincial Police vehicles, their lights flashing but their sirens silent as they approached the overpass. As the motorcade passed beneath us in eerie silence, we all turned to watch it continue on its way west until it disappeared into the setting sun.

The crowd silently dispersed, heading north and south off the bridge to cars parked along the road. As I walked to my car I noticed the number of license plates with the red poppy veterans insignia. Soldiers from a different time, survivors from a different war, come to pay their respects to young fallen soldiers from this time, and this war.

I fight back tears, as do many, in the walk from the bridge, thinking of the families of these brave soldiers. I wonder if they feel the outpouring of respect and support from all the people lined up, bridge after bridge along the highway. I hope they draw some sense of comfort from these strangers, and hope they feel a little less alone along their journey.

Since that day I have stood on that bridge in a winter storm when the air was so cold and the wind so harsh I could no longer feel my hands or feet. The repatriation ceremony was delayed, and our wait became painfully long, but no one left the bridge, no one gave up to seek shelter and warmth, because we had not yet done what we came there to do.

I have stood on that bridge and cried; the procession passing beneath us as a piper played "Amazing Grace."

I have stood on that bridge and watched as a military vehicle, travelling east to CFB Trenton, pulled off the highway and three soldiers made their way up to the bridge. They then shook hands with every person there, thanking us on behalf of all military personnel.

I have stood on that bridge with the mother, sister and friends of soldiers stationed overseas, all of them there to pay their respects, and hoping never to see the view of this bridge from a military motorcade.

And on one cold winter day I stood and watched the procession approach, and saw a child's hand, covered in a red mitten, extend out the window of the limousine to wave in acknowledgement to those of us on the bridge.

There is always some small occurrence to make each time on the bridge unique, and yet the feelings of sadness, of respect and of pride are always the same.

~Deborah Lean
Coburg, Ontario

26

Pilgrimage to Holland

They shall not grow old, as we that are left grow old;
age shall not weary them, nor the years condemn.
At the going down of the sun, and in the
morning, we will remember them.
~Laurence Binyon, "Ode of Remembrance"

I never met my Uncle Craig, my mom's only brother, but I felt I knew him because she, Nan, and Gramps talked of him so many times. A picture of him sat in a prime spot in our living room. Athletic and handsome, with blond wavy hair, Craig was a beloved son, brother and friend. Like me, Uncle Craig had loved to draw. Up in Nan's attic there was a trunk full of his old books and sketches from his childhood of deer, raccoons and rabbits. As he got older the sketches were of flags, guns, and soldiers in battle. But that wasn't surprising; it was 1939 and Canada was at war. Many of Craig's friends and neighbours were enlisting and going overseas. In July 1942, just shy of his twentieth birthday, Uncle Craig enlisted. After training he became a proud member of the Essex Scottish Regiment. He was a dispatcher and drove a motorcycle over the fields of the Netherlands and Germany.

Uncle Craig wrote home often. He loved the regular care packages Nan and Gramps and relatives sent — especially Nan's homemade white Christmas cake. Sadly, after serving three years overseas, and only weeks before the war ended — he was hit by mortar fire. He died on April 12th, 1945, and was buried overseas.

Shortly after his death, Nan and Gramps received a letter from Gerard and Soje Sanders in Dieren, Holland. Mr. Sanders was manager of the local hospital, where his wife also worked. They had no children. They had been given Craig's name, along with those of other young Canadian boys who were buried in the Holton Cemetery, fifty-six kilometres from their home. They asked my grandparents if they could look after Craig's grave.

That letter opened up an ongoing correspondence and instant friendship between our families. It began with black and white photos of the Sanders standing by Craig's well-maintained gravesite. The gravestone read: *Pte. C. Mclean Alles, Canadian Infantry Corps, 12th of April, 1945, Age 22.*

Our family sent photos of Nan and Gramps, Mom and Dad, my two older brothers and me to the Sanders, so they would get to know Craig's family.

Finally, in 1964, while on their first trip abroad, Mom and Dad made arrangements to meet the Sanders and visit Craig's grave. The following summer the Sanders came and stayed with us for a week. They were wonderful people, and the relationship continued to grow. In the early 1970s my oldest brother visited them while backpacking across Europe. But it wasn't until the summer of 1972, five years after my gramps had passed away, that Nan was able to make the trip to Holland to see her beloved son's grave in person. My mom and dad and I went with her.

We arrived in Holland on a bright sunny day in late August. The Sanders met us at the airport and took us to their simple four-room flat in Dieren. They served us homemade soup, neatly cut sandwiches and a pot of tea. After lunch, we drove to the Holton Cemetery.

Although Nan and I had both seen many photos of the cemetery and the gravesite, neither of us was prepared for that moment. It started with a long walk up wide, well-worn stone steps, and then through tall iron gates that opened up into the cemetery. The grounds were beautifully maintained. Freshly watered green shrubs and tulips of every colour filled the air with a sweet, inviting fragrance. But it was our first steps into the cemetery that hit us like a hard blow to the chest. There before us stood acres and acres of gravesites. Rows upon rows of simple white markers, each one honouring a young man or woman just like Uncle Craig. As we read the markers, we learned that the vast majority of these brave young soldiers were twenty-five years old and younger.

As we got closer to Craig's grave, I felt Nan's hand tighten in mine. She was shaking. My mom and dad each took one of her arms for support. Three feet from Craig's grave, Nan's legs gave out. She dropped to her knees. For the first time I saw my loving, courageous Nan weep openly. Over twenty-five years of pain burst open in a flood of tears.

Later that night, Nan tried to apologize for breaking down in front of me. "It's funny," she said. "My mind knew he was gone, but after all these years there was still a little part in my heart that hoped it was just a bad dream. Seeing Craig's grave today for the first time made it all so final. It felt like losing my son all over again."

The next day we met the Sanders at their flat for a light lunch before returning to the airport. Gerard and Soje wished us a safe journey and presented Nan with a delicate porcelain tulip broach. Hugging her through tears, this beautiful couple thanked her for her friendship. But mostly they thanked Nan for her son Craig, the heroic Canadian boy who like so many, left his loving family to travel thousands of miles to fight and do battle — in a country he'd never been to, for a nation of families he never met. All so they could be free.

"We are eternally grateful to you, our dear Canadian friend, for all you have sacrificed and given us," Mrs. Sanders said. At that moment, when Nan and Mrs. Sanders embraced, thousands of miles from our home, I was never more proud of Nan, my Uncle Craig, and of our country.

~Cheryl E. Uhrig
Newmarket, Ontario

Author's Note: I was seventeen years old when I made that visit to Holton Cemetery. I returned in 1996 with my thirteen-year-old son Michael, our dear friend Marie and her family. The Holton Cemetery is still beautifully maintained and we remain grateful to the wonderful people of Holland.

27

The Christening Gown

The greatest glory of a free-born people is to
transmit that freedom to their children.
~William Harvard

George Harbert lived in Montreal, Canada with his wife Gertrude, and their two daughters Ruby and Gertie. It was an exciting time to be living in one of Canada's greatest cities. But half a world away events were unfolding that would change their lives forever.

On August 4, 1914, Canada, as a member of the British Empire, entered The Great War. And, like so many brave Canadian men, George would be heading overseas to join the fight. It was always heartbreaking when a man had to leave his family and go to war, but it was especially heartbreaking for George because he had only recently learned that Gertrude was pregnant with their third child.

Canadians were quickly involved in the thick of the fighting in France. The conditions at times for soldiers in the front line trenches could only be described as horrific. Canadian casualties started piling up. Every time the newspaper was published, Gertrude would review the list of the men who had been killed and breathe a little easier until the next one.

Gertrude felt very alone as she approached the end of her pregnancy. She worried, too, because she had heard of wives who religiously checked the newspaper lists as she did and then received a telegram instead reporting their husband's deaths. So when a package arrived in the mail one day, from overseas, she was terrified. Were these her husband's personal effects?

But when she opened the package she discovered that George had sent her a beautiful christening gown for their new child! George was alive, and from the bloody battlefields of Europe, he was participating in the birth of his third child in the only way he could.

On February 11, 1915, Gertrude gave birth to a lovely baby girl she named Helen Catherine Harbert. And when Helen was christened she was wearing the beautiful new gown that her father had sent.

It was another three and half years before the war came to an end. At 11 a.m., on the 11th day of the 11th month of 1918, the Armistice was signed and the Great War was over. In Canada, November 11th came to be known as Armistice Day. Not long after that, George came home and was reunited with Gertrude, Ruby and Gertie. And for the first time, he got to meet Helen, who was now three years old.

George was lucky because 65,000 Canadians were killed in World War I, and 172,000 returned home wounded. That meant that of the 424,000 Canadian soldiers who went overseas to fight, more than half were either killed or wounded. From that day forward, all Canadians would gather on November 11th, Armistice Day, to remember their service and sacrifice. Their efforts in battles like Vimy Ridge literally put Canada on the world map. Government officials and veterans wanted to do more to remember a sacrifice so great, so Parliament changed the name from Armistice Day to Remembrance Day. They also moved our Canadian Thanksgiving from November into October to allow the focus in November to be totally on the soldiers who gave their lives for Canada.

And the christening gown? Well, generations of Harbert children have been christened in that tiny gown. Helen Harbert, the first to wear it, was my mother. Many years later I was christened in it. My son, James, was christened in the same gown and a few years back my grandson, Troy, was christened in it. And in November 2015, one hundred years after it was first used, my granddaughter Amber was christened in the gown that her great-great-grandfather George sent home from overseas during the war. Five generations of my family are tied together by this gown. For our family, it is this celebration of life that is the spirit of Canada.

~Chris Robertson
Fort Saskatchewan, Alberta

28

The Trouble with Dad

If the only prayer you say in your life is
thank you, that would suffice.
~Meister Eckhart

My sixteen-year-old brother had gone downstairs to work on a small motor. His glove caught in the flywheel, and when he emerged through the trap door that led from the cellar of our old farmhouse, his right hand was twisted at the wrist in an awkward angle. The shock on my mother's face told me something was terribly wrong. The urgency with which she hustled him off to the hospital fifteen miles away alarmed me, and I was left alone with Dad.

I was only four and I didn't know what to think. *Would they cut off my brother's broken arm? Would he die? Maybe you bled to death if you broke your arm. And what if Mom never came home again? Who would look after me?*

I so much wanted someone to reassure me, but I couldn't ask Dad. You didn't ask him stupid questions or he would get angry. And you didn't make noise when he was around either. And you never, ever let him hear you cry.

I didn't understand it at the time, but I had just encountered the first emotional roadblock in my relationship with Dad. He just sat in his rocking chair that day reading the newspaper as if nothing had happened, as if I wasn't even around. I huddled behind his chair, where I could be close, but not be seen as a bother. And I was still there, cold and cramped and hungry, when Mom came home.

I started school, and despite getting good grades and being an obedient daughter, Dad seldom seemed to notice. In a rare mood he would occasionally admire one of my achievements, then just as suddenly throw up another barricade when he sensed the gap between us closing.

My poor mother was caught between the husband she loved and the daughter who feared him. She started showing me things from his past, from his World War I service. This was how I would grow to understand his pain.

Hanging on a nail in the hallway of our house was a khaki bag with a red cross on it. In it was a picture of a young man in Army clothes that Mom claimed was Dad, although I didn't recognize him in his uniform. Also in the bag were a few bullets, a knife, and a fork with one tine missing. A black booklet had his regimental number and name in it, the creased pages officially stamped by Canada's Department of Defence. One tarnished shoulder badge he had earned for outstanding marksmanship was in the shape of two crossed rifles.

I fingered the items with curiosity, especially a small photo showing lines and lines of wounded soldiers lying in an open field in France. At one point my father may have laid among them when a piece of shrapnel severed two fingers of his left hand, but I never asked him about being wounded. You didn't ask Dad much of anything, and certainly not about the war. Oh, sometimes when a drink or two loosened his tongue, he and an old fellow soldier would start to reminisce about the rats in the trenches, the lice that drove them crazy, the scream of the cavalry horses among the din of battle, and Army rations so awful they either chose hunger or stripped the food supplies from the slain. "All except the butter," I remember him saying. "You couldn't stomach the butter from off a dead man."

I learned very early never to approach Dad quietly from behind. Only once did I forget, and the hammer he was using at his workbench came hurtling toward me. I ducked, and then fled back to the house in terror. "Shellshock," my mother explained. "Involuntary reaction to any unexpected noise or movement." Thereafter I tried not to approach him unless it was absolutely necessary. He seemed incapable of demonstrating any affection, of identifying with any of my emotions. Never once did I hug him or sit on his knee. I had a hunch such overtures, if not rejected, would certainly not be reciprocated.

Dad was law and order, Mom justice and mercy. As a teenager, I often wondered why, indeed, Dad was the way he was — not that I didn't give him my respect. He was, after all, my father, and my mother defended him to the last. Sometimes I begrudgingly saw her unfailing devotion as an admirable trait; at other times, I saw it as blind devotion to a man who was not at all like the one she married. She told me as much herself, years later. We were discussing what is now called post-traumatic stress disorder, and how severe trauma can forever change a person's outlook, personality, and even values.

"Just think of your dad," she said. "He was never the same after the war. The emotional pain he suffered was so great, that rather than risk losing the ones he loved, he built up a wall that nobody could penetrate. All I could do was try to understand."

Instead of understanding, I blamed him. I failed to see those emotional wounds he suffered, and the permanent scars he bore as a result. Forgiveness did not come quickly, but settled slowly into my soul as year after year on November 11th the haunting sound of a bugle played "Last Post" from the Canadian War Memorial in Ottawa. When the television showed jerky footage of soldiers in the trenches of World War I, I wondered if my father was among them. Watching those youthful faces contorted in misery, my resentment toward him was slowly replaced by deep gratitude for the sacrifice he had made, and for which I had never thanked him.

The only public recognition for military service he ever received was at his funeral, when a local lad in dress uniform marched up to his open coffin and smartly saluted the old soldier lying there. Beyond that, nothing was ever said. That's how he seemed to want it.

Last November, while hurrying out of the supermarket I saw a frail old World War II veteran selling poppies, his wrinkled hands blue with cold. He was a small man, about the size of my dad, with those same steely blue eyes. I stopped.

"It's a miserable day," I said, trying to make small talk as I rummaged around in my purse for some coins.

The old veteran didn't respond. I dropped some change into his box and pinned a red poppy to my lapel. And then, very deliberately, I took his withered, veined hand in mine. Looking him straight in the eye, I said, "Thank you for what you did for us in the war. Thank you."

He never said a word, but tears escaped those steel blue eyes and trickled down the creases of his face. Temporarily, the wall that a toughened old soldier had erected in defence of his emotions crumbled.

For him it may have felt like defeat. For me it was a bittersweet victory.

Having failed to recognize the symptoms of my father's posttraumatic stress disorder, neither had I understood his suffering, much less forgiven him. He was the one who went to war, but in extending gratitude, at long last I am the one who is at peace.

~Alma Barkman
Winnipeg, Manitoba

29

VE Day on Bay Street

*Never in the field of human conflict was
so much owed by so many to so few.*
~Sir Winston Churchill

As I went up to the sixth floor of the Bay Street building where I was working, there was a buzz in the air, a distinct feeling of heightened anticipation. The building was on the corner of Bay and Richmond in the heart of Toronto's financial district. The Toronto Stock Exchange opened at ten, but as part of a team assigned to audit this brokerage firm, we started at nine.

I had been discharged from the Canadian Army in 1943 for medical reasons, and had resumed my career as a student in chartered accountancy. I was now twenty-one years old.

It was May 8, 1945, and still early, but knowing something was about to happen, people had already started arriving. There had been new developments all week, and we knew that the Germans were on the verge of signing the peace treaty that would end five years of war. Like everyone else, I had lost a lot of friends in the war. A lot of guys I went to school with had been killed.

There was a Canadian Press Teletype machine in one corner of the office. The news would just keep ticking away during the day, and if there was something important it would go "bong" and then somebody would go over and have a look at it. People checked it regularly to make sure that the news item wasn't something that might affect the market. Today, as the minutes ticked by, and the anticipation built, like all the other offices on Bay Street we just watched, and waited.

Suddenly, around 10 a.m., that Teletype machine started to go bong-bong-bong-bong-bong, and just kept bonging away. Soon, everyone was crowded around that Teletype machine, we saw the words we had been waiting to see for so long: "GERMANY SURRENDERS! HITLER IS DEAD! THE WAR IN EUROPE IS OVER!" And we learned then as well that a peace treaty had been signed by an Admiral Dönitz, who was now head of Germany.

Pandemonium broke out in the room and everyone began to cheer. Like magic, bottles appeared from desk drawers all over the office. And then, because the office faced onto Bay Street, we all ran to the windows to see what was happening below. There was no air conditioning in those days, so all the casement windows on the buildings opened up wide. And as we watched, on this early spring day, the street began to fill with people as they poured out of the buildings, and the noise of everybody cheering got louder and louder. Back then, there was a streetcar line on Bay Street, and it was now completely blocked from Queen Street south, and the streetcars were trapped. Instead of traffic, rejoicing people filled the streets.

There was a ticker tape machine in the office for all the transactions made on the Toronto Exchange, and the ticker tape was in rolls. So the girls in the office grabbed the rolls and started unrolling the tape and tossing it out the windows, and we had a real ticker tape affair. And when they ran out of ticker tape, they started tearing up telephone books and throwing bits of paper out the windows. All down Bay Street, we could see people doing the same thing, as the cheering throngs filled the streets and headed up to Toronto's City Hall to gather and celebrate.

Everything, including the stock exchange, shut down then, and I don't think it ever even opened that day. The streets remained filled with people all morning, and no one did any work that day. Unlike today, when a television news team would have filmed the excitement, then we only had radio. You just had to be there that day on Bay Street, to really know what it was like.

Five years — five dreadful years — of war were over. The future lay in front of those of us who were left. There have only been a few days in my life since then that have compared: the day I married my wife of fifty-two years and the days my two daughters were born. May 8, 1945, was without question, one of the most unforgettable days of my life.

~G. Norman Patterson
Toronto, Ontario

All in Vain?

The living owe it to those who no longer
can speak to tell their story for them.
~Czesław Miłosz, The Issa Valley

I t was my granddaughter Celeste's idea that we visit the
National War Memorial in Ottawa. I had been to many other
Remembrance Day services at the memorial at home. There I
marched and stood in silence with my family, friends and comrades from the Canadian Legion. I paid my respects and remembered
the conflicts, those who had fallen and those who survived, scarred
for eternity.

But today would be different. It was only a short walk across the
plaza to the Memorial, but it seemed that with every step a memory
would resurface. Perhaps it was the weather. It was a grey day, with
dark clouds. The chill wind whipped around my legs. The damp,
bone-chilling cold that seemed to be reserved for every November
11th was miserable.

I shivered. It was like this when I was captured, barely alive,
surrounded by the shattered bodies of men and horses lying in the
bloody mud. We were marched as prisoners, in wooden shoes, herded
like animals across Nazi-controlled Europe. I escaped twice, was twice
recaptured and finally exiled to the notorious Stalag 13. But I survived.

Prompted by today's martial music and the flags snapping in the
wind, memories of "liberation day" brought back memories of the Allies
arriving to be met by cheering crowds. I was free — free to wander

from country to country, to work camps and resettlement camps, and finally to a job in the Netherlands. It was hard, menial work; but I met my Tilly and found love, marriage, children, family and hope. Then the Soviet KGB came. They wanted me and my language skills for their intrigues. We fled to Canada where we faced more challenges — another language and a new culture. But we found peace.

I squeezed Tilly's hand a little tighter as our family group made its way across the plaza, seeking seats in the public viewing stands. The Memorial dominated the centre of the civic square. I could see the rows of satin-ribboned wreaths, their red poppies fluttering in the stiff breeze, waiting to be placed at its base. Just as we reached the stands, an official looking woman approached. Were we in the wrong place? She spoke but I couldn't hear all her words. She repeated her query more loudly. "Veteran?" I nodded. She smiled and motioned for Tilly and me to follow. Rows of chairs had been arranged in a special area at the front. Some were already filled with men and women, in and out of uniform, people our age.

Tilly and I were seated like honoured guests. A warm blanket was laid across our laps, and we were given a commemorative book and special coin. I watched the final preparations from a new perspective. Commands were barked and rows of today's young soldiers snapped to attention. A children's choir, dressed alike in red and white, took its place and began to sing. It seemed strange, their young voices singing old songs — from past wars and from new ones, calling for peace. My fellow veterans who could still march filed past and stood in silence, waiting. The service was similar to the many I had attended back home, just on a larger scale. I could not hear all of the words spoken, but I knew them by heart.

The clock in the Parliament Hill Peace Tower struck eleven and we silently listened to the mournful sound of the "Last Post." The assembled artillery fired their salute and all eyes turned skyward as the jets flew over with an incredible roar. Then, as if a celestial command had been given, those threatening clouds parted and the sun finally shone. The orderly ranks became a moving mob, returning to everyday life. The rest of the family re-joined us and we began to make our way through the crowd to place our poppies on the Tomb of the Unknown Soldier.

I was still lost in thought. Each November 11th, I asked myself the same question. It was good that we remembered, but had it all been in vain? Then I felt a tug on the sleeve of my coat. I looked down and saw a little girl smiling up at me. Still dressed in her red and white choir clothing, she appeared to be draped in the Canadian flag. Her bright eyes sparkled as she spoke. "Thank you! Thank you for fighting for our freedom!"

My heart swelled; what better answer could I have been given?

~Walter Sawchuk
Orillia, Ontario

A Bloom of Friendship

No one is as capable of gratitude as one who
has emerged from the kingdom of night.
~Elie Wiesel

While studying in Ottawa in the early 1980s, I never questioned why our capital was host to the Canadian Tulip Festival. Like Winterlude and other seasonal events, it just was. But in 1995 I came to understand the festival's origins. That year marked the 50th anniversary of the Liberation of the Netherlands and, to highlight the significant milestone, hundreds of Canadian war veterans travelled back to Europe to revisit the Dutch people and battlefields they had known half a century earlier.

There was substantial news coverage of the commemorative celebrations, and Peter Mansbridge from the CBC was there reporting live. As our Canadian war veterans proudly paraded through their streets, the Dutch people cheered and celebrated. The palpable joy and gratitude emanating from my television screen moved me to tears.

That week I learned how Dutch children help take care of the war cemeteries where Canadian soldiers, who never came home, are buried. The children decorate the graves with flowers in the spring, and light candles and place them on each grave every Christmas Eve. I also learned that the genesis of our annual Canadian Tulip Festival was a gift of 100,000 tulip bulbs from the monarchy of the Netherlands in 1945. This offering was to thank us for having provided safe haven to members of the royal family during World War II and, more importantly, to thank Canada for the pivotal role Canadian soldiers played in liberating the people of the Netherlands from Nazi rule. Every year since, Canada has been given 20,000 tulip bulbs from the Netherlands, and we will continue to receive this bequest in perpetuity. Why tulip bulbs? During the last months of the war there was so little food left the people were starving; many of the Dutch ate tulip bulbs to survive.

My uncle, Thomas Delaney, was one of the thousands of Canadian soldiers who fought to help free the Dutch people. In 1944, at age eighteen, he had enlisted in the Army and was sent overseas. On the morning of April 8, 1945, he was shot in the hip by a German sniper. He was then recovered by members of his unit, and hidden in a barn owned by a Dutch family with young children. Like many war veterans, when he returned home he never spoke much about his experiences during the war. It was only after his return from the Netherlands in 1995, when he recounted the joyous celebrations he had attended, that he finally shared his war story with me.

While he was visiting the Netherlands, with the help of a local historian from Holten in the Dutch province of Overijssel, my uncle was able to find the barn in which he had been hidden fifty years earlier. "The barn was painted a different colour," he said, "but I recognized it immediately. With this historian's help," he continued, "I was also reacquainted with one of the daughters of the Dutch farmer who owned the barn. She remembered the event in detail."

Uncle Thomas returned to the Netherlands in subsequent years, and each time he was treated with warmth, respect and admiration by the Dutch people. Health issues prevented him from attending the 70th anniversary celebrations in 2015, but I know he was there in spirit. For all these reasons I resolved to preserve my uncle's story, and, in my own small way, help teach children in this country what Dutch children have been taught, generation after generation, of the sacrifices our Canadian soldiers made so many years ago.

My first children's book, *A Bloom of Friendship: The Story of the Canadian Tulip Festival*, was the result of this promise. If stories of our past are not recorded, they are lost when the voices that experienced them pass on. May our proud Canadian heritage never be silenced, and let us all endeavour to preserve the precious threads of our history.

~Anne Renaud
Westmount, Quebec

A Poppy for Remembrance

*What the soldiers gave us is freedom
and the air to breathe democracy.*
~Mark Cullen

When I first arrived in Canada from Michigan, one of my editors told me that come fall, I should look for poppies. I had no idea what he was talking about and soon forgot. Adapting to our new surroundings was my all-consuming challenge. Canadians and Americans appear similar until you scratch the surface. I was quickly face to face with dozens of cultural differences, from where you buy your stamps to what's on the extra-value menu at McDonald's.

It was nearly November before I remembered my editor's remark about poppies. But I didn't have to look for them; suddenly, they were everywhere.

I noticed it first shortly before Halloween, when people started arriving at storefronts and gas stations holding boxes of red plastic poppies. I didn't think much of it at first as there is frequently somebody collecting money for something outside of Canadian stores. This, however, was different. Unlike most charitable donation collectors, there was no pitch. I also quickly realized no one was trying to avoid them. I watched people stop at these vendors, purchase a poppy and immediately pin it on their jacket. One after another. I was aware that Canadians celebrate Remembrance Day on November 11th, the same day Americans celebrate Veterans Day. I had even purchased paper poppies before in America. I figured this was something similar.

But it wasn't. Poppy boxes soon graced every counter of every business. Day after day, without comment, poppies were purchased for a donation — and worn. When I saw sales material, which was rare, it was simple and without agenda: "In Remembrance." Then, unannounced and without request for payment, two more poppies arrived in the mail. My husband came home from work with one. My children came home from school wearing poppies. Poppies were slowly taking over the coats, jackets and sweaters of every man, woman, and child around me. Eventually, I was embarrassed not to wear one.

I was even more embarrassed to ask why this was happening. I purchased a poppy, pinned it to my jacket, and went home to research Remembrance Day.

Poppies, I learned, are the symbol of the fallen soldier, made famous in the poem "In Flanders Fields." The author, Lieutenant Colonel John McCrae, a Canadian soldier who fought and died in World War I, was born in Guelph, Ontario, less than forty kilometres from where I live. Since 1921, Canada and all the British Commonwealth countries have worn poppies on Remembrance Day. The proceeds from poppy sales go to assist veterans and their families.

While it's true that Americans make similar gestures and have similar symbols, they splinter into a hundred different expressions according to the individual. This was different. Everyone was united under one symbol — a simple red poppy secured by a straight pin on the left lapel. On November 11th there were special services and official ceremonies, but to me, nothing could be as sincere a tribute as an entire population quietly wearing this symbol of the fallen soldier — and remembering.

The poppies lingered long after Remembrance Day, slowly fading off lapels like real blossoms fade off trees — a little at a time. But I kept mine. After two years, this will be my last Remembrance Day here in

Canada. Next year I will be home, observing Veterans Day like my fellow Americans. Still, I plan to wear my poppy. It may be a Canadian gesture, but it's universal in its powerful meaning.

~Nicole L.V. Mullis
Battle Creek, Michigan, USA

33

The Night We Were All Just Canadian

Under this flag may our youth find new inspiration for
loyalty to Canada; for a patriotism based not on any
mean or narrow nationalism, but on the deep
and equal pride that all Canadians will feel
for every part of this good land.
~Former Prime Minister Lester Pearson

While driving home on October 22, 2015, I heard the breaking news. Corporal Nathan Cirillo, an army reservist from Hamilton had been shot and killed while standing guard at the National War Memorial in Ottawa. As the day progressed more information came in and, along with other Canadians, I experienced a deep sadness.

Nathan had been a typical young Canadian with a son and a loving family. His goal had been to become a full-time soldier but, in the meantime, he was active in the reserves. As he stood on guard, unarmed, at the National War Memorial, he was shot without having a chance to defend himself. He probably barely even saw his killer. It seemed like he could have been the guy next door.

Five days later we were out of town and heading back to our home in the western Toronto suburb of Mississauga. Our regular route was jammed with traffic, so we decided to take an alternate way back through Hamilton. The sun was setting as we got to Hamilton, and streaks of bright orange and yellow painted the western sky. As we drove along Highway 403 we noticed one of the overpass bridges was crowded with people, cars and emergency vehicles with their lights flashing. At first we thought there must have been a major accident, but we soon discovered it was the same for every bridge we passed under. On the third bridge we saw a number of construction vehicles including dump trucks and graders. There were also a couple of cranes with strings of white lights that were flying Canadian flags.

I turned to my wife Susan and said, "This is so strange. Why are these vehicles blocking every overpass across the highway?"

"I don't know," she replied. "Let's turn on the radio and see what's going on."

It took less than a minute to hear the news. We were travelling east on the same highway that Nathan Cirillo's funeral procession would be taking as it travelled west to the cathedral in Hamilton. At that point we were about half an hour away from the funeral vehicles that were heading our way. Over the next few kilometres we began to see cars stopped along the side of the highway, their drivers and passengers standing outside. The farther we went the more vehicles were parked on the shoulder of the roadway — from pick-up trucks to cars and utility vans. Some people were saluting, others just quietly standing. It had turned dark and the wind was cold, yet more and more people had stopped to stand and wait for the funeral procession.

The radio host kept us updated on the progress of the funeral cars, and by the time we entered Mississauga we were only about five minutes apart. We were on a six-lane limited access highway, but I had a strong feeling that we too needed to pull off to the side. I shut off the engine, and we sat in silence and waited. A couple of minutes later we saw the funeral cars and the hearse, followed by a couple of police cars with flashing lights. It felt like time stood still as we sat on the shoulder of the highway. A young Canadian soldier — one of us — was passing by on his last journey. He was just twenty-four, but he would never see another sunrise or hug his five-year-old son again.

Once the procession had passed we started our car and slowly moved back on to the highway. Other cars that had stopped began moving as well. About a kilometre away we were approaching our exit from the highway, and slowed down as we got closer. The entire overpass bridge was packed with people of all ages. Parents were there with babies and young children. A few seniors were in the crowd as well as small groups of teenagers. Every race and ethnic group in Canada was represented on the bridge; they had all come to say goodbye to one of our own. Everyone was quiet; there was no need to talk. Most were carrying or waving Canadian flags. Some people were hugging each other and more than a few were brushing tears from their eyes. Several police cars and an ambulance were parked on the bridge, and as their lights flashed they illuminated the crowd around them.

On the bridge were a number of construction vehicles with their drivers standing beside them. These were working men — covered with dust and grime, having come directly from their work sites to honour this young reservist. I noticed one little boy about eight who was carrying a Canadian flag and holding his dad's hand. Tears streaked his father's face and, as this little boy looked up at his dad, we could see the sorrow in his eyes as well. It was at that moment that a wave of emotion swept over me. Not only had we lost a young man from Hamilton who was serving his country, but for that moment in time we were all united as Canadians; we were one. Regardless of our age, colour or cultural background — we stood together. I felt my eyes filling with tears as I watched the solemn crowd moving past us. We drove home in silence knowing this would be a night etched on our hearts for life — a moment in time when all our differences melted away, and we were all just Canadian.

~Rob Harshman
Mississauga, Ontario

Chapter 5

The Spirit of Canada

We're All in This Together

My friends, love is better than anger. Hope is
better than fear. Optimism is better than
despair. So let us be loving, hopeful and
optimistic. And we'll change the world.
~Jack Layton

34

The 2010 Winter Olympics

Canadian pride may not rest on our sleeves,
but it resides in our hearts.
~Steve Miller

L ike most Canadians, we were excited when Vancouver hosted the Olympic Winter Games in February 2010. Generally during the Olympics we cheered for our Canadian athletes from half a world away. This time was different. Now they were competing in our own country. Sweeter yet for my husband Don and I... we were staying with our two granddaughters, Jordan and Lindsay, in Kelowna, British Columbia while their parents vacationed.

On that first day, we tuned into the Opening Ceremonies just in time to see Canadian snowboarder Johnny Lyall leaping through the giant Olympic rings. He sure got our attention! Then, after First Nation leaders welcomed the world to Vancouver, we cheered as 2,600 athletes entered the stadium. Vancouver's BC Place was suddenly transformed into varied Canadian landscapes, and the entire opening ceremony gave us goose bumps and left us with tears of pride. When it came time to light the giant caldron, four iconic Canadian athletes appeared — Catriona LeMay Doan, Steve Nash, Nancy Green and Wayne Gretzky. It couldn't have been better.

A few days later, twenty-two year old Alexandre Bilodeau, a

freestyle skier from Quebec, dazzled us with his superb performance on Cypress Mountain to win Canada's first gold medal of the games. It was Canada's first gold medal ever won on home soil! The crowd was delirious with excitement… and so were we.

Then we got a call from our son Doug and his wife Cathy, who had stopped in Vancouver on their way home. They had obtained tickets to some Olympic events and urged us to join them for a few days. We were all excited as we piled into the car with the girls and headed across the Coquihalla Highway to Surrey.

That night, after supper we took the Sky Train to Robson Square in downtown Vancouver. When we got off the train, the six of us joined a joyous mob of thousands, most wearing red and white, and pressed so tightly together you could scarcely raise an arm. "Stay close," Cathy shouted. That wasn't hard since we were practically glued to each other. Suddenly brilliant laser beams flashed along a zip-line stretched between two office towers about three blocks apart. Athletes in uniforms representing various Olympic events sped along it to deafening roars from the crowd. Gas jet cauldrons ignited periodically with a burst of Canadian colours. Then came the dazzling fireworks display followed by choruses of "ooh's" and "aah's."

Friday morning the rain began. Armed with umbrellas and wearing parkas, scarves and gloves, we boarded the Sky Train to connect with the Cypress Mountain bus for the snowboarding event. We had to dodge puddles for about half a kilometre along the slushy, icy trail before reaching the venue, then climb about 200 steps to our seats. The rain showed no sign of stopping so we covered up with some trusty plastic garbage bags while watching the athletes trying to manoeuvre their course in the relentless downpour.

The cold wind and fog made it difficult for the competitors at the top of the mountain, and one spectator predicted, "They're all going to get pneumonia." But the athletes, displaying amazing tenacity and determination, seemed undeterred. After about four hours we were wet and shivering, our fingers and toes numb. We trudged back to the bus and an hour later retreated to a downtown Tim Hortons for a welcome bowl of hot soup.

That night was the semi-final hockey game between Team Canada and Team Slovakia. Don sat by a man in a wheelchair, a para-Olympian named Joe. "You should be wearing a red shirt, buddy," Joe admonished, and then pulled a red Canadian jersey from his duffel bag. Don could have explained that his own red shirt was drying after our wet morning on Cypress Mountain, but instead he simply thanked Joe and pulled the shirt on while Joe smiled his approval. Slovakia was a determined team, but when Canada pulled off a narrow 3–2 win, it was bedlam among the joyous, predominately Canadian, red and white clad crowd. The win assured Team Canada of a silver medal, and the opportunity to play Team USA for gold on Sunday.

After Doug, Cathy, and the girls left for home Sunday morning Don and I headed back to Robson Square. We hoped to roam around the area while intermittently checking on the gold medal hockey game, which would be televised on a giant, raised TV screen in the Square.

With an hour left before game time we managed to find a deli with a vacant table that had a clear view of a TV screen. We couldn't believe our good fortune and promptly ordered coffee and a pastry.

What a game it was! In the third period it seemed Team Canada had it wrapped up at 3–2 until Team USA scored with 24.4 seconds left in regulation time.

"Oh no!" everyone groaned. "We can't lose now!"

Could Canada still win? With the game in overtime, Sidney Crosby — "Sid the Kid" — answered the question decisively when he slammed in the winning goal and everyone went wild. Unbridled joy erupted... clapping and cheering. "Way to go, Crosby!" someone blasted exuberantly. There were no sour faces in that crowd! It was a great day for Canada — and we were there.

It was a good day for the deli, too. Tips were generous, and appropriately so, since forty people had enjoyed good food, excellent service and front row seats to the "Golden Game."

There was euphoria in the streets, with cheering, hugging and high-fiving between total strangers. Kids wearing red and white make-up raced along the streets holding Canadian flags as big as they were. While waiting for our Sky Train a rich tenor voice began singing "O

Canada" and within seconds there was a choir. How delightful to experience such exuberant, spontaneous expressions of Canadian Spirit!

This bond of pride and appreciation that Canadians share for our great country — usually quietly, found full and joyous expression during the 2010 Winter Olympics. The committed, talented athletes who competed for Canada inspired us. We were overjoyed for those who won medals.

As Canadians, we don't generally boast to the world about our country. It's not our nature. But that doesn't mean we don't realize how privileged we are to live in Canada. I suspect most agree we live in simply the best place in the world. Perhaps it is that shared bond of pride and deep appreciation that constitutes the "Spirit of Canada," and thrives in the hearts of Canadians all year round.

~Gerri Nicholas
Sherwood Park, Alberta

35

The Flood of
the Century

We fought side by side with neighbours and friends;
Yet the Red River kept rising, without end.
~Darrell Scarrett

It began with a freak spring blizzard the first weekend in April of 1997. Winnipeggers were blinded for forty-eight hours as gale-force winds dumped a hundred centimetres of heavy, wet snow. By Sunday everything looked pristine and new. The cars in my neighbourhood were mounded snowdrifts, and shops and buildings were thickly caked, like fancy snow palaces.

It wasn't until Monday that the blizzard's significance sunk in. The first words I heard when I entered the newsroom at the *Winnipeg Sun* for my 5:00 p.m. copy-editing shift were: "There's gonna be a flood."

Several editors had gathered around a primitive graphics display mapping the predicted water levels of the Red River over the next ninety days. Several cities and smaller towns along its banks, including Winnipeg, were at risk. It was a sombre briefing. Our city desk editor stroked his grey beard: "With this much snow so close to spring, it's gonna go straight into the Red." He rapped his knuckles once on the meeting table, signalling the meeting was over.

From that point forward, the "crest" of the Red — its highest point — became the focus of all activity, discussion, and for some — even their dreams.

One night, ten days after the blizzard, the news desk phone rang. The editor answered it, his voice terse as he responded, "Are they safe now?" And then: "I'll contact them." The call had come about two reporters at our rival publication, the *Free Press,* who'd been sent across the border to cover reports of flooding in Fargo, North Dakota. When the road washed out they'd had to abandon their vehicle and make their way through waist-high water to higher land.

President Clinton had already declared the entire Red River Valley a disaster zone. Then the flood claimed its first lives. A woman and her little girl had also been on that road in Fargo. They too left their car and fled for safety, but perished in the raging floodwaters. In the days that followed I thought of nothing but the safety of my fellow journalists, who were being sent out to investigate stories that placed them at high risk.

A few days later the CBC shifted 100% of its regional programming to flood coverage. We stopped having contact with the rest of the world, our attention focused solely on the minute-by-minute details of the impending "Crest of the Red" and its potential impact.

Ten days later the Crest of the Red came barrelling into the downtown core of East Grand Forks, North Dakota. The deluge started an electrical fire, and downtown was destroyed, leaving 35,000 people homeless. I wondered if this would happen to us, too. We had seventy days to go before the crest was expected to hit us.

An all-out sandbagging effort was now well underway. Every day, before my evening shift at the newspaper, I joined thousands of volunteers who rode in school buses to farms and homesteads with our sandbags.

Each bag weighed forty-five pounds. If you kept moving them from person to person fairly quickly they weren't too heavy. "These weigh as much as my six-year-old son!" a woman beside me wailed, as a sandbag slid out of her arms and down her leg, leaving a muddy streak in its wake. I bent down to help her lift it back up, and showed her how to hold it level — with her biceps outstretched, and her forearms curled like hooks around the bag. The line stopped and waited patiently until we could resume passing them forward again.

Each site had a crew director at the front directing bag placement, with the strongest volunteers at either end of the line for lifting and unloading. Advice was freely offered: "Wear work gloves, keep your forearms covered. Take ibuprofen before you leave in the morning. Get some juice in you, you look exhausted. Did you bring a hat?"

Sixty days to go and we were still sandbagging, strangers looking after each other. Like everything else, there was a knack to it, a rhythm, and many tiny adjustments that once learned, made it easier. Despite the daily exhaustion, the unrelenting fear, I experienced something else that was deeply heart-warming, a kind of moral ecstasy that built up inside of me. I credit it with my ongoing ability to jump out of bed for another day of sandbagging despite the aches and pains.

The morning the Canadian Army, Princess Patricia's Canadian Light Infantry, arrived in downtown Winnipeg, I heard boats on the Assiniboine River beside my building. There were three of them — each packed with Army personnel — as well as a helicopter. All of them were heading directly toward me. I felt suddenly dizzy with anxiety; it felt like a war zone.

The troops pitched in, digging trenches and sandbagging along with the rest of us. Much to-do was made of their arrival in the national media, the Army's humanitarian assistance coming, as it did, in the wake of the Somalia affair.

With every conceivable weak spot for kilometres now sandbagged, and the Crest of the Red now a mere seventy-two hours away, a potentially fatal flaw in the city's fortification system was discovered. Pulling out all the stops, a last-ditch (literally) effort began to erect what came to be known as the Brunhilde Dike. A Z-shaped breaker-wall made of dirt, rocks, sand, crushed cars and even old school buses emerged from round-the-clock labour, and heavy digging and levelling equipment.

When the seventy-two hours were up, Winnipeggers held their breath as the water rose and the Crest of the Red arrived. Would the dike hold? With only inches to spare the water stopped rising — and the dike held. Winnipeggers collectively breathed out… and the majority of the city was spared.

It was the end of May, and the flood clean-up was well underway.

Those who had not escaped the water's damage set about restoring their homes and businesses. I boarded the Via Rail train for a much-needed visit to family back in Ontario. As the passenger cars full of Prairie dwellers pulled away from the station, a porter offered us all drinks with tiny umbrellas and everyone cheered. As the wheels of the train picked up speed, the talk in the car became light, woven with laughter. I reflected on how I had grown during the whole experience, starting as a confused twenty-something, and becoming part of a community that had united to preserve life and property for everyone.

~Erin McLeod
Sault St. Marie, Ontario

36

Bonding at the Rink

*I have a huge interest in hockey because I
grew up in Canada, where it's kind of the
law that you love hockey.*
~Matthew Perry

Hockey is *huge* in Canada, particularly in my hometown, where the Toronto Maple Leafs are an institution. Despite not winning the Stanley Cup since 1967, their games are always sold out and millions tune in to watch on TV.

But I grew up in a family that had no interest whatsoever in hockey. My parents were decidedly not athletic, and although I had skating lessons, I never really learned how to skate properly. I had never even seen a hockey game until I spent a Saturday evening with a friend's family and they were all glued to *Hockey Night in Canada*. Sometimes I felt I'd missed out on our national passion.

When I met my future husband, he had been divorced for about three years. Dave's ex-wife and two young sons lived nearby, and he saw the boys every weekend. I was uneasy when I first met nine-year-old Mike and eleven-year-old Scott, and they were understandably shy and cautious. But everyone soon relaxed and after a few visits we felt more at ease and enjoyed spending time together.

Dave and his sons were huge hockey fans, and both boys played on local teams. When Dave and I went out on dates, we often went to the boys' games first, before heading off for dinner. They were a lot of fun! Dave taught me the basic rules, explaining what "offside" was and what "icing" meant. Both boys played well, and we had so much fun cheering them on.

While everything seemed right between Dave and me, I was still a bit uneasy about the situation. It was quite a change from my single lifestyle and I wondered what the boys really thought of me, in private. Did they worry that I would try to take their mother's place? Did they resent the time I spent alone with their father? And I was very uneasy about what their mother might think. After all, I was stepping into her world.

When Scott's team arranged a father and son game, Dave was excited and eager to join. He had grown up playing hockey and was very good at it. Since we had plans for later that night, I went with Dave to the arena. But once he got his skates on and went out on the ice, I was left on my own.

The arena had a closed off, heated area for spectators, but I felt uncomfortable there by myself, so I wandered out along the side of the rink. There were a few benches there, so I sat down to watch the game. Everyone was having a lot of fun, and Dave often waved to me as he happily skated by.

Then a woman came out of the parents' area and started walking toward me. I had seen her with the boys several times, so I knew she was their mother, but we had never met. Her smile was warm and reassuring as she sat down beside me and said, "Hi, I'm Mary Lou. Scott and Mike have told me a lot of nice things about you."

"They are wonderful boys," I said, with a sigh of relief. "They are always so nice to me."

At that moment, Dave skated by, close to the boards in front of us. At first he smiled just at me. Then he noticed Mary Lou beside me and did a classic double take! His eyes popped wide open as he glided halfway down the rink. He turned back and opened his mouth to say something, and then slid right into another father.

Both Mary Lou and I laughed at his reaction, then turned toward each other again and continued our friendly chat. Dave kept on playing, but glanced our way often. He looked worried, probably wondering just what we were talking about!

Dave and I have been happily married for thirty-eight years now. Mary Lou and I have become great friends over time. We have two wonderful grandchildren, and we attend their hockey games together. As easy as it all has been, I have never once forgotten Mary Lou's kindness, consideration and warmth at that awkward time. For me, that one particular hockey game became a watershed moment, one that changed my life.

All we need now is for the Maple Leafs to win!

~Julia Lucas
Aurora, Ontario

37

Stranded at Big Sandy

*It is wonderful to feel the grandness of Canada in
the raw, not because she is Canada, but because she's
something sublime that you were born into, some
great rugged power that you are a part of.*
~Emily Carr

I tucked our five-year-old daughter, Gae, into the bottom bunk of our compact hardtop trailer. Her teenage brother, Brent, had already usurped the top bunk, and my husband, Leo, was helping four-year-old Glen snuggle down inside a sleeping bag on the floor. It was to be the last night of a two-week family fishing trip spent "north of 53," the parallel separating western Canada's wheat fields from its wilderness.

Parked on either side of us along the shoreline of Big Sandy Lake were six or seven other units. Behind our trailer was the bear-proof garbage barrel and beyond that, dense forest. Shivering from the dampness, I crawled into bed. I could hardly wait to get back to our comfortable suburban home the next night.

Little did I know that our most memorable vacation was just beginning, not by choice but by circumstance.

Two hours after we went to bed, a violent thunderstorm rocked our trailer. The wind was howling, lightning was illuminating the sky, and rain was pouring down. A tree crashed into the undergrowth nearby.

The storm lasted for hours. Leo and I kept vigil until the clouds finally rumbled off over the lake. When we surveyed the damage at daybreak we discovered the nearby bridge had been swept away. We suspected the same was true of several more. There were at least thirty of us, including several children, now stranded at the edge of Big Sandy Lake, with no cell phone coverage, cut off from hydro and with insufficient food supplies.

The kids and I had to wade barefoot through five inches of water to reach the outhouse. Broken branches littered the path to the pump where we got our drinking water. Two huge trees had fallen across the trail to the woodpile. "I'm hungry! When are we gonna eat?" Brent asked. He had a good point and that sent a wave of anxiety through me. As we crowded around the little table in our trailer, I doled out breakfast more carefully than usual. Four-year-old Glen rattled off the blessing. "God is great, God is good. Let us thank Him for our food." Little did we know how meaningful that little daily prayer would become.

"Anybody goin' fishin'?" an elderly man called through the screen door. Tycoon, the retired fellow camped next to us, was carrying his fishing rod and a huge scoop net. "Olga tells me I oughta git out and rustle up a little grub, seein' as how we're gonna be here a spell." Noting the size of Leo's much smaller dip net, Tycoon remarked, "Boy, I can sure see you ain't got much faith!"

That's my problem, too, I thought to myself as I watched them go toward the lake. Other campers soon followed. "Deadpan" began soberly trolling along the edge of the lake for pickerel. Lance was casting among the cattails for northern pike. Others had headed out for deeper water in search of trout. "Git the fryin' pan hot!" Tycoon called to me a couple of hours later, as he came shuffling up the path carrying a pail of pickerel fillets. "The others are still down in the filletin' hut dividin' up the bounty."

Catching enough fish was not our only concern. At 5 a.m., a bear, trying to pry open Tycoon's camper truck, had rocked the camper, leaving behind muddy claw marks. Fishing remained good, but even the smallest cloud made us worry. What if more rain hampered the bridge repairs? What if strong winds churned up the lake so we couldn't fish? Our refrigerators were out of propane, so even if we managed to catch enough fish to tide us over during more bad weather, how would

We're All in This Together |

we keep it from spoiling? I had brought along my preserving kettle in hopes of finding a good patch of wild raspberries. What if I used the jars we had emptied along the way and refilled them with canned fish?

The men found some dry wood and soon had a roaring campfire snapping and crackling under my old blue granite kettle holding seven pints of pickerel. As they stoked the fire, I overheard talk about further washouts and road repairs, about stretching food supplies and safety issues.

"I gotta gun," said Tycoon. "If that bear gives us any more trouble, we'll have bear steaks!" The bland diet of fish day after day was soon depressing. The kids roasted the last stale marshmallows over a campfire. They relished the last tin of pork and beans. To boost morale, the men tied a string between two trees and rallied the campers for a volleyball game. Come Sunday morning, a woman named Deidre invited us to a church service she had organized, conscripting my husband Leo as preacher.

Our family trooped up the gravel road to the appointed "sanctuary," a high knoll overlooking the lake with towering pine trees in the background. A teenage girl carrying her little white dog joined us, followed by a young couple leading two toddlers. Then along came Jean, Lance, Olga, Tycoon and all the others. "Say preacher! Ya forgot to take off yer fishin' cap!"

Leo read from Psalm 19:1: "The heavens declare the glory of God and the firmament shows His handiwork." After reminding us that God is with us in the storms of life but also in the good times too, he suggested we sing the first verse of "How Great Thou Art." That afternoon Tycoon organized a fishing derby. To tell the truth, after catching fish, smelling fish, filleting fish, frying fish, and eating fish, I was just plain tired of fish, and besides, there weren't enough rods to go around.

A twelve-year-old boy proved my excuse wasn't valid. He tied some castoff line to a short stick, hung a lead weight and a rusty hook on the end and tossed it overboard. Within minutes his line pulled taut, and reeling it in hand over hand, he landed a three-pound pickerel.

On the sixth day we heard the unmistakable chop of a helicopter bringing in two government employees, who told us the road out would be passable the next day. After packing up, and waving goodbye to the other campers, we slowly wended our way across the makeshift bridges and drove back down the road that had brought us all together. As we turned toward home, I caught sight of two bear cubs trotting along beside their mother. Somehow, even then they symbolized a vacation that would in retrospect be twice as meaningful as any others we have ever had.

~Alma Barkman
Winnipeg, Manitoba

38

Found in the Fire

*Today — our hearts and prayers are with the people
of Fort McMurray. Tomorrow — our hands,
backs, trucks, and tools will be with you to
rebuild. Stay Alberta Strong.*

~Worldviews Project

My husband Stewart and I stood by the river, watching the wildfire ravage Fort McMurray, a surreal scene that mesmerized the world. They were watching it on TV, but it was a very real and terrifying sight all around us. The hour before had been frantic: watching the orange glow of the sky as the fire approached; attempting to contact the kids at school; calling Stew home from work; trying to pack; and then hearing the emergency evacuation alert scream through the radio. We escaped our small subdivision just as the first flames were visible behind our house. It was chaos as tens of thousands of people fled the inferno, flooding roadways and the single highway heading south out of town.

We didn't want to be stuck in traffic, so we decided to take the exit to the college. We pulled into the parking lot in time to watch the forest behind our house engulfed in monstrous flames. Then, the fire moved rapidly toward the highway where people were sitting in their vehicles. Fear for their safety had my stomach in knots. The ash showered us, and smoke stung my eyes. It was hard to breathe — physically and emotionally.

We needed to move on so we got back on the road. Progress was slow, so once again Stew pulled over and parked along the riverbank. We watched the hill on the other side of our house burn. It took three minutes to burn from top to bottom, with a final huge plume of black smoke as it destroyed the houses. I stood in silent disbelief as Stewart uttered out loud the thought that was in my head. "That's it, our house is gone." Our home of twenty-four years was gone just like that.

We moved on to what was most important — our children. The safe haven where they were was now under threat and further evacuation had been ordered, so we joined the long line of vehicles continuing our escape. After we got the kids I felt surprisingly calm, almost content; we were together, we were safe. We were on our way north of the city now, deeper into the boreal forest but away from the imminent danger.

The hours we crawled along in the convoy gave me plenty of time to reflect. The book *A Course in Miracles* says there are only two emotions — love and fear — and all other emotions are derived from those two. I could definitely see those two emotions at play during those days of the fire. People had lost homes, vehicles, belongings, a sense of safety and security, and irreplaceable treasures. Most tragic was the death of two teenagers killed in an accident south of the city as they evacuated.

There was fear and severe loss to grieve, and yet I had witnessed so much good as well. Part of the healing process was finding the "good" or light in the darkness of this catastrophic event. What we found in the fire on May 3, 2016 burned long after the last flame was extinguished months later.

The purest and richest of human virtues had emerged in epic proportions. It was profound. It was powerful, and, yes, sometimes it was overwhelming — in a way that made my eyes tear up and my heart soar.

Courage and Strength: I observed the collective courage of people, not only in the early hours of evacuation when the threat and danger was imminent, but also in the many days after, as displaced residents adapted to unfamiliar surroundings and uncertainty about the future. The stories of courage and strength were remembered long after the crisis passed.

Compassion and Kindness: The gestures of kindness, generosity and compassion are all expressions of love. In a time when fear was naturally present, the light of these acts of love overshadowed that darkness. There were several moments that touched me deeply. I watched three young men stand in the food line ahead of us at the Dorothy McDonald Business Centre. Volunteers from the Fort McKay First Nations had put together an impromptu barbeque to feed the exhausted evacuees taking refuge for the night. When these three young men got to the front, they saw that supplies were running low and decided to step away, stating, "There are kids and families that need this more than us — let them eat." I so appreciated their sacrifice so that my children could be fed.

Evacuation centres popped up quickly around the province, overflowing with donations of food, household items, and clothes, from Albertans and from across Canada. I am especially proud of some of the young people we know — our nephew Daniel and his girlfriend Ashley who worked tirelessly to collect and unload donations at Wandering River, as well as buying vast amounts of food for a barbeque to feed thousands of people. And, two young men — Justin and Jon, who grew up in Fort McMurray, took the day from work to transport fuel from Bonnyville, helping stranded motorists, stepping in without question to help strangers — with no expectation of payment. They said it was simply "what we needed to do."

In the early hours after we had slept one night in our vehicle, we made it to the small village of Plamondon where the local co-op had been open for twenty-four hours to ensure the evacuees had access to supplies. When I thanked a woman for volunteering to bag groceries for patrons, she touched my arm and replied, "This is nothing compared to what you are going through." It was a moment of pure love and compassion.

Connection: People who collectively experience an event of this magnitude have a sense of camaraderie, like nothing they would experience in day-to-day living. In that same grocery store in Plamondon, when asked, "paper or plastic?" the lady responded, "Oh, I brought my own bags!" Another customer and I had a chuckle together as we recognized a shopping bag from one of our stores at home. I may not have had time to get much out of my house, but we did manage to escape with our rather large collection of re-usable grocery bags, because they were already in our car.

While the rest of Alberta hosted us in their cities and towns they got to experience the richest resource of the Canadian oil sands — the people. And in our fatigued, frazzled, and frustrated state, perhaps we were not at our best, but they graciously accepted us with open arms. For that I am grateful. I am also grateful that when we had watched the hills around our house burn, we had actually witnessed a miracle. We just hadn't known it at the time. Our house — and most of our subdivision — was damaged but still there.

When I reflect on our escape from the wildfire, Canada's largest natural disaster, and the record-breaking evacuation of 90,000 people — it was those small moments of courage, compassion, and connection that stayed with me and soothed my soul. After the fire was quenched, it was those embers of human spirit and love that continued to burn brightly.

~Carla White
Fort McMurray, Alberta

Conversation Circle

Recognize yourself in he and she who
are not like you and me.
~Carlos Fuentes

I t's Wednesday evening at the Windsor Public Library, and the Conversation Circle is gathering. We have all come from different countries and different ethnic backgrounds at different times. But we are all eager to practice our English with each other. Even our facilitator Wendy is an immigrant.

I came from Bangladesh as a landed immigrant, and joined the Conversation Circle in 2011. It had started fifteen years earlier when some ESL students approached Mongai, one of the librarians who was an immigrant himself, and complained they had no place to practice speaking Canadian English. Mongai started the Conversation Circle. All the teachers are volunteers, and most are first or second generation immigrants themselves. Julius, who was from China, was the founding participant. When I met him he was in his late eighties. He walked with a walker and used a hearing aid, but I never saw an older gentleman so enthusiastic and eager to learn. It was an amazing experience for me.

As time passed many teachers and students came, and then went on their way. Even Julius eventually stopped coming due to health reasons. Then Mongai left the library, but even now the group continues to meet every Wednesday evening. Some are old members, some are new. We discuss different topics like festivals, food, flags, and holidays in our countries of origin. We talk about how our home countries are different from Canada, and how they have changed since we left. As we speak English and share our experiences, we all have different accents and we struggle to find the right words to describe things. But we do our best to encourage and listen to each other.

As I watch the new participants struggling, I remember the early days when I first came to Canada and went to a job workshop. The speaker said to me, "You can't speak English like me because I was born and raised in Canada. But I can't speak your language like you. Always remember that language is just a means of communication. As long as you can *communicate*, you are okay in Canada." I never forgot her words of wisdom. Over the years I've shared them with so many people I've lost count. Her wisdom provided such encouragement for me, and then for others. Those words have become my mantra.

Every year we have a potluck Christmas party. We all enjoy it no matter what our race, religion, or ethnic background. Usually people bring dishes from their country of origin to share with the others. Before eating we always explain the ingredients of the dishes. We get to practice speaking and learn something new at the same time. It is always a lot of fun.

Perhaps one day, like Julius, I won't be able to come anymore. But I know the Conversation Circle will continue — it will always be there to help whoever wants to come.

It reminds me of one of my favourite Bangla songs, "*Coffee Houser Sei Addata Aaj Aar Nei...*" This song is about a group of friends getting together in the evening to chitchat over a cup of coffee in a café, and how their lives have changed over time. The café is still there, but as time passes a younger generation has taken their place at the same table to chitchat over a cup of coffee — just like they used to do. Long live Conversation Circle!

~Durre N. Jabeen
Windsor, Ontario

We're All in This Together | 163

Christmas Ice Storm

Having a place to go — is a home. Having someone to
love — is a family. Having both — is a blessing.
~Donna Hedges

My sister and I had already put up our Christmas tree, trimming it with strings of colourful lights, glass ornaments, and tinsel. My parents and my brother had decorated our home with outdoor festive lights and garlands, and had placed a Christmas wreath on our front door. The neighbourhood was decked out for the holidays as Christmas approached.

Then, on Saturday December 21st, we were hit by a severe ice storm in southern Ontario. The freezing rain fell continuously, and the ice began to build up everywhere. On Saturday night, somewhere in the distance, I heard the frightful sound of electrical transformers exploding. The lights flickered on and off, but I was relieved each time the power came back on. My mother went to the basement to find candles and flashlights in case we needed them. When my sister returned home from work that evening, she was soaking wet, and really cold. "The roads and the sidewalks are covered with ice," she exclaimed. "It's a miracle I didn't fall." My brother, who was visiting, decided to stay overnight, fearing the roads were too dangerous to drive home to his own apartment.

When I awoke the next morning the house was eerily silent. I realized the furnace had gone off, and we had lost power. We had no lights, no heat, and of course our electric stove did not work. The house was already cold, and we had no way to boil water or make coffee to warm up.

Outside, the trees and streets were covered with a thick layer of ice. It looked like the kind of winter landscape you see depicted on a Christmas card, with rooftops shimmering and trees encased in sparkling ice. However, the reality wasn't as pretty as the picture. As the freezing rain continued to fall, the temperature dropped steadily in our home. As the hours went by we waited, hoping for the power to be restored. A neighbour came by to help us scrape the large build-up of ice from our driveway and walkway. Another neighbour, who had a gas stove, came over to offer my mother a kettle full of tea. "This will help warm you up," she said.

With no radio or TV, we had no news about the extent of the damage, or when the power might be restored. My sister was scheduled to work that afternoon, but the slick, ice-covered sidewalks had grown even more treacherous overnight. She wasn't sure she could get there, so my brother offered to drive her.

It was now early afternoon. With no power to make a hot lunch, we settled for making sandwiches. As we were preparing them, my brother returned with some good news. He had passed by his own apartment and discovered that his building had power!

"You can't stay here — it's too cold," he said. "We'll have lunch at my place." We quickly packed up the sandwiches we had prepared, and left. When I opened the back door to my brother's car, a sheet of ice fell to the ground. As we drove through the city, there were fallen tree branches lying in the middle of roads and hanging dangerously from power lines. Some streets were closed with yellow police tape blocking off the sections made dangerous by fallen trees or electric wires. It was a strange combination. There was the frightful scene of downed power lines and branches and, at the same time, a picturesque scene of sparkling trees and glittering rooftops.

When we arrived at my brother's apartment we turned on the television and learned that the power outages were far more widespread than we'd thought. Hundreds of thousands of people were without power, we learned, and it might be several days before it would be restored. It was only three days before Christmas, and no one was sure if people would be able to return to their homes by Christmas Day. When I heard this, my heart sank.

From the beginning, Hydro workers worked day and night to restore power. Others came from all over Ontario and then from all over Canada, sacrificing their own Christmas at home with their family and friends to help Ontarians through this crisis. They worked fourteen to sixteen hours a day in cold and freezing rain to get the power back on in homes.

That evening we returned to our own home to see if the power had been restored. But it was still dark. There were no streetlights on in our neighbourhood, and there was no warmth in our dark, silent house. Using flashlights and candles, we gathered together some overnight supplies. We let the water run to prevent the pipes from freezing. To our surprise a glass of water which my mother had left on the kitchen table already had ice in it.

On our way out, my mother saw our neighbour outside. He had decided not to leave his home despite the loss of power. They had a gas stove, and were able to at least prepare hot food and drinks. His little granddaughter was at a relative's house, however, because her lips had turned blue in the cold.

"I wish I didn't have to leave," my mother sighed. "I've never had to leave my home before, especially at Christmas." She gave him a box of chocolates as a Christmas gift and asked him, "Please watch over our home, and call me if you see anything." He smiled when he saw the chocolates, knowing they would cheer up his granddaughter. "Don't worry," he said. "I'll let you know if I see anything."

When Christmas Eve arrived there was still no power in our neighbourhood. But we were all at my brother's, preparing our traditional Italian Christmas Eve dinner, a special meal made up of fish and pasta dishes. Despite the difficulties, we were all together and that was the most important thing. Just as we were about to sit down to dinner the phone rang. It was our neighbour announcing that the lights had come back on. We were ecstatic! Those hard working Hydro workers had restored power to our neighbourhood, and we could go home.

When we returned home, we immediately turned on the Christmas lights. As our neighbourhood quickly sprang to life, those lights seemed to shine more brightly that Christmas Eve than ever before. The Christmas of 2013 will forever be remembered in Toronto as the Christmas of the Great Ice Storm. Filled with Christmas spirit, everyone worked together to help bring about a Christmas miracle.

~Nada Mazzei
Toronto, Ontario

The Hunt Camp

*Walking, I am listening to a deeper way. Suddenly all
my ancestors are behind me. Be still, they say. Watch
and listen. You are the result of the love of thousands.*
~Linda Hodges

Going to the hunt camp, according to the men in our family, is a spiritual experience. The men think about it all year long. When a boy reaches his twelfth birthday in our family, if he has aced his gun safety course he gets to go with the guys. They hunt for partridge, moose, and deer. Apparently, they also hunt for the record for who can best hold their beer. They do all this at the family hunt camp built by our grandfathers.

Once a year, women are allowed. It's a known fact that there are women in our town who, while not actually seeing this as a spiritual experience, see it as a prelude to courtship. The rest of us are so over that. The men call us their "womenses." It rolls off the tongue much easier than their "better halves." Our one day at the hunt camp takes place in the fall, and it's as perfect as it can get. Our job is to simply show up. We bring our kids… even the babies.

We women come as close to lounging as we can while sitting on a tree stump. Sitting in a huge circle around the fire pit, we're treated like royalty. The men do the cooking and serve us fried fish, beans, and hot dogs. Once we even had cabbage rolls.

One time, on this one co-ed day at camp, we were all taught a valuable lesson. My son David was three years old. He and some of his little cousins had been having a great time gathering firewood. He came to me, pulling on the bottom edge of his shirt. He didn't say a word; he just kept yanking on his shirt. I pulled the shirt up and out flew a swarm of bees. His tummy was covered with little welts that were getting bigger by the second.

Now the womenses in our clan were like a mini United Nations. We came in all colours, sizes, and faiths, and between us, we carried a vast amount of knowledge. But the woman who helped us that day wasn't from our family. She was a neighbour, a native of our First Nations, who taught us to fry our fish in bacon fat, butter and a touch of soy sauce. Her name was Lily. She grabbed David and ran right into the lake. Then, she dug into the muddy, clay-like sand and smeared it all over his tummy. When finished, she handed his limp little body to me and told my husband to drive us to the nearest hospital. Lily then asked somebody for a make-up mirror and, handing it to me, told me to hold it under David's nose so I'd be able to tell if he stopped breathing.

I never took my eyes off that mirror. Things go through your mind at moments like this. Things for which you're grateful: family; friends; freedom; a country that has the best health care in the world; and places of worship — be it churches, temples, cathedrals, synagogues or sacred lodges.

And then, I added to that list: a hospital that was staffed by nuns; and the doctor who told us that what Lily did actually saved David's life.

Later that night, we drove back to the hunt camp and sat by the fire. Those who could… played an instrument, and those who couldn't… played the spoons. We all sang. We gave thanks. Grandpa gave each and every one of us a blessing, a tradition handed down to the family when his grandfather immigrated to Canada by way of France. But, the fact is, Lily's forefathers were the first ones in our land. They were here first, and we'll be forever grateful to them for sharing their country with us. Maybe the men were right after all; going to the hunt camp *is* a spiritual experience.

~Mary Lee Moynan
Callander, Ontario

We're All in This Together |

Keeping Up with the Newfies

*Gratitude unlocks the fullness of life... It turns denial
into acceptance, chaos to order, confusion to clarity.
It can turn a meal into a feast, a house into
a home, a stranger into a friend.*
~Melody Beattie

The first thing I noticed were the icebergs floating lazily past, with nowhere to be and nowhere to go. I couldn't help but envy those icebergs.

I'm always on the go. Things need to be done, money needs to be made, and things need to be bought. I rarely stop to enjoy what I have before I'm thinking about the next thing. I start planning my next trip when I'm still on vacation. I think about what has to be done around the house or what needs to be upgraded before actually taking the time to enjoy what I already have.

I wondered, would I be like this if I had these gleaming white beauties in my back yard every day, reminding me that it's okay to slow down and just be? Perhaps I would learn from the icebergs to enjoy the ride I'm on, instead of always thinking about the next one.

It seems to be working for the friendly people of St. Anthony, Newfoundland. I was lucky enough to visit their town with my mother, grandmother, and husband during the annual Iceberg Festival in June. My grandmother was in her mid-eighties and wanted to see every province of Canada. Newfoundland and Labrador was the only province we had left, so the festival was the perfect time for us to visit.

As a city girl I wasn't too thrilled about driving through Gros Morne Park to the other end of Newfoundland, but I was willing to do anything for my grandmother. My reluctance turned to excitement as the beautiful, rugged terrain began to reveal itself. The serene water was as deep blue as a sapphire, and a perfect contrast to the jagged cliffs of the rolling green and brown mountains. For the first of many times on the trip I was brought to tears by the exquisite beauty of nature.

As we drove the lone road up to St. Anthony I noticed that everything looked clearer, brighter, and simpler. The little fishing houses were tiny, but they were painted beautifully and well taken care of. You could almost feel the love the owners had for their homes. Then, just outside of St. Anthony, I noticed what looked like little gardens on the side of the road. Planted in the ditches, they had metal fences around them. They were nowhere near any houses. I had no idea what they might possibly be.

By the time we actually arrived in St. Anthony we were all starving. As soon as we were settled into our hotel I ran to the nearest Tim Hortons for coffee and doughnuts. I had read that Tim Hortons had a special doughnut commemorating the Iceberg Festival. As I waited in line a friendly man next to me said, "You aren't from here, are you?" At first I was a bit offended, but then I looked around and noticed that everyone seemed to look the same. The women all had similar no-frills haircuts and outfits to match. Here I was, long blond hair, wearing boots, leggings, and a scarf; I clearly looked different.

"You're right," I said. "I'm here for the Iceberg Festival with my family. We're just visiting."

"Well," he said, "the best way to really experience Newfoundland is to go to a kitchen party." He went on to explain that a kitchen party was a big party with dancing, drinks, and, if we were lucky, an appearance by some Mummers. When I asked him what a Mummer was, he said it was something I would need to see to understand. He then gave me the address of a kitchen party, and I headed back to round up the family.

I was a little nervous to go, but I knew we needed to try this new experience. And from the moment we arrived I knew it was going to be life changing. It was so far beyond anything I could imagine in my wildest dreams. We were served drinks that were chilled with pieces of iceberg instead of ice cubes! I could not believe I was literally drinking an iceberg! It was colder and fresher than any drink I've ever had in my life.

In the main room a traditional Newfoundland band was playing regional folk music. People were dancing and singing and having the best time. Everyone looked so happy as they passed around the "Ugly Stick," a traditional musical instrument made from household and tool shed items like a mop handle with bottle caps, tin cans, small bells and other items to make noise. It's played with a drumstick and produces a very distinctive sound. Everyone was given a chance to play it, myself included. I'm not sure I've ever felt happier than I did while I was banging the boot with the stick attached on the floor, the nailed on bottle caps clinking to the rhythm of the folk song the band was playing.

When the band took a break shortly after my turn with the Ugly Stick, I asked the people around me what it was like to live there. They explained their simple way of life, based around fishing. Everyone was a friend, and everyone looked out for each other. The gardens I had noticed in the ditch were planted by the residents, and each one had something different growing. They would all share the harvest with each other. Everyone went to the same hairdresser and shopped at the single clothing store, and that was why everyone looked so similar. And they were happy with it. It seemed to be a simple and idyllic life, and it worked for them. I don't think I have ever encountered a more friendly, genuine, and happy group of people in all my travels.

All of a sudden everyone started clapping and very upbeat music began. Out of nowhere, a group of little men in costumes ran by and started dancing. The Mummers were out! Traditionally, they come out on Christmas Eve and get everyone drunk, but they had come out for this Iceberg Festival kitchen party. People were dancing, yelling, singing, and having the most spectacular time. As I looked around, taking in the sight, I noticed there were no televisions, no designer clothes, and the women looked like they weren't wearing any make-up. Everyone was exactly who they were, in the raw. And they were so incredibly happy! I realized that I needed to stop trying to "be up on everything" that was the latest and learn to be happy just the way I was.

Today, when I find myself getting too busy or overwhelmed, I think back to the icebergs, and the people of Newfoundland. I remind myself that it's okay to relax, experience life as it is right in front of me, and just be myself.

~Patti Leo Bath
Tampa, Florida, USA

43

Helping Hands

When you are kind to someone in trouble, you hope
they'll remember and be kind to someone
else. And it'll become like a wildfire.
~Whoopi Goldberg

Jubilation marks the end of World War II. Hope flourishes as bells ring and people embrace. But my Russian parents are filled with loss: they have lost their families and their homeland. My mother is already pregnant as they trek from Czechoslovakia to Regensburg, Germany. Here they find refuge in a camp for displaced persons from Russia, Ukraine, and Poland, all victims of forced labour or prisoners of war. I would be born there.

My parents soon meet a destitute elderly woman who has lost her family. They take her in. Within a year my father finds work at a coal mine in Belgium. It is dangerous work, and in the barracks where we live the anxiety of the women waiting at home is palpable. I hear frightening tales of cave-ins and trapped miners.

But I have two parents who love me, rabbits and chickens in the small yard beside the outhouse, an army of dolls, and a large bear that I love. My clothes and those of my dolls are hand-sewn by the elderly woman who is now my godmother, and the only grandmother I will ever know.

In Belgium we learn to speak French and, knowing that French is spoken in Canada, my parents decide to emigrate like others from the mines. We receive postcards from those who have gone before us, and

I dwell on one in particular. It shows a man in a large feather headdress standing beside a tepee. I assume this is how we will live in Canada.

After four years there is finally enough money, and we take the train to Bremerhaven, Germany where our ship is docked. But we almost miss the ship's departure when the Canadian Immigration official wants to deny my grandmother boarding; she is not a true family member. At this I start to wail and cling to her with all the love and grief of a five-year-old whose life is already disrupted. Thankfully, the compassionate official writes her name in my father's passport as his natural mother. With relief, we board the ship, and our voyage to Canada begins.

It is a stormy crossing, and most passengers are seasick. Fortunately, my father and I escape that fate and enjoy the ship's cafeteria, watching the swirling outer world through portholes. We arrive late, but safely, at Pier 21 in Halifax, where we undergo health examinations. Customs inspectors cut away the canvas my mother carefully sewed around our two cardboard suitcases. They confiscate a dried salami but permit us to keep the jar of my favourite cherry jam. Next we board a train for Kingston, Ontario, where Russian friends from the mine have already settled. But because of our ship's late arrival there is no one to meet us. Nobody here speaks French either, and we are on our own.

We leave the suitcases at the station and begin to walk. It is December, almost Christmas, and snow banks line the sidewalks we follow into town. The joy I first felt at seeing so much snow is short-lived. It is a long walk, none of us has proper footwear, and the adults take turns carrying me. With ten dollars in his pocket, my father's first priority is to find food to feed his hungry child. We stop at a small corner store with glass cases displaying a variety of sweets. There is a delicious aroma from the fresh loaves of bread on a rack behind the counter.

Then a miracle happens. When the elderly couple waiting to serve us hear my parents speaking Russian, they exclaim excitedly, "We haven't heard anyone speaking Russian since we left St. Petersburg after the Revolution! Welcome, welcome!" They hug us as though we are long lost family. They take us to their living quarters above the shop, give us tea and cake, and invite us to stay with them until we have sorted out our situation. I am intimidated by the grand piano in the sitting room but soothed by the beautiful carpet hanging on the wall, Russian style, just as my mother decorated a wall in the Belgian mine barracks. Our suitcases are retrieved, and I am reunited with my beloved bear. Someone vacates a bedroom, and we spend our first night in comfortable beds.

A few days later we arrive at an old stone farmhouse outside the city. The heating is limited and I am frightened by the many rooms with closed doors. But I am happy to be reunited with another family from the barracks. They are the first in a series of unrelated people who become adopted aunts, uncles and cousins, since our real relatives are assuredly lost to us, even if any of them survived the war.

A few days later it is Christmas. Someone provides a tree, which my mother decorates with a few ornaments she brought. My grandmother cuts out delicate fairies from plain white paper. Someone else brings a cardboard box of gifts for me: mandarin oranges, candies and little plastic figurines of cowboys and Indians. I don't know what they are but the headdress on one is familiar and I wonder if a tepee might still figure in my future! All this is in addition to boxes of warm clothing, which we desperately need. So much is provided for us by the goodness of many hearts.

My parents begin new jobs while my grandmother looks after me. My mother, once a medical student, washes dishes in a restaurant. My father, an electrical engineer and military officer, drives a tractor cutting grass in city parks. Sometimes he works a second job as a bartender in the same restaurant as my mother. They work so hard that within five years my father is able to begin building our own house. The former coal miners who live in the same city share their skills, and help one another build homes.

Despite this abundant new life in Canada, my parents miss their homeland. They meet other Russian immigrants, sometimes in the evening sitting on blankets in a park. Someone brings an accordion and they sing the old sad songs, tears streaming down their faces. None of them can go back, and no one can discover what happened to their families. The Iron Curtain is impenetrable.

So strangers become a kind of family. My mother never forgets the compassion and generosity of those who made possible our new beginning, all members of the local Jewish community. Although not Jewish, she begins a life-long involvement with the synagogue, volunteering at fundraisers and providing food or companionship to the sick or elderly.

Just as they were welcomed, my parents have continued to greet newcomers to Canada with Russian words of welcome when they arrive at their door seeking help and advice. Soon they have leads on jobs, and help with learning the intricacies of banking, shopping and public transportation.

It takes a village to help establish bewildered or lonely immigrants. A village of compassionate people helped my parents create a new home, and provide a safe and happy life for the child that was born as a displaced person. My mother, at ninety, continues to inhabit this village, helping and welcoming when energy permits, as new refugees and new generations of children find the opportunity for a safe and happy life in Canada.

~Tanya Ambrose
Mallorytown, Ontario

44

When It's Maple Sugar Time

You can't buy happiness, but you can live in Canada
and that's pretty much the same thing.
~Author Unknown

I t never fails. It's been a long day at work. I'm trying to get the key into the lock, I hear the phone ringing, and my arms are full with a briefcase and a toddler. After ten seconds (although it feels like an hour) I get into the house, put my grandson Matthew down on the floor, and race for the phone, getting there just as the ringing stops.

I check the call display and panic sets in. It is 4:30 in the afternoon and I see my parents' number. My parents are frugal; their long distance savings plan does not begin until 6 p.m. Of course they did not leave a message. I brace myself for the worst and, with shaking hands, dial their number at the farm. My dad answers, "Hello?"

"Hi Dad," I say quickly. "What's wrong?"

Dad responds with some urgency in his voice. "Nothing is wrong, but I've tapped some trees and would like to do a few more. But now that I'm the only one left to do it, I need a bit of help."

***

A few hours later I'm on the road with my husband Jack, making the three-hour drive to the family farm in Sauble Beach, Ontario.

On the way, I think about my time at the sugar bush when I was growing up. During my childhood, in the early part of the season when there was still snow on the ground, Dad would hitch Nell, our Clydesdale, up to the sleigh and off we would go to tap trees. Later we'd return to gather the sap and then boil it down to make maple syrup. Finally Nell got too old, and Dad replaced her with a tractor.

As I grew up, I was able to trek to the sugar bush myself wearing snowshoes. And when I became a parent myself, I brought my children to the farm every year during March break to help their grandfather and enjoy the fresh maple syrup.

We arrive and we're out first thing the next morning. The sun is shining brilliantly on the small bits of snow that are remnants of a long hard winter. I walk to the sugar bush rather than riding in the tractor with Dad. I want to breathe in the fresh early spring air. I notice the walls around the fire pit are crumbling and old, but the sap pans are still sitting there waiting to boil down the maple sap. I see the wood neatly piled and ready for the fire, and then I see sap buckets hanging from the maple trees. Dad is already there.

I'm excited because, for the first time in my forty-something years, I get to use some of the tools. The rule was that only adults use hand tools, so I feel as if I have finally grown up. Dad's view on life is that you don't fix what isn't broken, so the tools are probably from the early 1900s. That's okay; they still work. It's all part of the tradition.

I take the brace and bit, a hand tool used to drill into wood, and drill my first hole into a maple tree. I insert the "spile," which acts like a tap, and hang a sap bucket on the hook. What I hear is music to my ears, the "ping, ping, ping" of maple sap dripping into the metal bucket. I watch Dad as he hangs a yoke around his neck with a pail hanging from each side. He carefully walks around to the trees that have already been tapped and gathers the sap to pour into the pans.

"It wouldn't be right if we didn't have a drink of fresh sap," says Dad. It is too sweet, but I relish the taste and the tradition. Jack too, savours the taste. It makes me happy to see Dad having his first sip of the season. He has a look of utter contentment on his face.

We're All in This Together |

Soon we have enough sap to start "sugaring off." It is a bit later in the season so there really isn't enough snow to make maple syrup toffee on the snow. Nevertheless we're going to have fresh maple syrup at some point this weekend. We stoke up the fire and, with his accurate eye, Dad determines there are forty gallons of sap in the pan, enough for a gallon of syrup. It takes hours, but eventually I can smell the fragrant maple aroma as the sap slowly boils down into syrup.

Finally the syrup is ready to be poured into a huge kettle, and taken to the house so Mom can finish it off. They have graduated from the old woodstove to an electric one, but the process is still the same. Mom stands there skimming off any foam, and eventually she strains it through cheesecloth. Finally, she pours the delicious fresh maple syrup into heated sterilized jars.

We are almost ready to eat and I am so excited! Am I hungry? Not really, but I am so happy to see my dad enjoying what he loves to do. I love to see his expression when he has his first taste of the finished product. My aunt Theresa, Dad's sister, calls from the next farm and says, "Bring the syrup, I'm making the pancakes." She doesn't have a fancy griddle, just the top of her old wood stove, which is greased and ready when we get there. The pancakes are not from a mix; she has made them from scratch. This special, traditional meal is delectable and filled with love. Dad comments, as he does every year, that "this will probably be the last year that I make maple syrup."

"Oh you say that every year," replies Aunt Theresa. "You'll be making maple syrup until you die."

* * *

It has been a long day at work and I'm trying to get the key into the lock. I hear the phone ringing, and my arms are full with a briefcase and a toddler. I get into the house, put Matthew down, and race for the phone, getting there just before the ringing stops. It is my cousin Earl, Aunt Theresa's son.

"I have bad news, Nancy," Earl says gently. "Your dad passed away this afternoon." Two weeks to the day from Dad's initial phone call, he is gone. I think he knew the end was near, but the memories of the joy he had in that one last sugaring off will stay with me forever.

~Nancy Loucks-McSloy
London, Ontario

The Spirit of Canada

Into the Wild

*I have vaulted over an immense land which is both
forbidding and beautiful and it took my breath
away. There are no people more fortunate
than we Canadians. We have received
far more than our share.*
~Marc Garneau

45

Storyteller Lost and Found

Stories have to be told or they die, and when they die,
we can't remember who we are or why we're here.
~Sue Monk Kidd

My parents met in a mushroom factory in Dublin in the early 1950s. They married, took a boat ride to Canada, which they called their honeymoon, and settled in Toronto. Five kids later we had our own pew at St. Patrick's Parish and were living in "Cabbage Town" in Toronto's "Inner City." We never met a relative while we were growing up as they were all still in Ireland and wondering if we were out of our minds living in igloos in Canada. Our friends told us my parents spoke funny and they could not understand a word they were saying. I would tell them my parents were Irish, they would ask what that meant and I would have to say I did not know. But, I thought it had something to do with having to go to church all of the time, and eating lots of potatoes, while my friends were out playing, eating pizza, or sleeping in.

When I finished high school I took a job with the Hudson's Bay Company. They shipped me to the Arctic to trade furs with the Inuit people who lived there. It was very cold and dark for six months of the year and I felt very alone, just as my parents must have felt coming to a new land. Most of the Inuit could speak basic English, which was good because their language sounded like Gaelic to me. There were very few non-native people there, and I longed to spend time with the Inuit and learn their ways. I found them to be a very likeable lot, not just because they never ate potatoes, but because they were always smiling and knew how to laugh at themselves. Many generations lived together under the same roof. They also knew exactly who they were. That's what I wanted to know myself: who I was and why I felt like a cultural orphan.

One spring day a group of old men knocked on my door and invited me on a hunting trip. They said we would be gone for three days hunting caribou, which I did not believe, because we had no tent or other equipment. We travelled the entire first day and half the night as, it being spring, it never got truly dark. When we finally stopped it was only because a blizzard had blown in and we had to build an igloo before we froze to death. For two days we sat in the igloo waiting out the spring storm. Two days!

To entertain us the old men took turns telling stories in both languages. The adventures went on for hours — danger, narrow escapes, great feats of survival and daring. And ancestors gone but never forgotten. Suddenly all became quiet. Everyone turned to me. It was my turn to tell a story.

I told them of my parent's journey leaving poverty behind in Ireland to find a new life in Canada. I told them of huge cities they could not imagine. I told them of never knowing a relative or knowing who "My People" were. I talked for hours. They looked at me and at one another in disbelief. One old man said it was wrong to let my people be forgotten, because our ancestors live on only if they are remembered in our stories. A long discussion ensued in the Inuit language after which the men broke into gales of laughter. (I was hoping they were not laughing at me). I was also thinking it would be nice to have a hot plate of mashed potatoes right about now.

I asked the old men to let me in on the joke. They told me their grandparents had told them about when white men came in great ships and killed the whales to take the oil. The whalers had taught them how to jig and introduced them to stories of the green island from which they had come. It was said that the Irish whalers were great dancers and even greater storytellers. The Inuit called them "*Sag-Li-Oonaat*" or "great liars." The people held the Irish in high regard. The men agreed that it was wonderful to have a young "*Sag-Li-Oonaat*" amongst them once again, and would I take them hunting on the green island if I ever went there.

After the trip I spent the next twenty years in Canada's north and now regale my own children and friends with stories of my adventures and the wonderful people I have met. The Inuit helped me find peace with who I was, where I came from and why. I am a descendant of the "*Sag-Li-Oonaat*," the people from the green island. As long as I can tell stories, all those who I have ever met will live.

And that is who I am.

~John J. Seagrave
Yellowknife, Northwest Territories

46

Chicken Soup for the Soul

A Taste of the Wild

*They danced a cotillion in the sky; they were rose
and silver shod; It was not good for the eyes of
man — 'Twas a sight for the eyes of God.*
*~Robert W. Service, "The Ballad
of the Northern Lights"*

The rattling yellow bus bumped to a halt as it careened into the gathering area in front of Camp Wright's mess hall. Doubtless the driver thought the four of us were out of our minds, taking fifty grade-six students into the wilderness at the end of January. Certainly that thought had crossed my mind more than once.

This was part of tradition at Ormsby Elementary School, though: three days in the wilderness in October, another three days in January, and three days hiking in the Rockies at the end of the year. If nothing else, these kids would leave elementary school with a taste of the wild.

The students grabbed their sleeping bags and backpacks and tumbled off the bus. It was their second trip here, and they knew the drill. Once they claimed the rest of their belongings from the luggage compartment, the boys headed west and the girls east. Little had changed since our last visit, except in January the world around us was white and black, with shades of grey.

With my teaching buddy, Anne, I headed toward the teachers' cabin, tromping through the snow. The knob turned easily enough, but it took a solid hip check against the door to break the ice that had sealed it shut. I unrolled my down-filled sleeping bag on the lower bunk, then sat down and pulled off my mukluks so I could put on an extra pair of wool socks. Zipping up my parka, I headed to the door. "We'd better check on the kids," I said. "I hope they remember their fire-starting from the fall; they're going to need it."

The only heat available would come from wood we burned in the fifty-gallon drum stoves in the cabins — rustic cabins with chinking missing from between the wallboards. Keeping the fires going through the night was critical, as the temperature was to dip to −30° C. We had worked on fire building, and trained the kids to handle axes and bow saws during the fall visit, but only a handful were truly skilled. Each cabin group had collected a bundle of firewood, but as I arrived to check the final cabin, the girls complained there wasn't much left in the woodpile. I called Garry, the lead teacher on this expedition, and we went to inspect the supply. We stared in shocked silence; whoever had used the camp before us had neglected to restock the wood. Any other time of the year, it would have been just a nuisance, but in January having a good supply of wood was essential for survival.

Garry quickly rounded up a chainsaw, half a dozen of the strongest boys, and George, the fourth teacher. The group headed into the woods to scout out deadfalls they could cut up and haul back to camp.

Camp Wright, southwest of Athabasca in northern Alberta, at the tip of Narrow Lake, was used as a survival camp for Army and Sea Cadets. It was a spartan camp, but perfect for what we wanted our students to experience. There was a generator to provide electricity to the mess hall, but that was about it in the way of services. For many kids, the visit to the fall camp was the first time they had ever used an outhouse — a real outhouse with pit toilets. We brought an ice auger with us, as any water we needed, including drinking water, had to be hauled up the hill from the lake.

It was a wilderness camp carved out of the boreal forest, miles from nowhere, and we were reminded of its wildness every time we walked through the mustering area. There at the edge, just north of the mess hall, stood a balsam fir permanently scarred with the unmistakable claw marks of a bear.

With the short supply of firewood, the afternoon of our arrival was spent cutting, chopping, and splitting the deadfalls that Garry and George pulled out of the forest. Anne and I kept busy by checking to see that every one of the fifty kids had enough clothing for the extreme weather. This far north, darkness would be upon us in late afternoon. By the time the shadows had lengthened, the cabins were stocked with enough wood to last the night, and every cabin group had managed to get a fire going. When the supper gong clanged, the kids streamed into the mess hall for a well-deserved supper of bread and steaming chili.

It wasn't difficult to convince our young charges to trek to their cabins after dinner and tuck in for the night. By the light of their flashlights, the kids donned layers of clothing and crawled into their sleeping bags. Stories were shared and jokes were told until all the exhausted children slipped into a deep slumber. The crackling fires gradually died down, leaving behind a heap of glowing coals to duel with the dropping temperature. We prayed the coals would win.

Sleep is a luxury teachers can't afford when they are responsible for a group of students they've led into the wild. We took turns slipping out into the night to check that no one was uncovered. I had just returned from my midnight check on the cabins when Garry opened our door. "Come out, you've got to see this!" he called. "And go around and get as many kids to come as you can."

We had no idea why, but we did as he asked.

About half the bleary-eyed kids slipped into their coats and boots, and together we followed Garry down the hill and out onto the frozen lake. We gasped as we looked up at the ghostly green glow above us. The glow morphed into dazzling bands of light — pink, green, yellow, blue, violet — swaying back and forth across the sky, like curtains in the wind. It was the aurora borealis, or northern lights, and they were putting on a show like none of us had ever seen. We stood there in awe, impervious to the cold, knowing we were watching something we'd never forget.

The morning dawned bright and clear. We had made it through the night, and although the temperature was still well below zero, the blue sky and sunshine lifted our spirits. It was a cold but wonderful day. I led the kids through the forest and across a beaver dam on snowshoes. With Anne, they skied across the lake and into the woods. Garry and George had them build a snow shelter called a quinzee. In the end, though, it was the unplanned that excited them. Rather than our carefully designed activities, they talked about working together to survive the brutal cold and tromping at midnight to the middle of a frozen lake to behold the mystery of the aurora. These kids had experienced a profound connection with each other and with the wild — a lesson that could never be taught in the classroom.

~Linda Mehus-Barber
Kelowna, British Columbia

47

Standing Bear

Regard Heaven as your Father, Earth as your Mother,
and all that lives as your Brother and Sister.
~Native American Proverb

For twelve years I guided canoe trips throughout Ontario and Quebec. My love of canoeing and camping is a large part of who I am. Whether it be feathering a paddle through a still lake to silently slip past a moose, manoeuvring through a roaring rapid, or lugging a waterlogged cedar-strip canoe over a steep portage trail, I feel at home in the Canadian wilderness. Many of my trips happened inside Algonquin Park, where much of the scenery is reminiscent of the work of the Group of Seven. I was always inspired by how well they captured "The Spirit of the Land" through their paintings. In fact, Tom Thomson Lake was one of my most frequently visited routes as we made our way from the access point to the interior.

One year, I was leading a group of twelve-year-old girls on a five-day trip at summer camp. With me I had two female counsellors, and Peter, a guide-in-training. Peter was eager to become a junior guide but was paranoid about bears. He and I were sharing a tent, and every night when I left the tent to make a final check of the campsite he would get concerned.

On the morning of day three we had finished breakfast, the tents were down, and the bags were all packed and ready to load into canoes. Peter headed toward the "thunder box" or "kybo," a wooden box toilet that sat over a deep pit about fifty metres back from the campsite. He returned in a frenzy, barely coherent and sputtering loudly, "b... b... b... bear!"

I told him to calm down, so as to not cause panic in our group. I instructed him to continue loading the canoes. "It's probably just a raccoon," I said. "But I'll go check it out." I grabbed my hatchet, just in case, and set off for the thunder box. I seriously doubted Peter's account.

But then I saw it. An enormous black bear was heading toward our campsite. I returned to the group and told everyone to finish packing and get all the campers into the canoes and out into the water. They would leave me one canoe and wait in the lake while I monitored the bear's advance.

I was concerned about the safety of our group, but also the potential for the bear to take our food supply. Being two days out in the wilderness makes having no food a serious issue. My goal was to ensure the safe evacuation of the site with all our belongings, and in order to balance the risk I needed to see what that bear was doing. I was still holding the hatchet, but as I approached within sight of the bear again, I realized how useless it would be.

I watched as the bear lumbered forward and reached the thunder box. At this point, I was probably fifteen metres away from him. He sniffed the wooden box and then, as if it were a pebble, swatted it sideways, sending it flying about ten metres.

Then, in a breathtaking moment I will never forget, the bear stood up on his hind legs, reaching a height of close to seven feet. He turned and looked right into my eyes. You know the line in that bear song, "He looked at me, I looked at him..." This powerful beast locked his gaze on me, but something happened in that exchange. In that moment I didn't feel any fear or aggression toward him. Instead, I felt awe and respect. I was overcome by the magnificence of this animal, and I believe my eyes told him as much.

His eyes told me not to worry either. After what seemed like twenty minutes (but was probably only a few seconds,) the bear lowered back down to all fours, turned his head and walked away. Then my heart started to beat again, and I was overwhelmed with the reality of what had just happened. I turned and headed back to the campsite. Everyone was waiting offshore, so I jumped in my canoe and paddled out to them. Of course I told them all what had happened, and how lucky I was.

Yes, I had been lucky — truly fortunate to experience this beautiful animal in his own habitat without fear or competition. Instead we shared an almost sacred moment of peace and recognition, with mutual respect and wonder.

As I paddled away from the scene of this encounter, the water seemed to sparkle in the sunlight a little more, the greenery of the pines looked somehow deeper, and the few clouds in the otherwise blue sky appeared as if they had been painted on canvas and placed there deliberately. I felt an almost timeless sense of the spirit of this land that had been travelled by those before me, from the Algonquin First Nations tribe to the Voyageurs and the French *coureurs de bois*. Perhaps, they too had had an encounter like mine.

This wasn't the first time I'd encountered a bear, nor would it be the last. But this experience stands out as a moment that established within me a sacred connection to the spirit of the bear that I carry to this day. The bear holds a space inside my soul that still fills me with wonder and gratitude that we are able to share this great land, in all its majesty.

~Bradley A. Rudner
Victoria, British Columbia

48

Four Seasons in Moosonee

The more I see of the country, the less I feel I know
about it. There is a saying that after five years
in the north every man is an expert;
after ten years, a novice.
~Pierre Berton

I guess someone should have warned us it wasn't a good idea to get married and start a family when neither of us was fully employed. After our third anniversary, I was pregnant, we had no full-time work, and we were both still in college in Toronto. It was then that my husband, Doug, decided to apply for a teaching position in the north.

Waiting is always hard, but finally he received the call, an interview, and an offer all in one day. He came home so excited. "I accepted a job teaching a grade five class in Moosonee!"

"Excellent." I said. "Where is Moosonee?"

"I don't know," he said. "Let's get out the map."

"Okay, straight north of us. That must be a two-day trip to get there. Looks good. But, wait, there are no roads going that far north. How do we get there?"

"By train," explained Doug. "Or, as my principal explained, we could ship our stuff by train and then fly in, but you know how much I like planes."

"So, train it is," I said. "Excellent."

Maybe not so excellent. Now came the warnings from family and friends: "You'll feel isolated so far from everything." "You'll experience culture shock in a tiny remote native community." "You may even feel some antagonism toward you, being one of the very few non-natives." "You will be homesick." But if this was going be my new home, I reflected, how could I feel anything but "at home?"

With our few belongings crammed into a crate, we boarded the train in Toronto for the all-day trip north to Cochrane. The next day we boarded the train called the Polar Bear Express for the rest of the trip. For six hours we bumped and lurched over the boggy terrain, filled with the excitement of this crazy adventure. Crossing many rivers, we surveyed an endless terrain of short and skinny spruce and tamarack trees.

Moosonee. A tiny community of mostly Cree natives. But the few jobs were filled mostly by outsider white men, like the newbies climbing down the steps of the train that bright, hot August day. Some of our wide-eyed fellow travellers, who were tourists, headed for the motel down by the wide Moose River. Our new home sat slightly behind the motel, but from our bedroom window we could still see past it to this ever-changing body of water. Being so close to the Arctic tidewaters of James Bay, only eighteen kilometres away, we saw the dramatic effect of the tide throughout the day. At low tide, the low, fast flowing river revealed a huge sandbar in the middle, but as high tide approached, the river swelled and then seemed to flow backwards. Fascinating!

The first day of school was soon upon us. Doug quickly learned that the dress code was not as formal as southern Ontario. Not formal at all, actually. But he easily and quickly fit in, especially since even the natives thought he was native, too.

One day, I agreed to meet him after school at the only store in town, the Bay. This Hudson's Bay store had a little of everything: clothes, furniture and food. Prior to this, it had always been so easy for me to find Doug anywhere. Taller than most men, Doug stood out with his raven black hair. But of course everywhere I looked here I saw tall men with shiny, raven black hair. It was not so easy to find him now!

As for me, I was maybe the only blond, short female anywhere here or in the small neighbouring town and reserve of Moose Factory, just across the river. Strange name, eh? In the early days of exploration, the Hudson's Bay Company sent out men to set up trading posts. These men were called Factors, and their home and shop was called "The Factory."

How were we going to make this unique community our home? It wasn't long before we'd explored all we could of the very limited roads on our bikes. We took short walks into the surrounding wilderness. We took the boat taxi over to Moose Factory. My new friend and neighbour walked with me every day to the post office. Some days the short walk involved a long detour around a hungry, dangerous pack of stray dogs.

In the fall, so many of the locals disappeared into the bush to hunt that school was closed for a week. So Doug took a gun safety course and got a hunting licence. He would only be allowed to go hunting with a native guide, though. In the past, the low marshy terrain and the fluctuating, unpredictable Arctic tides had taken too many lives. Doug quickly realized that he could not take the lives of those beautiful, innocent snow geese. Also, he had an extremely close call that almost took his life. So that was the end of the gun.

Doug played the organ for the Anglican church services. We sometimes attended the Pentecostal and Baptist worship services as well. Everywhere we made lots of long-lasting, faithful friends. While Doug took evening classes to learn the Cree language, I took a koolatuk-making class. A koolatuk is a very warm northern-style parka. I actually became somewhat artistic by designing my own unique pattern to embroider on both the inner and outer layers.

It turned out we really needed these warm coats. Winter arrived in a snowstorm in mid-October. During November, I checked the thermometer every day. But since it consistently read −20 C, it was a safe bet the rest of the winter was going to be well below that. Most people had snowmobiles, zipping up and down the roads and across to Moose Factory over the five-foot-thick ice covering the river. For the few cars, at every parking spot the store provided a pole with an outlet in order for customers to plug in their vehicles. At the usual −40 C it doesn't take long for a battery to freeze.

We started hosting youth group meetings. The kids made their excitement and gratitude evident at having something positive to do, to counter the substance abuse that had become a serious threat.

When the warmth of spring arrived, we learned about the gigantic blocks of ice that would jam together and potentially cause flooding. Around that time our baby was born in the Moose Factory hospital. Now that we had a baby in this tiny, isolated, northern Ontario town, it felt like home.

Summer brought a hot sun and swarms of shockingly enormous moose flies. But the youth assured me those thick swarms were not dangerous. The Polar Bear Express once again brought tourists to the motel down by the river. And although I did not look like I belonged there, I was most assuredly *not* a tourist. This was Moosonee and this was my home.

~Elizabeth Kranz
Killaloe, Ontario

49

Where Ravens Fly Backwards

You have not seen Canada until you
have seen the North.
~Former Prime Minister Pierre Elliot Trudeau

As the floatplane circled lower over the Payne River, the pilot pointed to a cluster of houses. "That's Payne Bay," he said. "The tide's out so we'll have to land a ways out, clear of the rocks. Don't worry, they'll come out and get you." After we touched down in the water I stepped onto the pontoon and into a waiting motorboat. I had arrived — 100 miles north of the tree line in Arctic Quebec (Nunavik), at the Inuit village known today as Kangirsuk on the western side of Ungava Bay. The shore was lined with elders and children who had halted their play to come and greet their new teacher. I returned their smiles, but heard no English until Jim, the principal, stepped forward to welcome me. It was August 1969 and I had just turned twenty-two.

Knowing nothing about my accommodations, I was pleasantly surprised when Jim took me to my own house. He pointed out the water tank that was filled daily by a community worker, who in winter would also bring blocks of ice from the nearby lake. At the bathroom door Jim motioned to a metal bucket with a toilet seat mounted over a sturdy garbage bag saying, "that's called a honey bucket."

"I'll be fine," I grinned. "I used an outhouse as a child."

I was glad to see the well-stocked pantry and freezer, proof that my Montreal order had arrived on the summer ship, unlike my trunk of clothes.

"Don't worry," Jim assured me. "It'll probably be on the next plane." (It wasn't but I managed).

"That's my house over there," he pointed. "My wife will have supper ready at 6:00."

The next day I saw my classroom, which contained just blackboards, neat rows of desks and the same *Dick and Jane* books I had read in grade one. In a cupboard I found flip chart pads, crayons, and paints. The youngest in my K through 4 class only spoke Inuktitut so I was overjoyed to meet Anna, my Inuit assistant. Anna was responsible for teaching basic English. She also made hot chocolate, delicious and essential for dipping vitamin biscuits.

At the first sound of a plane the children would rush to the windows but, on one particularly windy day, I was the one who took a second look when I saw a raven flying backwards. That became my measure for gale force winds.

I purchased a parka at the Co-op, and the Hudson's Bay store had most essentials. There was only one radiophone in the village, and to call home I had to connect with an operator in southern Quebec who then rang my parents in New Brunswick. The protocol was to speak, say "over" then wait for the relay and response. But we forgot, talked at the wrong time and laughed until tears threatened to flow. Calls were too short, a high followed by the low of goodbye.

Mail arrived by plane, but just before freeze-up came a period when planes couldn't land on the river because spray would freeze on the wings, and the ice in the lake was not yet thick enough. Then my only connection with the South was CBC's Northern Messenger on my short-wave radio. Letters were sent to Montreal to be read on air, connecting teachers all around Quebec's Arctic coast. We learned of engagements, family reunions and new babies, and became one family. I don't think the broadcaster appreciated the humour when my mother included hard-to-pronounce place names like Lake Magaguadavic, and I wasn't amused when she responded to a lack of letters by inquiring if I had broken my arm or perhaps the post office had burned down.

I loved the treeless landscape and spent my spare time climbing hills, picking my way over rock fields and jumping small streams. I purchased an over-and-under (single shot 22 and 20 gauge shotgun) at the Hudson's Bay store and proudly carried it as I wandered the tundra. I jumped when ptarmigan flushed near my feet and marvelled at my first snow geese, but after I shot a Canada goose I stopped hunting. Geese mate for life, and the plaintive honking of the flock haunted my every step home.

Winter brought new adventure when I acquired an older 10 horsepower Skidoo. It wasn't fast or powerful, but I loved that little machine and the freedom it brought. Cold demands respect so I never left the village alone. David, the principal's administrative assistant, became my Skidoo buddy. We sped along valleys, drove on thick river ice cracking and shifting with the tide, and I learned to skirt the dangerous inland ponds.

In March I was thrilled when David invited me to join an overland trip to Koartac over the Easter weekend. But I had never driven for eight hours straight, and became uncertain as I watched the Skidoos being checked and the komatiks (Inuit sleds) loaded. Then, on Tuesday, a storm blew up, and my indecision increased with the swirling snow. Mid-morning on Good Friday the wind dropped, but the sky remained grey and all traces of the trail were gone. Nevertheless, I was on one of ten machines that left for Koartac mid-afternoon.

At 6:00 p.m. we stopped for hot tea and cold meat. I revelled in the holiday mood, pleased that I had no trouble keeping up. *There are no stars,* I reflected, *and every rocky hill looks the same. It's amazing — I wonder how they find their way?*

At 9:00 p.m. we halted again. This time three men drove their machines in a big circle, their headlights shining out into the darkness. Then they consulted, each pointing in a different direction. I had no idea what they were saying. This was repeated about every hour and I became more anxious with each stop. *Were we lost?* Cold and fatigue seeped in and my knees resented climbing back on the Skidoo.

Finally at 1:00 a.m. David told me we were going no farther;

Into the Wild |

they were afraid of running out of gas. I watched as both men and women tramped snow in two big circles. Long knives flashed cutting blocks and, just like that, two traditional igloos emerged! A woman motioned for me to enter one, and gave me tea she'd made on a small burner. She quickly turned it off because the roof was dripping. I laid my sleeping bag down on caribou hides, took off my outer clothes and gave in to exhaustion.

I awoke at first light to the sound of excited voices. Apparently we had gone too far west and were now on the wrong side of the bay. Breakfast could wait! After loading up, everyone chose their own path racing across the ice, meeting the searchers who by now had set out from Koartac. I was elated. I had done it!

Monday we returned home on a clear trail, and I had learned two new things. I don't like muktuk (whale blubber) and one should never have two cups of coffee where there are no trees and you are wearing a one-piece Skidoo suit!

I left Payne Bay after two years but the experiences have never left me. My soul expanded in that open Arctic land, and the accepting Inuit taught me to embrace Canada's diversity. On cold winter nights the memories are still as vivid as ravens flying backwards.

~Rose Burke
Rusagonis, New Brunswick

50

Season of the Fly

*And the black flies, the little black flies. Always the
black fly no matter where you go. I'll die with
the black fly a-pickin' my bones. In North
Ontar-eye-o-eye-o, In North Ontar-eye-o.*
~Wade Hemsworth, "The Black Fly Song"

I n 1961 my father decided it was time to introduce our family to
the joys of "wilderness" camping. Not one to undertake mod-
est adventures, he chose for our week-long holiday the mighty
Algonquin — the famous 7,652-square-kilometre Provincial
Park on the doorstep of Ontario's wild north. I was nine and my
brother seven. Although raised in the country, we'd never ventured
beyond our tamed landscape of rolling pastures and tidy dairy farms.
Our father's descriptions of the wonders of watching bears rummag-
ing through dumps and deer begging at cars on roadsides intrigued
us, although our curiosity was tempered by some past experience
with Dad's exploits.

He fancied himself a yet-to-be-discovered inventor, business mogul
and explorer, worthy of the National Geographic Society; he rarely
let his inexperience get in the way of his enthusiasm. Dad did some
checking and discovered the very best time to camp in Algonquin was
May. Few people booked campsites at that time of the year, and it was
dirt-cheap. Dad put this down to the stupidity of the common man
blind to the value of a good bargain. So book he did, and the family
prepared for our great adventure.

My parents cleared out our blue and white Volkswagen bus and restocked it with a mattress for the floor, blankets, tarps, boxes of food and utensils, a cast iron frying pan, clothes, fishing gear, rubber boots, soap and sundries. We did not pack sunscreen or bug repellent.

We arrived in the late afternoon. Strangely, there were no other campers in our vicinity. My father was delighted — he regaled us with tales of Iroquois warriors stalking the lonely pines, and described wild trappers cloaked in furs, muskets in hand, hunting bear and wolverine.

The first clue as to the real trouble we were in came after my mother and I left to fetch water. With the sun close to the horizon there was some urgency in getting settled for the night. As we crossed a grassy patch toward the waterspout, our way was blocked by a vast black cloud of dancing dots. My mother laughed at my hesitation. Bugs were part of camping after all. "Just keep your mouth closed," she advised, "and forage on."

Oh, the courage of the innocent! The moment we stepped into the maelstrom we were blinded by thousands of tiny buzzing insects. They gleefully scrambled into our eyes, ears and nostrils, no doubt amazed to find some warm-blooded fools openly crossing their green valley on a cool May evening. We thrashed our arms around wildly, drew our shirts up over our heads and stumbled to the tap, where we poured out a thick mixture of water and insects. We then ran all the way back to the bus, the black cloud accompanying us. Thus began our memorable encounter with north Ontario's little black fly.

Sitting outside by a campfire was out of the question, despite my father's assertion the smoke would drive off the buzzing horde. After two minutes of slapping, wriggling and shrieking we cried defeat and retreated to the bus. After we desperately stuffed clothing into all the openings to the outside we huddled together like terrified rabbits. After a miserable supper eaten out of cans we retired early.

It was a restless night. What we didn't know was that the black fly army had found its way in despite our blockades, and feasted on our sleeping bodies the whole night long.

The next morning, Dad got the fire going, and my brother, mother, and I headed out on a bathroom run. Again we were besieged by flies.

Again we jumped and swatted like a family that had lost its collective mind. In an open area with tall grass my mother stopped in her tracks and told me to lift my hair. For some reason, my mother had always insisted little girls' hair looked best if grown as long as possible. Apparently it made them look sweet and demure. As a result I had a mass of blond hair hanging to my waist. My brother was shorn, as it was believed long hair on a boy would tangle during daily exploits in trees and swamps and while battling cowboys, Indians and pirates.

Now, as I lifted my tresses for her to examine my back she gasped in horror. Black flies had made a home in my hair during the night, and had left bloody carnage from nape to waist. That was the last straw. An hour later we were packed and speeding back to the sanctity of home, my father's dream of wilderness camping fast eroding under my mother's angry tirade against the evils of dragging sweet and innocent children into Black Fly War Zones. We never did see dump bears or begging deer.

It turns out that I did inherit my father's sense of adventure, and my significant other and I have explored much of this magnificent park. Gone are the dumps, and moose have replaced deer as roadside attractions since the park has been carefully allowed to return to a more natural forested state. In spring (yes, I'll still visit the park in May), I've often seen and pitied tiny moose calves covered in swarms of black flies, their hides shimmering under the onslaught. How they must love the hot summer months when the little brutes finally die off. As for me, I also inherited some of my mother's common sense. I never go camping without my insect repellent. Thank the gods for Muskol lotion!

~Bonnie Lavigne
Etobicoke, Ontario

51

The One That Got Away

Sometimes when the water is quiet you can
almost hear the fish laughing at you.
~Author Unknown

It was a windy morning. Not cold, just windy, and sunny. Rainy Lake rippled like a dark blue flag creating a perfect "walleye chop" as we prepped for our daylong fishing trip. It looked to be a spectacular day for fishing.

I plopped into the old, red metal motorboat along with my dad, my cousin Sam, and my brother Jake. We began the bumpy trip across the lake to our favourite fishing spot. I loved the brisk, clean smell of the open water. A couple of Canadian loons bobbed not far off the coast of our island — diving and playing as we passed. Recent laws preventing non-Canadians from owning property here meant that very few Americans owned a piece of this beautiful wilderness. But my grandparents had purchased our island many years earlier, so our family was allowed to keep it.

As we neared our destination the landscape began to change. The shallow, sloping shoreline turned to steep rocky cliffs, and the lake began narrowing into a point. We began moving against a current as we entered the mouth of Canoe River.

Rainy Lake is a large, inland lake that straddles the Canada — U.S. border between Ontario and Minnesota. The water level is controlled by a series of dams on the several rivers that feed the lake. We were heading toward the water below the Canoe River dam; the relatively shallow water there creates a perfect spawning ground for many fish species, resulting in some of the best fishing anywhere. The only problem is that not many large fish actually live in the river—they're back out in the lake. We'd always caught a lot of fish here, but they were always smaller.

My dad slowed the boat as we reached our fishing spot, then cut the engine. Silently we readied our poles and lines. I put on a golden spinner, and noticed my brother and my cousin doing the same. These spinners were perfect for luring shore fish like bass, perch, and the occasional northern pike. Deep-water fish, like walleyes and muskies, rarely ever decide to bite one of these shiny shallow-water skimmers.

I noticed my dad attaching a strange lure shaped like a frog to the end of his line. "Do you really think you'll catch anything with that abomination?" I asked.

"It's never caught me anything before," he replied, "but you never know."

I thought using that lure was a waste of time, but decided to say nothing. I figured if he wanted to waste his day pulling that thing through the water without a bite, he could go right ahead!

By now, the unrelenting wind had pushed our little boat into a small, sheltered bay. Without the wind, I could smell the "wormy" scent of nature, of decay and good soil. This would be a good bay to cast our lines into. There were sure to be some bass and northern pike hiding amongst the fallen logs and huge rocks protruding from the water.

I made my first cast into the shallow, murky water. Almost instantly a medium-sized bass hit my lure. It's hard to describe the exciting, adrenaline rush of having a fish on the line. Reeling in a fish is an art. Keeping that fish on the line while pulling it toward you requires a lot of skill and finesse. Luckily I had learned from some pretty great teachers. I took a deep breath and began reeling in my line. The key to landing the fish is to keep the tip of your rod pointed up toward the sky, and to reel in the fish at a smooth, controlled rate. Eventually, I pulled the beautiful bass into the boat with the help of my dad, who handled the net. I removed the hook, then measured and weighed it. Then I put the slippery, flopping fish back in the water. Suddenly my cousin Sam called out, "I got one!"

The next hour and a half went roughly the same. With someone catching a fish, calling it out, and then bringing it into the boat with the help of someone netting it. Soon we had caught a total of seventeen fish: six for me, five for my dad, three for Jake, and three for Sam. Although we'd caught a whole variety of species, no one had yet netted a walleye. This was disappointing, but not unexpected. All the fish we'd caught were either small or medium sized.

Suddenly Dad yelled, "Got one!" There was a flurry of movement as everyone tried to get their own lures into the boat so they could help net Dad's fish. I was ready first, so I was put in charge of the net. Stepping over open tackle boxes and coolers I made my way past Jake and Sam to the back where Dad was now standing at work, reeling in his fish. As I reached him, I realized the fish he was battling wasn't some little perch. His rod was bent almost completely in half, and his arms gleamed with sweat from the exertion of holding the pole steady.

As I readied the largest net I prepared myself for whatever was about to emerge from the icy water. I suspected it was a very large northern pike, because the fish had taken his hook near the surface, and the line wasn't showing the spastic movements of a struggling bass.

As Dad brought the fish in closer to the boat, in a quick flash of scales I could see it was longer than a bass, but without the sleek build of a northern pike. Suddenly the fish was right next to the boat, and I quickly plunged my net into the water. For one brief second it appeared I had succeeded in netting the fish. I felt a sudden weight as I attempted to heave the end of the net out of the water.

What happened next will be forever burned into my memory. I managed to successfully heft the net out of the water with the huge fish in it, but the net was still over the water. I realized then that the fish was not a northern pike, but instead the largest walleye I had ever seen. Its tail and head hung over each side of the three-foot diameter net. The incredibly muscular body suddenly stiffened, turning the fish into a rigid pole. Suddenly it was no longer lying in the net, but instead it was lying on top of the frame. Then, with what seemed like a knowing look in its old, wise eye, the monstrous walleye easily rolled off the frame and slipped back into the icy waves. It spit out the hook a second later, and disappeared.

Silence swept over us like a wave over the rocks as each of us realized what had happened. We had just witnessed possibly the biggest walleye in the river, and we had no proof of it. Nobody spoke for the rest of the outing. We were all too busy thinking about the one that got away.

~Mitchell Kastanek
Amery, Wisconsin, USA

52

My Log Home Critters

*If you talk to the animals they will talk with you and
you will know each other. If you do not talk to
them you will not know them, and what
you do not know, you will fear.*
~Chief Dan George

Perhaps, like many Canadians, you have dreamed of owning a cozy log cabin, surrounded by snow-capped, majestic
peaks and nestled among pristine ski hills. Or maybe your
dream cabin overlooks a shimmering ocean, teeming with
aquatic wonders and graced with a coastal outline of magical islands.
That was my dream, and after parting ways with my husband, I went
and found my dream log home. On the Sunshine Coast in British
Columbia. Near the ocean. Complete with critters.

Now, no one mentioned to me there would be coastal critters,
especially my real estate agent. If she had said, "Fran, there are bears,
cougars, raccoons, deer, ants, termites and woodpeckers who will want
to live with you," I would have been forewarned and stayed glued to
Langley, where I'd lived for twenty-seven years.

Finding a suitable home, with a perfect suite for my then 100-year-
old mom, took many ferry trips and over fifty home viewings. But I
found it — a large, rustic, three-storey log home in Halfmoon Bay. The
warmth and textures of the various logs and woods wrapped one in a
sense of safety, cosiness and grass-roots comfort. When we moved in
it seemed like my dream had finally materialized. Ah, home: just me,

my mom, my dog Timber, and two cats. I do vaguely remember the home inspector mentioning something about birds nesting in the eaves and evidence of termites. But in my excitement, it didn't really sink in.

We moved in during late October 2009. With winter fast approaching I already felt somewhat isolated. Ensconced on my half-acre hilltop property, surrounded by sentinel-like groves of cedar and pine trees, I began to experience some niggling doubts. It sure was dark at night. At times, the evening stillness felt suffocating and eerie. *What on earth lurked in my garden beneath this silent shroud of darkness?*

Timber needed bathroom breaks every couple of hours. Out there in that ebony evening, Timber rarely barked. Yet one night, around 10.30 p.m., just ten days after we moved in, she began barking constantly. I grabbed a flashlight and opened the door just a crack, peeking out into the black void. *What was out there?*

Timber continued her incessant barking. Puzzled, I opened the large window blind, shining the flashlight into the night. There! Right at my fence line, the light caught two beady eyes staring back at me. Beady eyes belonging to a large bear cub, happily investigating my neighbour's nearby compost bin. Only a decrepit four-foot wire fence separated us. My light then caught the magnificent, shiny black coat of the biggest momma bear I have ever seen. Well, I'd never actually seen one to compare her to, but she was truly huge.

Apparently, Momma Bear, with cubs in tow, regularly toured the neighbourhood's compost bins and garbage cans in search of the fifteen- to twenty-thousand daily calories needed to help her through hibernation. With trembling hands and a pounding heart, I picked up the phone. Then put it down to first quickly pour a glass of wine, which I chugged down. Then I called my neighbour to warn her.

"Susan," I blurted when she answered. "There's a huge bear and two cubs in your driveway!"

"Really, Fran?" she replied calmly. "Thanks for telling us; we'll take a look. They won't hurt you. Come on, Stephen," she called to her teenage son. "Let's go look at the bears."

Look at the bears? I thought, downing another glass of wine while manoeuvring the large spotlight with my other hand. *Are they crazy?* I watched my neighbours saunter onto their deck, investigate the bear situation, then bang on a couple of pot lids. Momma Bear looked up, not particularly frightened, gathered her two sleek, shiny black cubs and sauntered down the driveway to the next neighbour's house. My other neighbour seemingly sat calmly in the kitchen, watching while the cubs played "roll in the garbage can" as Momma Bear nonchalantly supervised playtime.

That was my first introduction to my log home critters. My second critter invasion arrived along with the first sign of spring. A loud drilling noise sat me bolt upright from sleep. Apparently, woodpeckers used to nest in my roof. A damaged soffit had presented an ideal opportunity. Although now repaired, tell that to determined woodpeckers intent on revisiting their old haunt. In our attempt to reduce the growing row of holes and neatly drilled cedar planks along the eaves, my house soon became laughingly known as "Fran's Party House." Three stories up, the pest control man hung large salmon fishing lures along with flashing CDs, all sporting luminous orange and green streamers that twirled in the breeze to deter the uninvited house-eating guests. When I sold the place six years later, the party favours remained dangling.

My first year introduced me to the rest of the coastal critter delights. Thousands of swarming termites teemed in my mom's suite. Ants marched in, raccoons roamed nearby, and deer demolished delectable plants. Cougars crouched within a few hundred feet and bears reigned supreme, enjoying the neighbourhood's veritable feasts of fruit and gourmet garbage.

I slowly learned acceptance and how to live with my fears. My dog needed a daily walk. Armed with air horn, whistle and ski pole — not unlike preparing to go to war — I walked with vigilance. I did not explore the surrounding trails but stayed on the roads. My fears didn't leave me but luckily the wild critters didn't attack.

Now, living back in suburbia, I no longer pack my armoury when I walk. There is no need to fear bears and cougars. Instead, I watch traffic streaming by, leaving its trail of pollutants and swirling dust.

Now, I stare with fondness at the photo of my dream log home on my office bookshelf. I reflect on warm family Christmases and celebrations, snow-covered gardens, and Christmas lights twinkling in alpine-like postcard perfection. I remember thousands of stars in the crystal clear night sky. As I recall the spicy aroma of cedar trees and the soothing sound of the ocean lapping at pristine shores, I miss it all, even those log home critters.

~Frances R. McGuckin
Abbotsford, British Columbia

53

Tattler Lake Tales

The one who tells the stories rules the world.
~Native American Proverb

M y husband is Irish but he came to Canada for me — for better or worse. So I try to help him fit in, even though he doesn't play hockey and only knows two words for snow. In July 2011 I took him canoeing, which included portaging in Algonquin Provincial Park. Portaging is an activity that involves carrying a canoe on your head, at least when there is no river or lake to paddle in. You can spend a few hours or several days using this traditional method of travel to get deep into the Canadian wilderness to camp. Or in our case, to get to an old Ranger cabin on Tattler Lake.

I thought it would be a romantic way to share the beauty of my country with my husband. As it turned out, it's a wonder we are still married.

I kept a journal of the experience.

Day 1, July 27, 2011. I'll get my complaints out of the way first:
1. We went in the wrong direction, right from launching the canoe.
2. The bugs at this cabin are beyond my worst nightmares — like Freddy Krueger sort of nightmares. Currently, I am refusing to leave the cabin.
3. Swimming is disgusting; trod through weeds and ankle-high gunk while dodging horseflies that threaten to carry away small

children. Once again, have decided to stay in the cabin, and small children are on their own.

Now, on the brighter side:
1. Found a cool "Trip Log" in the cabin that dates back over ten years. Lots of fun entries to read from previous campers who have stayed here. Wildlife sightings recorded include moose, mice and snakes. Also a couple who claim to have done it on the picnic table outside (not without bug repellent, I hope).
2. Spring at end of short trail has beautiful, cold clean water. Will send husband out to get more soon as still refusing to leave cabin due to complaint #2.
3. Trip out from the Shall Lake access point an easy one. Took about four hours to get here with one 90-metre and one 550-metre portage. Should have been easier but jerk at outfitters gave us the wrong canoe. It weighs a ton and moves like a beached whale through the water. (Hold on, maybe I have a fourth complaint!)
4. Husband brought back yummy cold spring water.

Day 2, July 28, 2011. No mice, no moose, one snake. Bugs became manageable last night with a good fire. Made the mistake of reading trip log entry from October 3, 2003 about "Old Log Cabin Man/ Ghost of Gulaf" before going to bed, resulting in "nervous nelliness" that irritated usually understanding husband. Revenge was had when husband arose at 5:30 a.m. and knocked over pee bucket.

Day 3, July 29, 2011. Awoke this morning to husband swearing like drunken sailor about bugs. Cannot make decent cup of tea on picnic table without swarms of biblical proportions.

"Let's skip breakfast and just go," he pleaded.

"But we haven't seen a moose yet," I whined half-heartedly. "Or the resident groundhog."

I thought about the Tattler Cabin visitors who'd had infinitely more interesting experiences than us. They almost all had multiple moose sightings. Some had seen the Northern Lights. They'd cooked gourmet meals by firelight and done industrious things like taking out all the cabin windows and washing them in the lake. They'd made love on picnic tables and had mice spring from the food cupboard. They'd rebuilt the fire pit and seen bears while using the outdoor latrine they called the Thunder Box. Basically, these people had surpassed us in almost every single way.

Here are some fun entries from the Trip Log that we found in the cabin, in no particular order:

June 18, 2011: A little fun in the sun on the picnic table (Don't worry — on a towel).

Sept 16, 1993: It rained all day but we were still stupid enough to come here. We saw two moose and five ducks yesterday and a Great Herring today. We are eating our lunch of tea biscuits that my mom finally didn't burn.

Captain's Log Star Date 598: Spock and I stayed here over night. Mosquitoes so bad Scottie beamed us up.

Date unspecified: A strange combination of striking beauty and obnoxious friends. We appreciate the hospitality of dry bum wad.

Sept 28, 1999: We got drunk enough to solve all the problems of living with women. So you can imagine how drunk we were.

Aug 9-11, 2003: House Party — Dean made a dead rat dance.

Aug 2007: My brother's friend and I carved swords out of sticks. After, we started duelling. We made the ends of big thick sticks sharp and hit each other. Majority of the time we hit each other's sticks so hard that they broke. We also hit each other. Ryan, Age 12.

How could we leave Tattler Lake without experiencing something extraordinary and writing it down for future cabin inhabitants to read? How could we admit that all we saw was a beaver and a frog, and that we hid in the cabin most of the time and ate dehydrated turkey tetrazzini out of a bag? Someone had to be mauled by a bear this morning

over breakfast, or we would go down in history as the most boring couple that ever stayed here.

I explained this to my husband as he stood in the doorway swatting at deer flies. "Give that to me," my husband said, pointing at the Cabin Trip Log. He furiously scribbled in it for a couple of minutes and then handed me back the following entry:

July 27-29, 2011: After a short canoe ride of four to five minutes, with time out for a five-mile hike, my wife and I arrived at this cabin to find five moose dancing with a groundhog while a beaver played the harpsichord. Shortly afterward, I had flagrant relations with my wife several times at the fire pit, while the Ghost of Gulaf looked on and took notes. The following day, while my wife cooked beef bourguignon from scratch, I tore down the cabin and rebuilt it myself using only one nail and my teeth. This, after we had driven every last snake out of Tattler Lake and murdered every mouse in a four-mile radius. My wife skinned all the mice and made a lovely mouse fur blanket out of them for future cabin visitors to enjoy on cold nights.

"Ready to go?" he said. I was packed in less than five minutes. My husband may not play hockey or know twenty different words for snow, but he knows how to tell a good camping story, just like all Canadians.

~C.S. O'Cinneide
Elora, Ontario

Up Close and Personal

My dad taught us Trudeau boys how to paddle a canoe
pretty much as soon as we could walk. And like many
Canadians, I've spent loads of summer nights
out under the stars, beside a campfire...
getting eaten alive.
~Prime Minister Justin Trudeau

As I shifted the canoe into a more comfortable position on my shoulders, I thought to myself, *it wouldn't be so hard to take if it wasn't for the buzzing.* It was the fourth day of our backcountry canoe-camping trip in Halfway Lake Provincial Park, and I was finally starting to find a certain rhythm in traversing the portages, those narrow trails that get you from one lake to the next. Even the motion of hoisting my end of the canoe to my shoulders was much smoother than it had been on day one.

It was hot, especially in my rain gear, but I'd take sweating any day over the threat of those itchy little needles wielded by the swarming mosquitoes. As I plodded along, my vision a bit restricted by the fact that I was at the back end, a cloud of hungry insects hovered.

Small blessings, I thought to myself. *Focus on the small blessings.*

Fresh air and a break from the city were what my friend and I had come for. Halfway Lake is northeast of Sudbury in Northern Ontario. We hadn't realized the downside of canoe tripping this early in July was twofold: first, it was prime time for mosquitoes, and second, many of the portage trails had not yet been cleared. This meant occasionally having to step over huge trees that had fallen across the trail, not an easy task when carrying a canoe or a heavy backpack.

Still, there had been rewards. This far north there were few other canoe trippers and we had seen plenty of wildlife, although no moose as yet.

There was a definite feeling of accomplishment when we finally slipped the canoe back into the water at the end of the portage, loaded up and headed out on the last leg of the day's journey, our destination a campsite on a point of land. After arriving, we unloaded our gear and became quietly engrossed in the myriad tasks involved in setting up the campsite.

That's when our visitors appeared.

I sat on a weathered pine log, barely breathing, and watched as a female moose made her majestic way into the small cove adjoining our campsite. I'd seen these mighty mammals before, but never this close, and never for this long. I wanted to fully savour the experience.

After a few minutes we noticed a disturbance in the underbrush near the shore and, suddenly, a second slightly smaller moose with small, fuzzy antlers emerged from the woods with long, gangly strides. His coat was changing — part of it was light brown, and part a dark brown, almost black. Despite his messy appearance the moose calf captivated our attention as he waded through the still, shallow water, hauling out lily pads and eating them with obvious relish. As his mother watched indulgently, he at times plunged his head into the water up to his ears to pull out particularly tender specimens. As he fed, he gradually drew nearer to our campsite, occasionally lifting a dripping snout to glance around, until he was about 100 yards away.

Much as we enjoyed observing the moose, we needed to get our camp in order before darkness fell. As we resumed our work, I accidentally stepped on a twig. In the serene and silent surroundings that little noise resounded like a gunshot. I shot a quick look at the young moose just as he flung his head in alarm and scrambled awkwardly onto the shore.

When nothing happened, a few moments later he cautiously waded back into the water to continue his meal, and we in turn resumed our nature observation.

Our canoe trip ended the next day, and we headed back to the city. Still, the magical memory of watching two moose up close and personal has lasted for decades.

Creatures like moose personify the wonder of the Canadian wilderness. Being fortunate enough to see them up close underscored for me how fortunate we are to live in a country that still has open spaces where such creatures can live and move freely.

~Lisa Timpf
Simcoe, Ontario

The Spirit of Canada

Chapter 7

Rising to the Occasion

You were created to overcome every obstacle,
to rise above every challenge. Not just
to survive — to thrive!
~Joel Osteen

Perspective by Fire

*Wherever people are suffering, make
it your task to serve them.*
~Pope John Paul II

In just the same way a rolled up newspaper flashes, fully consumed when tossed into a campfire, I watched a family's home explode into a ball of flame. Then the neighbour's place flashed — and the next one on the street — and the next. I stood watching them burst into flames, falling like dominoes. In a matter of seconds an entire city block had succumbed. And my job was to help stop it.

On May 3, 2016 a relentless forest fire raged through Fort McMurray, taking with it ten percent of the town's structures. What a day to be a firefighter. A city of 100,000 was entirely evacuated. The RCMP was in the streets, pulling people from their cars and telling them to run as fire approached the road. Parents ran with suitcases rolling behind them and babies on their backs. Empty cars sat with doors wide open as bikes, wagons, scooters, and foot traffic weaved chaotically between them. It was like an Armageddon movie. But it was happening before my eyes.

My first assignment was the hospital. Hot embers and smoke were blowing across the highway, and the high occupancy building was a priority. I hopped into a pickup truck with a few other firefighters and raced to the hospital. We set up sprinklers around the building as nurses hurriedly loaded patients onto city buses. I climbed to the roof and opened one of the hallway standpipe systems, stretching out the hose and giving the end a quick tug to start the water flowing. I began soaking the roof as burning flakes rained from the sky. When I finally looked up, I nearly dropped the nozzle.

My city was burning.

The high roof of the hospital provided a surreal view of the inferno. Time seemed to slow down as sirens, the whir of helicopters and emergency radio chatter all blurred together. Smoke billowed from Beacon Hill, just to my left, where my childhood home stood. My parents had retired to Lacombe, Alberta, and I'd been living in the house while renovating it for them, and all my things were there.

I knew the odds weren't in favour of it lasting. Embers from Abasand, a small hamlet to the west, sailed past my helmet as I stared, stunned. For all I knew, these were pieces of my own Abasand condo falling around me.

I punched in my dad's number and the answering machine beeped: "Hey Pops, I'm not sure if you're watching this on TV or not, but, um… the fire has gotten into the city. Looks like the house is gone. I'm gonna be busy, but I'll call you when I can. Love you."

My next task was to fight my own despair, to keep working despite knowing that I had just lost everything I'd ever worked for. No one can ever teach you how to do this. I wanted to crumple into a useless heap of futile tears, but I knew — if I had the smallest chance to keep others from suffering their own losses, I had to take it.

On the second night, at 3 a.m., the fire jumped a river and ignited some grass next to the water treatment plant. *If that thing lights up*, I thought, *we lose*. There would be no more water for our hoses. Also, just up a steep hill about a kilometre beyond the plant was another neighbourhood, still untouched.

We moved into the third day of the fight. We had put water on more burning houses in the last thirty-six hours than many firefighters see in a whole career. My eyes burnt, from a combined lack of sleep and the relentless stinging of smoke. The blisters on my feet throbbed, threatening to burst with every additional step. Everything hurt. I felt like I had just run a marathon carrying sandbags. At this moment, pulling a fully charged hose-line up that hill looked like scaling Mt. Everest. It was the last thing I wanted to do. I felt a lump grow in my throat, and a warmth flushed my face. *I can't do it… Dear Lord, I don't have anything left.*

I dropped the hose, gasping for air — defeated.

Then I glanced up the hill and I saw one of my officers. Earlier I had seen him wrapping his entire foot in bandages, replacing blood-stained pieces of cloth with fresh ones. His feet had looked raw; most of the skin was missing. But there he was, dragging hose up this hill with quiet diligence.

The fire caught the first tree on the forest line and it flared up. I coughed and squeezed my eyes tight to clear my vision. Swallowing hard, I pushed down the knot in my throat. Lifting the hose over my shoulder, I started to climb. *If he can do it, so can I.*

Not one of the houses in that neighbourhood was lost. Neither was the water treatment plant.

A couple of days later I saw my childhood home for the first time. As I neared the plot of land that held so many memories, I thought I would cry. I stepped out of my car, still in bunker gear. My boots left footprints in the white ash that dusted the driveway, looking just like those left by astronauts on the surface of the moon.

Then it started to come back. This was where I set up my first lemonade stand, which taught me my first lessons about money. This driveway was where I fell off my bike, scraping my knee countless times trying to learn how to ride. The number of jump shots on that bent, melted basketball hoop had to be in the millions. That lawn I hated to mow, but taught me about responsibility, still showed a few bits of green. The brick chimney still stood, and the fireplace at its base sat charred, reminding me of the stockings that hung above it every Christmas. I learned how to kiss under that tree in the yard, how to pray in that living room, and how to cook on that stove that was now nothing but a warped shell.

I stood there, a defeated firefighter who had lost both his family home and his condo to the very thing he trained every day to fight. All I had left was the time I had put into the relationships in my life. The love I had given. The time spent on others. Now was the test of how much that would come back.

Standing there, I could still almost feel the incessant buzzing of my cell phone against my leg while I worked on that hospital roof. My phone battery died quickly that day, trying to keep up with all the messages, phone calls, notifications and concern from people who loved me.

Maybe, I realized, I hadn't lost as much as I thought.

~Anthony Hoffman
Fort McMurray, Alberta

Running Water

It takes nothing away from a human
to be kind to an animal.
~Joaquin Phoenix

It was a hot summer evening in July, and I had accepted an invitation from my friend John to visit him and his family on their farm. Driving out from my home in Port Alberni earlier in the day I had been able to appreciate the full beauty of the place, nestled beneath the Beaufort Mountain Range in the middle of Vancouver Island's west coast.

The family showed me around their dairy farm, home to about thirty black and white Holstein cows. The fields were quiet and tranquil on this lazy Sunday afternoon, and the creek that poured down out of the mountains sparkled in the sunlight as it ran through their lush green land. Now it was evening, and I listened with curiosity as they told me that one of their cows had gone into labour out in the field. I was very interested in seeing the birth of the new calf, and really wanted to stay, but it was Sunday night and I had to get home and prepare for work Monday morning.

I walked out on the sundeck and gazed out over the field, watching as John's dad rounded up the cattle to bring them in for the night. I then went to say goodnight to everyone. It was getting late and I had a half hour drive home.

On my way out the door I heard John's father yelling frantically from the field, "Bring the John Deere! Bring the John Deere!" The family became very excited and everyone ran out on to the deck to see what was happening.

We could see their dad down by the bank of the creek. Apparently the cow in labour had wandered away from the herd and managed to slip down the muddy bank of the creek into the cold rushing water. The bank was steep enough that the tractor was needed to pull her out.

We all ran through the field to the creek while one of John's brothers raced to the barn to get the tractor.

As we reached the creek we saw the poor cow was submerged up to her neck, with the cold water rushing around her. By now there was some panic because the tractor needed to pull the cow out was very slow, and still had some distance to cover from the barn to the creek.

Suddenly one of the girls yelled out: "The calf is coming. Look, see the hooves!" The cow was now in full birthing mode, in the middle of the creek, and the calf was being born under water.

Everyone was now panicking as they tried to get a rope around the cow to pull her up on the bank, but the fast running current kept taking the rope downstream.

Again I heard someone shout: "The calf is coming. Someone has to jump in and help!"

It had been a hot day, but by now the family had changed into jeans for the evening. As the only one still wearing shorts, I was chosen to jump in! When I entered the water I was shocked at how cold it really was and, as I waded out to the cow, I found myself in ice cold rushing water up to my chest. At that moment I realized the calf was really coming — and right now.

Within minutes a sixty-pound calf was born right into my arms! But when I realized the little guy's head was still under water I began to panic and started yelling for help. I knew that calf would not survive unless we could get his head out of the water. I heard a splash, and moments later another pair of arms arrived to help. We got his head out of the water, and then because the creek bottom was muddy and uneven we needed more help to carry the calf to safety. So a third person joined us in the icy water, and the three of us managed to float/carry the newborn calf to safety. The tractor finally arrived, so the rest of them were working on getting the cow out of the creek.

Now our next major concern was trying to get the calf warmed up. I was shivering, but the brand new calf was in real danger. One of the boys took off his T-shirt and handed it to me. I began rubbing the newborn with it to warm him up. I was cold, numb and excited, but also now fearful that the calf would not survive. As I rubbed him fiercely, my thoughts were totally focused on getting him warm so he might have a chance of survival. The others had managed to rope the cow and were pulling her up with the tractor, while a few of the boys got behind and pushed her up the creek bank to safety.

The cow was now safe, and the calf was still alive. Now we had another problem. Because the cow had given birth in the creek, her afterbirth had washed away, and along with it her scent. The new mother would not acknowledge the calf she had minutes ago given birth to. There was nothing we could do but get them both back to the barn, and hope that in a while she would accept him.

It was now 10:00 p.m., I was tired and very cold, and knew I just had to go home. I said goodbye to everyone, including the new baby I had been midwife to, climbed into my car and headed home. As soon as I arrived I called and got the great news! Once in the barn, the cow had taken only a short while to decide that this was indeed her calf, and the little guy not only survived, but was now busy guzzling away. We talked about what they might name him, and one of the boys suggested that he be aptly named "Running Water!"

I went to work the next day tired but exhilarated! All I had wanted was to see the birth of the calf, but to participate as fully as I did was one of the most wonderful experiences I've ever had!

~Carla Crema
Port Alberni, British Columbia

57

This Is How We Do It

He who would do great things should
not attempt them all alone.
~Seneca Proverb

I t was July 2, 2015, another scorching hot summer day. I caught the radio broadcast that a half-hectare fire was burning up the Sechelt Inlet. Just two kilometres away lay the village of Sechelt on First Nation's land. "It's only an acre," I reassured myself. "They'll put it out."

At my home in forested Halfmoon Bay, close to Sechelt on the Sunshine Coast, I lived in constant fear of fire. With Highway 101 being the only road out and limited firefighting services, my fears were real.

Unfortunately, the wildfire took hold quickly. When I awoke early on July 5th the winds had changed, and a strange red glow lit the sky. With no morning chorus of birds and an eerie silence, my world felt frightening and ominous. Ash rained down. Minuscule particles coated the coast in a deathly white shroud, spreading further than Vancouver. With these strong, gusty winds, I knew Halfmoon Bay could be threatened.

I started to panic as I heard the reports on the radio. The fire was spiralling out of control. Just seven years before, when I lived in Langley, I had stood by helplessly as my large workshop, horse barn, and half a houseful of priceless possessions burned to the ground.

With scant information available, the media reports were sketchy. That afternoon a friend called and told me about a new Facebook group devoted to the fire. A hundred kilometres away in Powell River, Ken White, a volunteer rescue agent for the Canadian Forces and Canadian Coast Guard, had launched "The Sechelt Forest Fire" Facebook page. I saw in amazement that nearly 2,300 people had joined the group so far.

The next day the monster fire had grown to 250 hectares. Quickly named the Old Sechelt Mine Fire, it burned uncontained, fuelled by hot weather, tinder-dry forests, and unusually strong winds.

Anxious for good news, I checked my iPhone early that morning. Instead, I was saddened to learn the fire had claimed the life of John Phare, a sixty-year-old Sechelt Indian band member. An experienced tree faller, John had worked feverishly to help contain the blaze. But amidst the noise of the fire and the helicopters overhead he hadn't heard the tree behind him falling.

Stretched past its maximum, the British Columbia Wildfire Service began contracting firefighters from everywhere to help. Fire fighters began arriving from Burns Lake, Duncan, Campbell River, Ontario and even Australia — but to few amenities. So Ken launched another Facebook page, "Sechelt Forest Fire Support Services for Firefighters," coordinating meals and supplies for them. Action photos and fire videos filled both Facebook pages.

I couldn't go outside without a mask due to the ash and smoke so I stayed inside and found comfort in the Facebook pages. I read countless reports of people sharing their fears and praise, and their willingness to contribute whatever they could to help the firefighters. I was deeply touched.

"I live by the fire, thank you for keeping me safe," posted one nine-year-old girl. "I guess what I am trying to say is "THANK YOU FIREFIGHTERS!!""

"I can barely put food on my table," wrote a struggling mom, "but does anyone reckon the firefighters need their clothes mended?"

"My husband's fighting the fire," posted another woman. "Do you know where the crew could eat at six in the morning?"

To which Selina August, of the Sechelt Indian band replied, "We want to help!"

What happened next was a true miracle. Selina, along with five other band members, jumped into action and started the incredible effort rolling. Hour by hour, it unfolded on my screen, gaining massive momentum. The Sechelt Indian Government District offered to provide firefighters with breakfast and dinner. Immediately the First Nation's people were inundated with donations of food, drinks, cash, shopping, freezers, cooking and personal supplies, gift cards, accommodation, entertainment and meals.

Starting the next morning at 4 a.m., dozens of volunteers prepared daily feasts for all the firefighters and paramedics at the band hall. The people of the Sunshine Coast united to help with a strength that attracted media attention across Canada — becoming heroes in the process. We watched online, fascinated. And helped when we could.

My friends Mokie and Mike Burnham owned the Sechelt Fish Market. When Mokie learned the Burns Lake forestry firefighters, including their son, were heading to Sechelt, she asked the fire centre manager if they could drop off homemade treats at the line. He agreed, so Mokie sent texts to two friends to help bake cookies. When they posted it on Ken's Facebook page, things went crazy. Within hours their fish market was swamped with food donations. The crews were overwhelmed, posting, "Thank you, thank you, but no more, please!"

Volunteers collected, cleaned and mended clothes. Businesses donated, organized and delivered supplies. They made T-shirts, bumper stickers and erected huge signs along the highway thanking firefighters, and honouring the fallen John Phare.

By July 12th the fire had exploded to 423 hectares, although it was forty percent contained and, luckily, burning away from Sechelt. That day, the province finally set up a base camp to serve the firefighters. The last meal was served at the Sechelt Indian band hall, with an abundance of leftover food donated to the food bank. Ken continued soliciting personal items online for the remaining firefighters. He is truly an unsung hero, creating this remarkable Facebook phenomenon.

That same day I read a post by Martin Ca of the Sechelt Indian band that brought tears to my eyes: "What started out as six individuals coming together for a great cause turned into an outpouring of kindness, togetherness, and inclusion of LOVE from the ENTIRE Sunshine

Coast Community. The Sunshine Coast is a great place to live and call HOME. We are ONE. Thank you very much."

By July 22nd our community was thrilled to learn that the fire, although still burning vigorously, was fully contained.

Meanwhile, another Facebook page was created as a memorial for John Phare, with condolences posted from all across Canada. Nearly 1,000 people attended his memorial service. John was later posthumously awarded the first British Columbia Medal of Good Citizenship by Premier Christy Clark.

November 10th was a big day. The fire was officially declared completely out. For four long months members of our community opened up their hearts, uniting through disaster — and death. In the process I learned the true meaning of the words humble, giving, and "community spirit." I honour and thank the firefighters, our First Nations people, Ken White, and the heroes of Sechelt and the Sunshine Coast.

~Frances R. McGuckin
Abbotsford, British Columbia

58

The Bad Marmot

*There is something that all Canadians know, the feel
of the wild even in the heart of the city.*
~Wade Davis

It was a lovely spring morning in Kelowna, and the dogs were going crazy. "There's a marmot in the driveway," announced my husband Carl. Here in the Okanagan Valley these rodents grow to somewhere between eight and twenty pounds — the size of a beaver. They are not uncommon, especially as we live next to an orchard and are accustomed to seeing wildlife, including deer, coyotes, and raccoons.

We headed out in my car to the dog park and when we returned the critter was still there — standing next to Carl's car. Then, just as we pulled into the driveway he disappeared up into the car.

At this point we were not very concerned. It wouldn't be that difficult to just shoo him out, we reasoned.

We opened the hood and quickly spotted him and knocked and yelled in attempt to scare him out. It was amazing to see how small a space he could squish himself into. Concluding we had frightened him into lying low, we retreated to the house and kept an eye on the car. Sure enough, he eventually came out. After letting him get a few feet from the car, we ran out and quickly moved the car into the garage.

At this point we did not realize that marmots *really* like cars.

As the garage door was closing he ran down the drive and, with us watching, he jumped into *my* car! I was not prepared for how indignant

I felt. Carl's car was one thing, but my car? How dare he? I went into battle mode. We tapped and banged on the car, to no avail. As before, we retreated to the house and then watched through the window.

We never saw him climb out of the vehicle.

For the next three days we tried everything we and our neighbours could think of. We bought a live trap and filled it with carrots. We drove to the park and left the car in spots we thought he would like. We heard marmots didn't like air fresheners so we emptied a can of Febreze into my bumper. I nearly asphyxiated myself — but he was still there. We even tried power washing him out. Yup, still there.

Taking a new approach, we phoned our car dealership. With a laugh, they said yes, they had encountered every kind of rodent problem this spring — no worries, bring it in. Why hadn't I done this right at the start? I was so relieved. I drove my car in, and Carl drove us home.

Two hours later the service manager called and said, "Lady, the biggest, angriest marmot I've ever seen is in the bumper of your car, and my guys won't touch it."

We decided it was time to bring in the big guns. The trapper from the pest control company agreed to go to the dealership while the car was up on the hoist. This next part I know because one of the mechanics took a cell phone video of the whole thing. The trapper used a long pole with a lasso and managed to snag the critter and drag it from the bumper. After finally wrestling him down to the floor of the shop… the giant rodent escaped! Mayhem ensued as the mechanics ran around shrieking. The trapper was in hot pursuit and the marmot, as it ran through the lot and saw all those new cars, was squeaking something to the effect of, "So many choices, so little time!"

The trapper, hero of the day, finally snagged the marmot again and this time successfully loaded him into the trap. We were left with about $1,000 in damage, immense gratitude to the critter-trapper and the service guys in the dealership, and a commitment to always, always park the cars in the garage!

~Jane Everett
Kelowna, British Columbia

Rising to the Occasion | 237

The Greatest Goal

All summer I was a calm and graceful
lady, then hockey season started.
~Author Unknown

M ath was never my favourite subject at school. I barely passed, and to this day I'm intimidated by anything more complex than adding or subtracting numbers. However, I could rattle off the jersey numbers of every player in the NHL and I knew the stats of every player on my favourite team.

I was in grade nine, growing up in the small logging community of Sooke, British Columbia. My two best friends and I were avid hockey fans. While the other girls fretted over their hair and make-up, we took a shop class and played on an all-girls floor-hockey team at school.

Our favourite NHL team was the Montreal Canadiens and my idol was the up and coming superstar, Guy Lafleur. I took great interest in every game and followed his career with a statistician's precision. I was devastated when my idol was not selected to play on a team that saw NHL stars pitted against a selection of Russian players in a friendly eight-game exhibition called the Canada–USSR Series.

The series was played at a time when cold war tensions were running high. I wasn't interested in the politics of the games, but I knew our nation's prowess in hockey, so I was convinced our guys would dominate. Hockey was, after all, Canada's game! When Russia beat Canada soundly 7–3 in the first game in Montreal, my friends and I were as shocked as the rest of the country.

When the fifth game shifted to Moscow, my friends and I wore giant Team Canada jerseys and proudly displayed Canadian flags in our bedroom windows. We looked forward to seeing our team win. But there was an unforeseen problem — the time difference.

We'd been able to watch the first four games on television because they had been played in Canadian cities. But the final four games were in Moscow, so those games would be telecast in our time zone early in the mornings — the exact same time we were supposed to be in Mr. Ruxton's math class!

A black and white television was set up in the school library for students with spares so they could watch the fifth game. We could hear their cheering while we were in agony trying to concentrate on integers and fractions. When an audible groan arose from down the hall we learned that Russia had won 5–4. I all but blamed Mr. Ruxton for the loss.

My friends and I had a sleepover so we could watch the Sunday morning game six. Team Canada was up against the formidable stick handling of Yakushev and Kharlamov, as well as the brilliant goaltending of Vladislav Tretiak once again. When Team Canada won the hard-fought game 3–2 we breathed a collective sigh of relief.

Later we huddled together to figure out how we could follow the action in the last two games at school the following week. We decided to bring our transistor radios and listen using headphones. We knew we were taking a huge risk but it was worth it!

I hid my transistor radio under my jeans jacket and camouflaged the ear buds under my long hair. Game seven had already started when I put my head down in math class and tried to look as studious as possible. With the score tied 3–3 close to the end of the third period, my friends and I exchanged forlorn glances. I felt like crying. Then with less than three minutes to play, Paul Henderson deked out the Russian defenseman, Tsygankov, and scored on Tretiak! My two friends and I sprang from our seats screeching, "Yahooooo!"

Mr. Ruxton jumped from his desk and glared menacingly at me. "What is the meaning of this outburst?"

Without hesitation, I said, "I just LOVE math!"

He shook his head while the rest of the class giggled. Then he motioned for us to show him our radios. We sheepishly obliged and then he asked, "What was the final score?" Turns out he had been on to us from the very beginning!

On Thursday, September 28, 1972 in an unprecedented move, Mr. Ruxton dismissed math class early so we could join the rest of the school in watching the eighth and final game of the Summit Series on television. My statistician brain was adding up the facts. Heading into that final game each team had three wins and three losses and one tie, but the Soviets were ahead in goal differential by two.

It didn't take a math genius to figure out that Team Canada had to win this crucial last game in order to win the series. With the Soviet team ahead 5–3 at the end of the second period, I glanced over at Mr. Ruxton, who looked as subdued and depressed as the rest of us. Surely even going back to math class was better than watching Canada go down to defeat.

Then, midway through the third period, Phil Esposito scored to put the Canadians within one goal. When Yvan Cournoyer scored soon after to tie the game, everyone around me went wild! All eyes were fixed on the time clock maddeningly counting down to the last minute of play. In those last few seconds I held my breath. No one moved; no one blinked.

It looked like it happened in slow motion. With only thirty-four seconds left to play, Esposito shot the puck at Tretiak only to have Paul Henderson pick up the rebound. Tretiak went down, Henderson lifted the puck and then Foster Hewitt yelled, "They score! Henderson scored for Canada!"

The cheering around me was deafening as I grabbed my two best friends and we twirled in a circle, holding each other in a frenzied display of unabashed joy. We were crying and we were laughing, teachers and students alike.

Mr. Ruxton looked over at me and winked. I hated math, but in that moment I loved Mr. Ruxton! While the players shook hands there in Moscow, we all burst into the spontaneous singing of "O Canada," and I knew I had just witnessed a moment in history that would never be repeated.

~Lynn Dove
Cochrane, Alberta

The Night the Lights Went Out

*I have travelled around the globe. I have seen the
Canadian and American Rockies, the Andes, the
Alps and the Highlands of Scotland, but for simple
beauty, Cape Breton outrivals them all!*
~Alexander Graham Bell

"Distinctive little village tucked on the west coast of
Cape Breton renowned for its hospitality, beauty,
and culture." That's all I knew about Mabou.
Once there, we discovered the famous Red Shoe
Pub, owned by the Rankin family, purely by chance. A "cool one"
sounded pretty inviting after driving the beautiful but winding roads
of our new summer vacation territory.

My friend Linda and I sat sipping our cold drinks, enjoying the
friendliness and soaking in the down-home Scottish music and atmosphere. Our waiter asked in his strong accent, "Are you goin' to the
cèilidh (pronounced kaylee) tonight, my lassies?" We soon heard that
Buddy MacMaster would be playing at the hall across the road and
everyone was going.

We didn't know who Buddy MacMaster was, but we learned that
he was a well-known, old-time fiddler of the Island and had been
invited to Scotland several times to teach the Celtic fiddling that had

been lost in the old country. Everyone in the pub seemed to know him and his family quite well, displaying great respect and admiration. I certainly knew of his niece, Natalie MacMaster, and her famous fiddling performances.

We were sure we wouldn't get tickets at this late date. And even if we could, how much might they cost? But we forgot we were in Cape Breton. We next learned that the cèilidh started at 7:30 p.m., and tickets could be bought at the door for seven dollars! Reasonable, casual, and so Cape Breton. No question — we would go.

We had about an hour until the show started. In the meantime, we were eager to share a Nova Scotian Alexander Keith's beer and treat ourselves to a local seafood chowder. Two fine young fiddlers performed. We wondered if the concert could be any better than this, but figured we'd give it a try.

At about 6:30, all of us at the pub gathered up our things, said goodbye and thank you to the staff and entertainers, and walked merrily across the road to the concert hall. Linda and I found seats in the fourth row! We exchanged quick hellos with a pleasant couple next to us from New York, who told us they loved to visit the island every summer — just for its music. That little hall, packed to capacity of about 300, soon hushed and we all settled in our seats. At 7:30 sharp, three musicians — Buddy MacMaster, Joey Beaton and Karen Beaton — walked up the eight steps onto the stage. The crowd applauded as they took their positions and plugged in their instruments — the fiddles and electric keyboard, and set up the microphone. Joey Beaton, also emcee, grabbed the microphone to begin.

Just at that moment, before one single note was played, before even one word was spoken, the power went off. The lights went out. There were no backup lights. Once again we remembered — we were in Cape Breton. Still, we were stunned. What now? What band can perform nowadays with no electronic equipment? But again, we forgot we were in Cape Breton.

Joey put the microphone back on the stand. His voice was strong and carried well. Laughing, he announced in true Cape Breton fashion,

"I guess we won't be needing this tonight. Well, you will be lucky. You'll get real music — pure sound. There will be only one change to the program. Our guest step-dancers will perform nearer the beginning because… we want you to see their feet."

Joey's wife, Karen, removed the dark curtains from the two little windows at the back of the stage, thus letting in the remaining summer evening light. The three entertainers moved to the other side of the stage, as if it had been planned. Joey sat down at the old upright piano, and the fiddlers, Buddy MacMaster and Karen Beaton, plopped down their wooden chairs next to him and began to play. All was well in Mabou.

To our amazement, the dancers performed and the jigs and reels continued. As the sun went down the hall grew darker, but we didn't notice. Each tune lightened our souls. All the performers were so professional — top drawer entertainers giving their all. Sometimes I could only see their silhouettes, but the music kept streaming out among us, mesmerizing us in this dark little hall.

Joey announced there would be a short break, and a few brave audience members ventured cautiously to the washrooms. He laughingly added that Buddy had found a penlight flashlight and was willing to talk and sell DVD's at a little table near the stage. I went to meet him and found a man as delightful as his fiddling. He autographed my purchase, and asked if I played. When I told him I had just started learning from an eighty-four-year-old gentleman, he said, "That's like me. I will be eighty-four in October."

Soon enough the performers took their places and the music resumed. A camper in the crowd had given Joey a headlamp so he could see the keys of the piano. The two other musicians admitted they could do some of their best work in the dark and everyone had a great laugh. After two hours of nearly continuous, joyful music, the cèilidh came to an end. Someone kindly shone his car lights to help the rest of us fumble our way out of the building. As we stumbled away to find our car parked in the pitch-black street, we knew we had been part of something truly unique. We'd been part of a special night in Mabou. The night the lights went out. We knew we were in Cape Breton.

~Glenice Wilson
Barrhead, Alberta

Rescue on Penn Lake

*Good is something you do, not something you
talk about. Some medals are pinned to
your soul, not to your jacket.*
~Gino Bartalli

"Can I go out fishing after supper? I'll stay close to shore," I promised.

"Okay, but you need to stay in front of the cottage where we can see you," replied my dad.

"And wear your life jacket," added Mum.

I lived in or on the water for these two weeks every summer, and this was not the first time I had done this. I put my fishing rod and tackle box in the bottom of the old blue wooden rowboat, buckled up my life jacket, and cast off. I rowed out just far enough and dropped anchor. I waved to my watching mum and dad, and tossed my line into the water.

I was ten years old, and in my element. It was a gorgeous Canadian summer evening at the cottage. The wind had dropped, the water was calm, and the lake was quiet. On the shore I could see the four old green cottages belonging to the Turnbull family. We rented Cottage #2 every summer. My grandparents took #1 — the Point Cottage — and I could see my grandmother sitting in a lawn chair watching me.

In one direction I could see the Deerhurst Inn, and in the other was the Farnsworth Farm — the cows grazing peacefully in the pasture that went right to the shoreline. On the right side of the bay I noticed a group of red canoes from the Camp of the Blue Ox — a boys camp on the other side of the lake.

With a deep sigh of contentment I cast my line out a bit further. This was my very favourite place in the world, and all was well in my world.

I heard the motorboat before I saw it, then watched as it sped toward the bay. Cutting a wide sweeping arc into the bay and then back out again, the driver waved to the boys in the canoes, and they waved back. I noticed that the driver was still looking at the canoes, and not watching where he was headed. Which was now directly toward me.

I was sitting on the middle seat and facing backwards, as you do when you row. With the certainty of youth I knew for sure that boat would turn away soon. But it kept coming straight at me. Closer and closer it came, the bow bearing down on me. It did not turn, and I finally realized it was not going to. At the last moment the boat veered slightly to the left, smashing into that old wooden rowboat about a foot in front of me with a loud crash, sheering off the back end.

Time stood still for a few moments and everything became silent. Stunned, I looked down and saw water where only moments before had been the bottom of my boat. There was the reel of my fishing rod caught on the last wooden crosspiece, the tip dangling in the water. My green tackle box was caught there as well.

Tears were running down my face from the shock, but I stood up then, and looked around. Part of me was scared, but another part of me was curiously aware and thinking clearly. Time started to move again, but in slow motion. *What should I do?* This boat was going to sink right under me.

On the shore I could see my sister sitting on the lawn and my father racing toward the water in total panic. I saw my grandmother running in their direction, her long dress catching around her legs.

Should I jump in and swim back to the dock? I had my life jacket on — it was not far, I could easily do it. But then I realized that old boat was made of wood — and was not going to sink. And I remembered the rule: "In a boating accident, stay with the boat and don't panic." So I sat down again, stayed calm, and waited.

On shore I saw my frantic father run to the boat at the next dock and try to start the little motor. But of course it would not start. At some point I became aware of the red canoes from the camp now heading out of the bay in my direction. One canoe was way out front and racing toward me. The motorboat, I was vaguely aware, was hovering off to one side. Suddenly the red canoe was beside me, and a young man was asking if I was okay. I said yes, and with no hesitation he plucked me from the shattered rowboat, set me in the bottom of his canoe, dug in with his paddle, and in seconds had me back on the dock in the arms of my parents.

By some miracle I was not injured — not even slightly. We later learned the driver of the boat had been drinking. Many years later we learned he was so shocked by the event, and what *could* have happened, that he never drank again. He also never drove a boat or a car again. Once my family realized I was unharmed, everyone calmed down. Before the canoeist paddled away my dad spoke with him, thanking him and shaking his hand. His name was Digby.

The next day my father and I drove around the lake to the camp. I was truly fascinated, as we had only seen it from a distance. He asked for Digby and, when the young man appeared, thanked him again and handed him an envelope containing a handwritten commendation for his quick thinking and responsible action. My father was the national accounting manager for one of Canada's big retailers, and he understood the value of a personal reference like this for a young person. It made me feel good to know he had done this for the young man who had rescued me.

I will always be grateful to Digby, from the Camp of the Blue Ox. Digby, local hero.

~Janet Matthews
Aurora, Ontario

All You Need Is Duct Tape and Beer

*What sets a canoeing expedition apart is that it
purifies you more rapidly than any other...
Paddle a hundred [miles] in a canoe and
you are already a child of nature.*
~Former Prime Minister Pierre Elliott Trudeau

I t truly was the crack of dawn. We expected thirty-six hours of summer daylight over the next two days. We intended to use it all on our annual *Deliverance* re-enactment trip, a mid-July run down an isolated section of a river in northern Ontario. Loaded to the gunwales with gear, we had seven paddlers convoying in three canoes: two canvas-over-cedar strips, and one fibreglass canoe. Our plan included fishing, shore lunches, and an overnight camp-out with unlimited adult refreshments. We also planned to challenge our canoeing skills by running the numerous sections of white water we would encounter.

Black-fly season was over, a light breeze was keeping the mosquitoes at bay, and the water was warm and crystal clear. The downstream current was gentle and we easily "shot" the first two sets of rapids, getting the kinks out of our muscles and scraping the rust off our paddles. As the current increased, so did the complexity of the rapids. The few level-2 runs tested our skills a little more, but we succeeded and became bolder. When we approached a narrow chute with a small waterfall we figured it had enough water to run. It did, barely. With paddles slashing, and our hull rocking wildly and slamming rocks hard and often, my three-man crew banged and clanged its way to a quiet pool below.

All three crews arrived upright, but were now much more focused. We stopped to re-secure our loads, do a bit of fishing and enjoy a delicious pan-fried trout breakfast. Only the sound of a helicopter transporting a section of metal to build a cell phone tower disturbed our peace.

As the day wore on we ran several other rapids, dancing around rocks and shoals and thoroughly enjoying ourselves. When we reached the marked portage the river was clearly too rocky to risk running loaded, so we carried our gear to the base camp below and set up. But after a quick analysis all three crews decided to give that stretch a "canoes only" run.

In the wilderness you can only flirt with danger so long. Disaster struck. It was a high water year, and while trapped in a challenging section of the chute our canoe was smashed sideways into a rock shelf and slid diagonally across it. The canoe was swamped. We ended up in the water, life jackets protecting us, as the rushing water bounced our bodies to the pool below. The canoe stayed jammed on the rock. I swam back far enough to acquire the tether rope and yanked. The hull released and thumped and banged its way to the pool. There it sat partially submerged: severely damaged with a yard long gash in the fibreglass hull and numerous holes below the waterline on both sides.

The two wooden canoes suffered bumps and scrapes and broken ribs but they were still seaworthy. Unfortunately, that didn't help. Carrying seven people in the two remaining canoes, even with just some of the gear, was not possible. We had to fix the canoe.

The fire pit glowed, cans of brew were distributed and the discussion began. Several ideas were suggested and discarded; then one of the crewmembers came up with a truly Canadian solution. In addition to food, we modern day voyageurs had carried with us two other truly Canadian necessities: duct tape and beer. Add some alcohol-inspired ingenuity and we had a solution. Our inventive friend used his utility knife to cut the ends off an empty can of Molson Canadian beer, and split it down the seam. Presto! The flattened metal cylinder made a patch. We applied the aluminum patch with duct tape, and a hole was covered. It worked! With salvation at hand, the members of our group responded to the challenge. We persevered and toiled late into the summer night, managing to empty more than enough cans, to complete the task.

In the morning our newly christened "Canadian" canoe passed its floatation test with flying colours. We enjoyed another full day on the water, continued our adventure and were able to complete the trek down the river. We made a successful — and dry — rendezvous with our pick-up vehicles. With our canoes loaded on roof carriers we headed for home. The customized "Canadian" canoe drew honks and waves from passing motorists and a flurry of questions at each highway stop. What could be more reflective of Canada's "spiritual" heritage than having coffee at Tim Hortons while telling a story involving canoes, white water, duct tape and beer?

~John Silver
Orillia, Ontario

Dancing a
Northwoods Ballet

*To touch, to move, to inspire. This
is the true gift of dance.*
~Aubrey Lynch

I felt trapped in a six-foot tall lanky body in a world designed for smaller women. Failing ballet at a young age and always feeling like a wallflower at dances had not helped my self-image. So I channelled my deep desire to move gracefully into recreational activities like windsurfing, cross-country skiing and canoeing. But I was still fascinated by dancing. When I confided this to a friend she responded that it made perfect sense. "You are fascinated by movement," she said, "and that's why you like tracking and wandering around in the bush so much." I had never thought of my love of the Canadian outdoors in this way before, but it made sense.

Years later, I found myself working in an isolated First Nation community just west of Thunder Bay. Here, feasts and festivals were frequently accompanied by dancing. The men would sit around a large drum and sing while the women danced in their jingle dresses. Sometimes I would join in, but I always had trouble matching my simple steps to the drumbeat. I knew I was like every other white person I had ever seen trying to dance powwow-style.

I had been in this remote northern Ontario community through winter and was still there as the ice broke up in the spring, a very important marker of the changing season. A few Native women had explained to me the origin of the jingle dress. It was considered a healing dress because it came from the dream of an ill woman. Her husband made the dress she described, cutting up many cans to make the hundreds of jingles that gave it the special tinkling sound. After the woman wore the jingle dress to her community's powwow, much to everyone's amazement, she became well. Soon the other women were making their own jingle dresses.

I was fascinated and amazed when I heard the sound these dresses made when the women danced. It was just like the sound of all the little pieces of ice that tinkle along the shoreline during break-up and freeze-up. I loved to walk, or paddle a canoe slowly along the shoreline, frequently pausing to just listen to this incredible sound, and watch the tiny little ice crystals bob up and down as if in their own dance.

In the spring it became a daily event after dinner to attend a gathering in the middle of the community, on the shore of the lake. Under a little cream coloured canopy the men would begin drumming and singing, and the women would dance. I often joined the event, still struggling with my dancing. A few women had offered to lend me a jingle dress, but I had always politely declined. I was very afraid I would look like a real fool with my tall body dancing awkwardly in a jingle dress that fit me more like a mini-skirt.

One night as we caught our breath between dances I sat next to a friend who was approached by one of the elders in the community. They spoke in Anishinabe and glanced at me, but I did not understand their words. Although I had never spoken with this elder, I had joined the younger women when they had joked and commented upon how even in her seventies this woman had more energy than even the youngest dancers. The elder then left, and my friend turned to me and said: "She has gone to get you a dress to dance in."

Oh no! I thought. *How can I refuse this kind woman?* I did not speak her language, and I really didn't want to feel pressured to dance in a dress that was far too short for me.

The elder returned holding a large brown paper bag and handed it to me with a broad, toothless smile. I accepted it and smiled back, unable to find a graceful way out. The other women urged me to put the dress on. I opened the bag, and felt the jingles tinkle all over as I pulled out a beautiful dress made in one of my favourite colours of blue. I slipped it on over my T-shirt and much to my amazement it fell down to well past my knees — the proper length for one of these dresses. I'll never forget the feel of the dress going on — it was like donning a rattle. The feel of hundreds of jingles moving and tinkling accented each little move I made.

The men started drumming again and the women got up to dance once more. As I joined them I was amazed by what my feet began to do. For the first time they were moving in rhythm to the drum! They felt spry and light and my whole body tingled with energy from the gentle caressing of the many jingles. Each little movement radiated outward through the jingles swaying.

I danced that night like I had always wanted to dance. I was surrounded by friends, in a community nestled deep within a forest. The sun was setting a magnificent red on the far side of the lake. The dance floor was the bare earth itself and I felt its pulsing with each step. Within me was the rhythm of the ancient seasons cycling round and round, break-up after freeze-up after break-up. On that night, I danced a kind of Northwoods ballet with the others. We all jingled together on one big dance floor, sensing the movements of the ice crystals, and the ancient rhythm of the seasons.

I often think about that elder with her long grey hair and toothless smile as she gave me that most precious gift. I occasionally still see her dancing at powwows and we continue to exchange smiles. We never did speak in words, yet to me she was a prima ballerina of the Northwoods ballet. She shared with me her ancient traditions and ancestral secrets — how to feel the dance of water on a lakeshore, deep in the heart of the Canadian Northwoods.

~Zabe MacEachren
Kingston, Ontario

The Sourtoe Cocktail Club

There are strange things done in the midnight sun,
By the men who moil for gold;
The Arctic trails have their secret tales,
That would make your blood run cold.
~Robert W. Service, "The Cremation of Sam McGee"

In 1990, my husband and I crossed Canada, from Montreal all the way to Dawson City in the Yukon. It was the kind of trip you take when you're young and adventurous. We took our time, taking four days to cross Ontario alone, stopping to camp at some of the most beautiful national parks in the country, waking to early morning mist off of Pancake Bay, visiting the port in Sault St. Marie (also known as the Soo), spending a day at Fort William in Thunder Bay where the Sleeping Giant lies, and tasting homemade moonshine on a derelict campground in Manitoba. In Vancouver, we stayed with a friend and walked along rugged beaches that were covered in kelp.

From there we headed to the Northwest Territories, one of the most spectacular sights I'd ever seen. The Klondike Highway is narrow and endless. Rest stops are far and few between and when you see one, you'd better stop, because if you don't, you will most certainly run out of gas. Every gas station had a helicopter, a restaurant and showers. We slept in the car on this two-day trek, barely getting any real rest because of the midnight sun; the days never get dark. We drove to the closest gas station and took a shower for a dollar while we waited for our bacon and eggs. In Whitehorse, we stayed at the cheapest hotel we could find and decided this would be our turnaround point. It was time to go back.

The next day, as we were looking for a bite to eat, we ran into a fellow from New Zealand who was hitchhiking through Canada that summer. His name was Peter Cooper. We chatted for a bit and when we told him we were heading back home the next day, he said, "Oh, no, you must keep on to Dawson City."

"Yeah, that's what my father told me on the phone yesterday," I said.

"If you do, you must go to the Eldorado Hotel and ask for Captain Dick," Peter Cooper insisted.

"Why?" we inquired.

"Because that's where you will find the Sourtoe Cocktail," he answered, and refused to tell us more. So we bought him a cup of coffee and chatted about his country for a while. When he told us he would be in Montreal a month or so later, we gave him our phone number.

"Feel free to stay with us, Peter," we said. This young New Zealander had piqued our curiosity about our own country.

That night, we decided to continue on to Dawson City. We drove by Lake Labarge on Highway 2, the very lake featured in the famous poem "The Cremation of Sam McGee" by one of my favourite poets, Robert Service. I just had to have a picture of myself standing next to this section of the Yukon River. And then we drove north to Dawson City and rented a little cabin on the outskirts of town. When we entered the town, it felt like we had driven backwards in time. The raised sidewalks were all warped from permafrost and the façades looked like they were left over from gold-digging days.

We didn't have to look far to find the Eldorado; it was in the very heart of Dawson. We walked in and asked the bartender where we could find Captain Dick. He pointed to an old fellow sitting at the back of the bar. He was rolling a cigarette and minding his own business. I walked right up to him, put out my hand and said, "Hi! I hear you may be Captain Dick and you do something called the Sourtoe

Cocktail. A fellow from New Zealand told us about you, believe it or not. Are you Captain Dick?"

"That's me," he said, barely looking up from the cigarette he was rolling.

"Can you tell us about the Sourtoe Cocktail?" I asked. He took out a tiny jar, placed it on the table. It was filled with salt, and something brownish sticking out from the top... it was a *toe*!

Both my husband and I took a step back, disgusted by the sight. Captain Dick smiled. He told us that if we gave him five dollars, and if we dropped the severed but sterile human toe into our cocktail drinks and drank up until the toe touched our lips then he would give us a membership card stating that we were officially members of the Sourtoe Cocktail Club.

We'd come this far, I thought, so why not? I took the challenge and watched this toe slide toward my tightly closed lips as I gulped down my Bloody Caesar. This small act of bravery would make me member 8,349.

"Where did you get it — the toe I mean?" I asked.

"That one was the result of a lawnmower injury," he replied. It seemed Captain Dick had a few in stock, donations from all parts of the country. He told us countless stories of this tradition he had started in 1973 when travelling from Nova Scotia to the Northwest Territories to work as a ferryboat conductor on the Yukon River. Chuckling, he told us that some German tourist had misunderstood and had actually swallowed the horrific thing. Another tourist had stolen the toe and he'd had to resort to the RCMP!

"Well, you won't be more of man than I am, so I'll give it a go too," said my husband. The toe was then plunked into his glass of beer, which immediately started to fizz. He drank his beer in one shot, making sure the toe only touched his lip. We were now both official members.

The next day we began our drive home with one hell of a story to tell, a story I still tell my students today. What a great icebreaker to begin a class! And all this thanks to a Kiwi — who would visit with us a month later — who told us Canucks about this odd northern tradition.

Today, The Sourtoe Cocktail Club lives on in Dawson City. The Eldorado Hotel has been renamed the Downtown Hotel, and Captain Dick Stevenson is gone, to be replaced by Captain River Rat or another. The Toe is usually dunked into a glass of whisky, perpetuating this initiation rite of becoming a true blue "sourdough," a tough survivor of the Great White North. As the words of the poem go, "There are strange things done in the midnight sun…"

~Julie Hamel de Belle
Pincourt, Quebec

Chapter 8

The Spirit of Canada

Living a Dream

*Canada is a country built on dreams. Dreams of
men and women who came here from many of the
countries I have traveled through. If you combine
the richness of the country with the spirit of the
people, our potential as a nation is unlimited.*
~Rick Hansen

The Ice Pond
of My Dreams

God gave us the gift of life; it is up to us
to give ourselves the gift of living.

~Voltaire

I was ecstatic as I left the Lounsbury Company in Moncton, New Brunswick, my arms wrapped tight around my parcel. It was 1959, I was twenty-five years old, and I had finally purchased my very own skates, known as "Reachers." Since I had moved to the city to study nursing and learned that skating at the Forum was the new "in thing," buying the Reachers had become my goal.

Skating was my passion, but I loved everything about winter. The first crackle of frozen puddles under my feet was music to my ears. While others dreaded the harsh winds blowing off the Northumberland Strait, I loved our little fishing village on the southeastern shores of New Brunswick the most when it was covered in a blanket of snow. It wasn't that I didn't like swimming in the ocean in summer, but in winter I could build snow forts, have snowball fights with my brothers, and experience the thrill of skating on a frozen ice-pond after clearing away the drifts of snow.

At school, the only subject I enjoyed was geography. By the end of the school day, I was staring out the window, planning how I could make it home before my brothers. With eight kids, our family could afford few luxuries, so my father bought one pair of Reachers — in the largest size — that we all had to share. The smaller children had to stuff the toes to make them fit. Whoever got home first got the Reachers. If I missed my chance it meant an afternoon without skating, and I'd have to stay inside doing chores with my mother and two sisters. I much preferred spending time with my five brothers; I was determined that anything they could do, I could do better!

When I arrived home and claimed the Reachers, nothing else mattered. Any hardships were quickly forgotten; there was just me and my frozen ice-pond dreams. I became a beautiful figure skater like Barbara Ann Scott as I imagined skating on all the beautiful rivers I'd learned about in geography class.

When I moved away from home I didn't know how I'd survive without my frozen ponds and the exhilarating winds off the Northumberland Strait. But I left with a goal and a dream: finish nursing school, find a job, and save enough money to buy my own Reachers.

Well, now I had the Reachers, and the moment I skated onto the ice at "The Forum" in Moncton, my passion was renewed. Once again I imagined I was skating on the most beautiful frozen ponds in the world.

Life moved on, and I became a wife, and eventually a mother of five. My dreams of travelling and skating on faraway frozen ponds disappeared as fast as the melting ice in spring.

Yet, as my children grew I became even more of an "outdoor freak." During snowstorms, I'd bundle up my children and we'd sit on the veranda, enjoying the storm. When it was over we got out our skates and headed down to the Richibucto River with our shovels to clear away the snowdrifts, revealing ice as smooth as a mirror. Chores were ignored as I taught my children the joys of winter, and especially, skating.

The years passed, and one by one, my children skated off on their own. As I watched their wings unfold, somehow a new vision formed in my mind — a new dream. I'd heard about millions of people skating on the world's largest naturally frozen skating pond — while eating beaver tails. This magical activity happened every winter in central Ottawa.

More research revealed that the cleared length of the Rideau Canal

Skateway was 7.8 kilometres, and it had the equivalent surface of ninety Olympic ice hockey rinks! It was open twenty-four hours a day, and I heard it was not unusual to see someone skating towards Parliament Hill with a briefcase. I completely fell in love with the idea of skating on the Rideau Canal.

Even as I became a grandmother, I held on to my vision. When my son, Ricky, landed a job in Ottawa, I realized I could visit him and skate on that canal!

On a cold February morning, I boarded an Air Canada jet in Moncton and headed for Ottawa. In my suitcase was my original pair of Reachers, purchased in 1959.

The very next day my two grandsons, Cole and Logan, accompanied their eighty-year-old grandmother to the Rideau Canal. I couldn't believe I was finally there. I sat down on a bench, took off my boots, and laced up my Reachers. Then, I glided onto the ice pond of my dreams... with my two grandsons by my side. Cole and Logan suggested we take it slow, but I had a plan. I wanted to skate the whole 7.8 kilometres — and along the way enjoy a beaver tail pastry. These pastries are covered with cinnamon sugar and individually shaped by hand to resemble the tail of a beaver.

Not only did we skate the entire length, but we stopped, rested, ate our scrumptious beaver tails, and then skated the whole way back!

That night as I lay in bed I was as ecstatic as I had been fifty-five years before when I walked out of the Lounsbury Company with my new Reachers. My dream had come true! But I realized I wanted more. The next day I told my son I wanted to skate the Canal at night when it was all lit up — and have dinner at the restaurant overlooking the Canal. And for sure I wanted a beaver tail for dessert.

That night my son escorted me back to the Rideau. I was enthralled

by the lights that sparkled on the ice along the length of the Canal, and that second skate, at night with my son, was even more fabulous than the first. As we skated, memories took me back to my fishing village and my childhood dreams, and I was so grateful for the spunk my brothers had given me.

Although my dreams had become misplaced through the struggles of life, I reflected, here I was at the age of eighty, and the magic and spirit were still there. I loved every minute of it: the cold toes and fingers, the taste of cinnamon and sugar on my lips, the lights, the other skaters, and sharing this experience with my son and grandsons. Closing my eyes, I could hear the swoosh of my Reachers on the ice. Silently, I offered a prayer of thanksgiving to God for the physical health and mental ability to live my dream. I had persevered, and the gifts of life were indeed spectacular. Maybe, just maybe, there are still unknown ponds to skate!

~Lorette Smith
Richibucto, New Brunswick

66

The Viking Voyageur

*The first step to getting the things you want
out of life is this: Decide what you want.*
~Ben Stein

Many years ago I attended a meeting for one of those get-rich-quick schemes. About twenty well dressed people sat in a large living room in a stately home. Dressed in a T-shirt and faded jeans, I knew immediately I didn't belong.

The presenter asked, "What would you do if you had a million dollars?" After hearing answers about buying yachts, sports cars, big homes etc., I said the first thing that came to mind: "If I had a million dollars, I would get a Viking ship." Well, the room broke into laughter, and the gentleman hinted that I should leave. So I did.

Years later I had a vision for another kind of boat. Taking a chance, I borrowed money and bought a used thirty-four-foot replica voyageur canoe. The Canadian canoe was an aboriginal creation made originally of birch bark, but my canoe was made of fibreglass and was a replica of the *canot de maître*, which during the era of the fur trade crossed Canada carrying trade goods and beaver fur pelts. My canoe also had a detachable mast with a large square sail and several red bladed paddles.

My plan was to run an ecotourism business called The Governor's Canoe from the marina in downtown Kingston, Ontario. I planned to give thousands of people a chance to be a voyageur and paddle into Canadian history. After getting the necessary approvals and permits,

I was in business.

Each customer received a life jacket and paddle, and a voyageur costume consisting of a loose printed shirt, a knitted toque and a *ceinture fléchée* — a traditional colourful woven belt. Once aboard I gave them a brief paddling lesson. In full costume myself, from the back of the boat I steered the vessel, sang traditional voyageur songs, told stories, and gave my "crew" a fun, educational, and satisfying adventure.

I told stories of how the hardy French Canadian and Mohawk voyageurs risked their lives paddling and portaging their canoes and ninety-pound backpacks over hundreds of portages along their route. I talked about how they were tough yet jovial men. I also told them how many voyageurs fought for the British during the War of 1812 against the United States. As soldiers they lacked discipline, and British officers were aghast at their behaviour and appearance. Even so, the Corps of Canadian Voyageurs played an important role in the War of 1812, as they were naturally suited to the kind of skirmishing that frequently occurred.

In the mid 1990s I was invited to Gananoque, a small town about twenty kilometres east of Kingston, to take part in a summer festival. Four tall ships and hundreds of people were gathering to be part of a historical re-enactment. Some friends helped me sail my canoe down the St. Lawrence River through the Thousand Islands to Gananoque. With the square canvas sail hoisted, the big canoe ploughed through the waves and actually created a wake!

Once we arrived I began offering Voyageur Canoe adventures from the Gananoque dock. I frequently headed out into the St. Lawrence with a canoe full of paddlers bound for Half Moon Bay in the rocky Admiralty Islands, just across the channel.

One evening a group of volunteers from the upcoming tall ship event approached me. The Commodore in charge asked, "How would you like to include your canoe in a re-enactment of a War of 1812 naval battle? You just need to show up for a briefing the night before." I happily agreed, saying I'd represent the infamous Canadian Corps of Voyageurs. But on the night of the meeting I had paying customers and couldn't make it.

On the morning of the re-enactment, again I had two trips booked. The planned naval battle was to take place in an hour, but I had a young couple, three teachers from France and my sister Betsy and her husband Ken with me. How was I ever going to participate in this naval re-enactment? Then I came up with a plan.

I'd missed the meeting, but I asked my new crew of "voyageurs" if they'd be willing to remove their life jackets and paddle right into the War of 1812 re-enactment. They all agreed enthusiastically, so we paddled off to Half Moon Bay until we heard cannon fire in the distance. At that moment we turned the canoe around and paddled hard toward the action. Once we could see the battle through the haze of smoke, we removed our life jackets. Then I raised the Union Jack flag on the stern and we paddled as fast as we could toward the tall ships. Musket fire and cannons blasted all around us, and the smoke seemed to cover the fact that I had no muskets aboard, nor any military moves planned, except to make a lot of noise and blast out a loud reveille on my old bugle!

On the shore was an audience of about a thousand people who'd gathered to watch the action. The MC was broadcasting a play-by-play over a loudspeaker while a Jolly Boat full of British marines fired muskets. Winging it, I yelled something about the Canadian Corps of Voyageurs fighting in His Majesty's service, and then we paddled furiously through the smoke to the port side of the American ship. We shouted and yelled and waved our paddles as if we were actually doing something. More musket shots rang out, and then I turned the canoe toward the shore in the direction of the audience, before paddling back to my home dock. I didn't look at the organizers or the Commodore on shore. Having improvised our military manoeuvres after missing the briefing, I figured I was in big trouble.

Back at the dock, the young couple declared they'd had a blast. And the three French teachers — well they never thought their trip to Canada would include paddling into the middle of a historic naval battle. Later that evening, as I tied my canoe up for the night, I saw the Commodore and his party walking along the docks towards me. I thought I was going to get "raked over the coals" for what I'd done, and be banned from all future re-enactments.

As they approached I prepared myself for the words I knew I deserved. But the Commodore grabbed my hand and shook it, and with a big grin said, "That was excellent! Nice show!" Boy was I relieved. At that moment I realized I was a true voyageur! In my own lack of discipline I had won my own battle, just by sheer instinct combined with a bit of acting and pageantry.

The next day I headed back up the river to Kingston under full sail. This time I was alone, so I loaded big rocks into the canoe to act as ballast. As the summer breeze filled my sail I imagined I was steering a Viking ship between Greenland and Vineland. Then I remembered that meeting I had attended years ago, where everyone laughed at me because I wanted a Viking ship. But I had the last laugh because I had achieved my dream Viking ship after all — just with a Canadian twist!

~Peter G. Elliott
Mount Pearl, Newfoundland and Labrador

67

Sampo Girl

*Feel the flame forever burn, teaching lessons we must
learn, to bring us closer to the power of the dream.*
~David Foster, The Power of the Dream

I glanced behind me at the sea of red and white jackets. Excited chatter filled the air. As we strode around the oval track in the stadium, I searched the stands for our coaches. There they were, small red and white dots madly waving small flags and cheering us on. *This is what it must feel like to be an Olympic athlete*, I thought. Suddenly, I was filled with pride. I had, after all, never expected that something like this could happen to someone like me.

"You'll love it," my mom had said after enrolling me in a class at the Sampo Rhythmic Gymnastics Club in Sudbury, Ontario. At the age of five I was a little overweight and a lot shy, and my mother not only wanted to get me moving, but also to help me interact more with kids my own age.

I had entered the first class with trepidation. "Come and sit in the circle," the coach said, motioning for me join the group. I tugged at my scratchy royal blue leotard and crossed my plump legs, glancing at the eager faces of the girls around me. Before long we were up and moving, twirling and spinning in front of the wall-to-wall mirror in the basement of the Finnish Hall on Antwerp Street. I soon forgot about how awkward I felt and how afraid I was to talk to anyone. I just let the movement and the music take me into another world.

A few years later, I graduated to the upstairs class with the "big girls." The hall was surrounded by long tables and stacks of chairs and even had a small stage with curtains. On weekends the hall was used for dances, weddings and concerts. Now, our coach used the stage as a barre for ballet practice. We leapt and turned diagonally across the dance floor to her counts. "Point those toes," she called. "Opposite hand to foot." I can still hear the creak of the wooden floor under our bare feet and the "dum-de-de-dum-dum" of her hand-held drum as she struck the beat.

Year after year, my mother drove me to and from classes. I worked hard to master the carefully choreographed routines and manipulate the balls, ropes, ribbons, clubs and hoops, like the older girls. I loved the smooth texture of the ball as it rolled along my fingers and the weight of the ribbon-stick in my palm as the fabric spiralled and snaked through the air. Although by now I towered over the other gymnasts in my class, in my imagination I was as graceful as a ballerina.

By the time I was thirteen, however, everything had changed. One day I pulled an oversized T-shirt over my leotard and hoped my coach would let me wear it in class. Any confidence I had gained seemed to have vanished into the floorboards. I still loved my sport, but maybe it was time to leave.

"I want to quit gymnastics," I told my mom as we drove home after class one evening. The fall season had only just begun, but I didn't want to go back. I had the same coach as the year before, but most of the gymnasts were new.

"Well, I've already registered you, so you'll just have to finish the year," she said. "If you don't want to return next season, that's fine with me." I nodded and held back my tears. It wasn't the first time my mom had told me to finish what I'd started. She wasn't going to let me quit.

My coach must have realized I was unhappy, so she kept finding me tasks to do, like helping someone learn a new technique with the ribbon or demonstrating a body wave. With her encouragement, I started enjoying the classes again and pushing myself to get better. One day near the end of the year, the coach pulled me aside. *Was I in some kind of trouble?* I wondered. Instead, she asked, "Would you like to join the competitive team next year?" I was astounded. I had felt like there was really nowhere else to go for someone like me. The gymnasts in the competitive stream were tall and thin, and moved with such grace and flexibility.

"Of course I'd be interested," I said. I couldn't wait to tell my mom on the way home. Unfortunately, the competitive coach retired and, with no replacement, the competitive stream ended before I could join. Instead, the club created a performing group with the most promising gymnasts in the club, and I was included in that, too! Still shy and introverted, I began to blossom. I loved being on stage and performing with my teammates. We began travelling and performing all over Ontario and Canada. My coaches started giving me more responsibilities; I assisted with warm-ups and even helped with choreography. Eventually, I took my coaching qualifications and started teaching the little gymnasts, seeing myself in their eager young faces. Like my coaches before me, I tried to encourage their participation and bring out the best in each of them.

When I was nineteen, along with gymnasts from all over the country, my performing group was chosen to represent Canada in Amsterdam at the World Gymnaestrada, the largest non-competitive gymnastics event in the world. I was thrilled to be travelling overseas to perform and watch innovative artistic and rhythmic gymnastics routines.

"Who do you think they will choose to be the flag bearer?" my teammate asked a few days before the Opening Ceremonies. We'd arrived early in order to recover from our jet lag before the event. I shrugged my shoulders.

"Probably someone from one of the big Toronto clubs," I said. Ours was a small club from Northern Ontario. Who would even notice us? The Sampo girls were just thrilled to be there.

The next day, our coach arrived to announce the flag bearer. We all waited, but with no real hope. We crowded into our assigned classroom, trying not to trip on the mattresses and blankets spread out on the makeshift bedroom floor.

Turning to me, my coach beamed and said, "Congratulations Liisa. You will be our team's flag bearer!" I was truly floored. Soon after, I was ready to enter the stadium, holding our flag, with my teammates anxiously lined up behind me. I took a deep breath—this was our moment! Stepping out I waved the huge Canadian flag and smiled at my coaches. Even a Sampo girl from Northern Ontario could feel like a Canadian Olympic athlete, if only for a day. It wasn't until that moment that I really understood what it meant to have pride in one's country, one's team and oneself.

~Liisa Kovala
Sudbury, Ontario

68

The Best Play
He Never Saw

The biggest adventure you can take is
to live the life of your dreams.
~Oprah Winfrey

When I was twenty and dreaming of becoming an actress, my father and I made our annual pilgrimage to the Shaw Festival. At sixteen I had stumbled upon a tiny ad for the fledgling festival, and the following summer we rode out to the historic border town that had repelled an American invasion in 1812. When we first discovered it, the old Upper Canada fort of Niagara-on-the-Lake, situated on the shore of Lake Ontario twenty-six kilometres from Niagara Falls, was noted more for its prettiness and historical significance than for its cultural life. But when a local wit posted a sign in front of his cottage that read, "Shaw's House," the old fort town hosting the festival came to be referred to, in our house, by the name my father gave it: "Niagara-Falls-on-the-Lake, where Shaw lives."

When I discovered the Festival, the main stage productions were held in the renovated courthouse; lunchtime theatre was housed in the town's original theatre, the Royal George. The large, modern Festival Theatre was about to be constructed, and that's where we saw Kate Reid play the title role in *Mrs. Warren's Profession*. At her first entrance, the audience gasped. A character actress known for her cello-toned voice, alcoholic binges, swollen body and out-sized talent, Reid had whittled down to a shadow of herself. Her large dark eyes, always luminous, seemed to bulge out of her head now. For the moment she was on the wagon, channelling her demons into a performance so searing that it left the festival audience sitting in stunned silence.

A passionate twenty-year-old, I needed no prompting. I leapt to my feet and began to applaud. My father, embarrassed, tugged at the hem of my skirt. Too late. Granted permission, the audience followed my lead. The Festival Theatre audience was on its feet for Kate Reid.

We left the theatre and got into the car. We were staying in Toronto, two hours away. On the steering wheel, my father's hands were trembling. He drove no further than the outskirts of town when he stopped, overcome by what he had witnessed on stage.

"I can't drive that far. I won't make it." Daddy turned the car around, and we rode back to Niagara. It was late September, and nearing midnight. The wind was howling, and mustard-coloured leaves rained to the ground. Queen Street, the main street, was empty and quiet, except for the after-theatre cabaret performing upstairs at The Buttery, and table lamps that glowed through the window of a bistro called Captain Brassbound's. We were the only patrons at Captain Brassbound's. My father ordered a bowl of vegetable soup. When it arrived, he cupped his hands around the bowl to warm and steady them. My loquacious dad had been struck dumb. He lowered his head in contemplation. Steam rose from the bowl. Across the bare wooden table I reached out my hands to his.

"Now do you understand, Daddy? This is what I want to be able to do. It's my dream."

* * *

I loved not only the theatre productions at the Shaw Festival, but also the laid-back ambience of the unhurried town. Though, initially, my dad attended the Festival in order to be with me, he soon grew to love it as much as I did. Still, Dad wasn't a hard-core fan. If I had arranged to see two productions on the same day, he'd attend the evening performance with me, but pass on the matinee. Instead, he would stretch out under a tree at the edge of the lake. I imagine Dad would interrupt his reverie to regularly check his wristwatch. As the time drew near, he would rise and saunter down an increasingly touristy Queen Street in order to meet me at the theatre when the show let out.

One shimmering Saturday in mid-summer, Dad's choice cost him. He missed the most rollickingly mirthful production I can recall of any season, ever. The actors set off a three-hour laugh fest that had a full house screaming with glee. At five o'clock, as the sun broke through a cluster of clouds, the audience floated through the theatre exits as if on a cloud. Emerging with the throng I could see Dad standing near the main entrance, waiting for me. As I inched my way toward him through the crowd, I saw Dad alert and receptive to the radiant expressions on the faces of audience members. Laughter still rippled through our ranks, and it was impossible not to overhear the glowing remarks.

By the time I reached Dad, he was tsk-tsking with his teeth and vigorously shaking his head. "That's the best play I never saw." Caught off-guard, I took the bait.

"But Daddy, you didn't see it."

"Well that's what I said!" Dad beamed, surprised and delighted to have fooled the one person he felt he couldn't fool. Then he reiterated, rubbing in the punch line, not only for me, but for all who cared to hear: "That's the best play I *never* saw!

***

We had already purchased our tickets for the season of 1983 when Dad died suddenly, in early spring. My mother and I decided to honour him by honouring the tickets. It was a bad idea. It was too painful for us to have Mum sitting in the seat we both knew had been intended for Dad. We never went back.

After my father's death I went to work in the family business with my mother to ensure that my younger brother would finish medical school. I was thirty-five when I finally returned to the pursuit of my youthful dream: working in the theatre.

My range had broadened and deepened. Soon I was playing large parts in small venues. At age thirty-eight I was offered a one-woman show. At forty, I played the lead in a play presented in a local auditorium. At the end of the performance the audience sat in stunned silence before leaping to its feet to offer me an ovation. As I was leaving, a woman ran over and grabbed me by the wrists. "Oh my dear!" she cried. "What a powerful performance! Look at me! I'm shaking! You don't belong here! You should be performing at Stratford! You should be playing at the Shaw Festival! Oh my dear, I'm going to dream about you all night. Look at me! I'm shaking so hard, I don't know how I'll be able to drive home!"

I trembled too, hearing an echo from that autumn when I was twenty. I returned to my apartment by bus, alone. Collapsing onto my bed, I flung my arms over my eyes, yet tears filled them, anyway. In the stillness and the silence I whispered, "Daddy. I did it. That was for you."

~S. Nadja Zajdman
Montreal, Quebec

69

The Red Mittens

Everyone had them as a kid. Red mittens with strings.
We all had them. That's why they were designed into
the uniform. One to give them a colour pop, and two
because it's an iconic Canadian piece.
~Mark Kinnin

"I'm on a quest for a pair of those red mittens," I said to Chris. We had travelled to Vancouver from Michigan for a conference of Meeting Professionals International. By nature, I'm pretty simple. I don't require trendy clothes, certainly not outerwear. But I had to have a pair of those mittens, even though it was July. They represented all that was wonderful about Vancouver and the recent 2010 Winter Olympics. I had been so moved by the event, from the opening ceremonies to the closing ceremonies, and how people bonded through trials and triumph.

I had seen those happy Canadians on TV — all wearing those mittens, smiling and celebrating. I remember the huge excitement — and I felt it myself, marvelling at the simple red mittens that came to symbolize the spirit of the Vancouver winter games.

As we boarded the sightseeing trolley in Vancouver I hoped to learn more about those red mittens and find out how I might get a pair. My dream became real as the tour guide spoke. "If you look to your left, you will see the Hudson's Bay Company. This is the place those famous 2010 Winter Olympic mittens came from — right here in Vancouver!" Exactly what I had been waiting for! Now I knew where to go. My heart did a little dance — I was actually going to get a pair! Then the guide continued. "Though you can still buy a pair of similar mittens, the first run of those 2010 Vancouver Winter Olympic mittens sold out many months ago."

What? I'm thousands of miles from home, as close as I'll ever get to purchasing those mittens in the very city they're from — and they're sold out? My heart sank. Knock-off replicas, no matter how nice, would not do. I wanted mine to be from the first run of mittens from the Hudson's Bay Company.

A meeting planner is also a creative thinker, so while I was sorely disappointed, I wasn't giving up. I had one more opportunity. I signed up to attend a session presented by the marketing people of the Olympic Planning Committee. During that session, the OPC members shared with us their intense but incredibly organized planning for the event. At the question and answer period, they passed around the Olympic torch, which was amazing and awe-inspiring. This was the actual torch that was lit in Olympia in October 2009, travelled to Canada over the North Pole, and then carried by about 12,000 Canadians, many of them celebrities, reaching over 1,000 communities before arriving at Olympic Stadium. Each runner, I learned, wore a pair of those coveted red mittens while carrying the torch, including the one that lit the Olympic flame that illuminated those Winter Olympics! I was thrilled!

As the torch made its way around, Chris and I admired its sleek and unique design. Of course we had our pictures taken with this special icon.

But even so, for me it was all about those red mittens. I had to try once more. The timing was finally right for me to ask my important question of the very people who might have the answer. I stood and asked, "Are there any mittens left?" And then I held my breath.

"Well, yes, there are," said the committee chair, "I have a pair."

A pair! All I needed was one pair, and I was willing to buy them. "Sir, what would be the cost of one pair of red mittens from the 2010 Vancouver Winter Olympics?" I realized the original $10 mittens would likely cost a bit more several months later, but I was willing to pay a little extra.

"About three thousand dollars," said the man. Then he smiled and asked me to meet him after the session.

Three thousand dollars? Really? Well, I didn't have three thousand dollars, and if I did, as much as I wanted those mittens, I didn't think I was prepared to invest that much. I anxiously waited for the session to end, and hoped the marketing committee chair would remember he had asked me to meet with him. He did, and when I approached him later he asked, "Would you like to see the mittens?"

Would I like to see the mittens? The elusive, famous, sold-out red mittens? You bet! As he handed me the mittens, I felt my heart race. They were beautiful — knitted in the red of the Canadian flag with the 2010 Olympic logo embroidered in white on the backs, and a white maple leaf stitched into the palms. As I slipped them on I saw they were still connected, with the tag on them. Those red mittens were warm and soft against my face, and I imagined what it must have been like to stand among the thousands of people who had been there, experiencing history being made, cheering, applauding, and waving with their Canadian red mittens!

Now you might want me to say that the committee chair gave me those mittens, and I would have to tell you — I wish I could say he had. But he didn't. You see, they were his to keep — he had earned them. His planning team brought the world a tremendous gift when they hosted the 2010 Winter Olympics in Vancouver. He deserved this last pair of red Olympic mittens. So after I finished admiring them, I took them off — and gave them back.

Although those red mittens didn't come home with me, for the few moments that I had them I felt the magic of them woven into my soul. I felt the spirit of Canada — through a simple pair of red mittens that mirrored the warmth of their country and stole the heart of the world.

~Sherry Taylor Cummins
Livonia, Michigan, USA

70

I Just Wanted to Play

Street hockey is great for kids. It's energetic,
competitive, and skilful. And best of
all it keeps them off the street.
~Gus Kyle

I leaned against the railing of the VIP suite surveying the playing surface below me. The television lights glinted off the polished cement floor, highlighting the freshly painted red and blue lines and the multi-coloured logo that dominated the centre zone. Celebratory bunting was draped from the box seat facades and, when I raised my gaze, I marvelled at the number of nations represented by flags hanging from the rafters.

I was a guest at a Canadian icon, the famous Maple Leaf Gardens in Toronto, awaiting an honour I had never sought let alone thought possible. I read the inscription on the orange ball I was holding: "World Championship." At my left stood another honouree, my best friend Paul. I handed the ball to him. He smiled and responded, "Did you ever think it would come to this?"

Playing road hockey is a "rite of passage" for young Canadians. A ball, a hockey stick, a street and enough players to form two teams were all you needed. Despite flying pebbles, lost balls, road rash and the need to move nets for "Cars!" we are passionate about the game. During my teen years, if I wasn't in school or participating in other sports, I organized neighbourhood street hockey games whenever I could. Then it all came to a halt. I became a young man with more pressing responsibilities; but I never lost my love of the game.

Many years ago I had stood leaning against a less ornate railing, in a much smaller arena, surveying a dull grey floor with no markings. The winter ice had just come out and, as a part-time "rink rat" I was contemplating summer rink activities and asking myself what would it be like to play ball hockey on that empty floor? The answer… "Why not?" Indoor ball hockey is essentially the same as ice hockey, but without the ice, using an orange plastic ball in place of a puck.

At age twenty-one I was finishing my second year as an elementary school teacher. The extra income from my part-time work at the local arena was helping pay for my post-grad degree courses. Had this extra job made me the right person, in the right place, at the right time? I approached the arena manager with my "Why not?" idea. Playing street hockey in an empty ice rink, in summer, had never been tried. I volunteered to launch this new activity in our arena's controlled setting, and he gave me the go ahead.

It was a humble beginning. We had just four teams and no sponsors. The young adult players paid a fee to cover the cost of their team sweaters, the balls, floor rental and the officials. My wife Carol and I managed literally every aspect of the league: scheduling games and officials, keeping statistics, and handling accounting. In addition to playing I wrote some basic "adaptive" rules. In particular, body checking and fighting were forbidden, and penalized with banishment.

To our amazement, our indoor street hockey was so popular we actually had to turn players away! The players loved the game and the unique format. With no skating required, it was hockey in which almost anyone could participate. It was fun, safe and encouraged terrific fitness.

Paul was the goaltender on my team, and he and his wife Lynn volunteered to help with the organization. We became life-long friends. The following year I transferred to a school in the north of Ontario and started a league in my new city. Paul took over managing the original league.

Media coverage of this revitalization of a Canadian cultural tradition prompted a stampede of young adults seeking to recapture some of the joy of their youth. New leagues spread like wildfire: provincially, nationally and then internationally. As a founder I was pressed into service in increasingly complex leadership roles, dealing with the good, the bad and sometimes the ugly events that occur when a new sport expands rapidly onto the world stage. The endless volunteer work and travel began taking its toll. By then I was a father of two young children and an educational administrator. Paul and I passed the torch to a new management team. The sport had grown so much that it was now run by a paid staff. Our volunteer management days were over.

But now Paul and I were holding the torch again, for the night.

"Gentlemen, it's time." Someone had arrived to escort us to the playing surface. We walked a red carpet to the face-off spot. The announcer introduced us as "founding fathers" and the crowd applauded. The Canadian and Russian teams, standing on their respective blue lines, tapped their sticks on the floor in salute, and the captains came forward for the ceremonial ball drop. I took my position, raised the ball high and waved to the crowd. Paul put his hand over mine and together we dropped the ball.

It was amazing how the sport had grown in forty years. Off the floor, a photojournalist posed the standard question: "How do you feel about all of this?"

"Years ago I had an idea for a new sport," I said. "Today I'm watching the world's finest players vie for international honours in a truly Canadian game, at one of our country's most hallowed sporting venues. I feel honoured and very proud; but also a little disappointed."

"Disappointed?" repeated the interviewer. "Why?"

I nodded toward Paul and he smiled, anticipating my reply.

"Because I would rather be playing. That's all I ever wanted."

~John Karl Forrest
Severn, Ontario

71

A Canadian First

Everything you've ever wanted is
on the other side of fear.
~George Addair

ne day earlier this summer, I sat down at Tim Hortons, my favourite reading and writing haunt. I was distracted by family issues, almost overwhelmed with worry. I tried to read but to no avail. I happened to look over at the woman sitting at the next table, and we made a connection. She gave me a big smile, and all I could do was smile back.

"I love coming to Tim's to read and also write," she said. I agreed, as I noticed her sparkling blue eyes and wondered if they reflected a happy spirit. She was wearing a bright pink jacket and maroon striped ankle boots.

She quickly introduced herself as Dyane, and invited me to join her. We soon discovered we had many things in common; besides being proud Canadians we both had Celtic roots. "I feel like I have come full circle," I shared. "I was born right here in Vancouver, and now I work at the same hospital where I was born."

"How interesting," Dyane laughed. "I came to Canada from Ireland as a twenty-two-year-old landed immigrant, originally for six months. That was fifty-one years ago. I've had many challenges and opportunities here, and each one has helped me become stronger and overcome the fears and self-doubts I grew up with in Ireland."

Walking home after our visit, I felt my spirit grow lighter and

Living a Dream

brighter. Dyane was good for me!

We met again, and our friendship grew. As the summer grew warmer we decided to meet for a swim and visit by my apartment pool. That afternoon I noticed Dyane had a tattoo on her ankle. This did not surprise me, as by now I had learned this seventy-three-year-old woman had a seriously adventurous spirit. I noticed the symbol on her ankle was encircled by a Canadian maple leaf.

"Tell me about your cool tattoo," I said, leaning in for a better look.

"Well," she replied, looking at her ankle with a mixed expression of humility and pride. "This is the Canada Ironman logo. In 1983, I was the first female to compete in the first Canada Ironman Triathlon. This symbol is to remind me that I am courageous and strong, and to never give up."

Then she explained. "The first Ironman Canada was held in Penticton on August 20, 1983. There were twenty-five of us in the race. Twenty-four males and me, the only female."

Smiling impishly, Dyane held up her leg so I could have a closer look. "Wow! Dyane," I whispered. "What an amazing challenge." I slumped back in my chair stunned.

Dyane spoke slowly. "I will never forget that early August morning as I stood on the sand beside Okanagan Lake in my one piece swimsuit and an orange swimcap with the "Canada Ironman" lettering. I thought of swimming as a sacred task that would put me in touch with my inner resources. In training, I had learned to be focused and present, and to accept my strengths and weaknesses."

"I don't know how you did it," I murmured.

"It took concentration," she said. "I closed my eyes and felt each breath filling every cell, organ and limb in my body. I breathed in a prayer. I was ready. I heard the splash of the water, the noise from the men. They breathed loud, grunted and groaned. I even felt a kick in my side because we were swimming in such a close pack. I had to resist the urge to panic."

"No way I could have handled that," I said.

"I had trained for it," Dyane said. "I knew they didn't mean to kick me. I focused instead on gliding. I swam on and on. As I came to the finish of my swim, I felt the buzz of the crowd, and I was so happy that I had completed the first phase." Dyane took a breath. She smiled, and I could feel her excitement as she relived that day.

"The second phase of my journey required cycling. The swim had set me up. I was energized and prepared for the challenges of the hilly 112 miles. In the bike race I focused upwards on my intuition and intelligence, and downwards on the muscles of my legs. I pumped the pedals, leaned forward, and kept my eyes on the road ahead."

She smiled as she remembered. "When I climbed off my bike, I put on my running shoes, gulped down another banana, and moved toward the gate to start the marathon. I was trembling by then, but somehow it was a relief to know that all I had left was a marathon!"

"Only a marathon?" I said. This woman was incredible.

Dyane said, "I was tired and sore, and my mind was numb. I wasn't in a good place mentally. By the time I finished, it was dark, and I basically limped over the finish line. There were times I wanted to stop, but as the only woman in the race I could not quit. I remember cheers when I finally finished, and someone hung a lei around my neck."

After listening to Dyane's story I felt exhausted — even though I had not moved from my chair! I had many questions that I would hold onto until our next visit, but there was one I had to ask now. "Dyane," I said, "how did you feel, and did completing such a challenge change you?"

"Well," she began, "because of the Ironman Canada triathlon, I've been able to accomplish things I would never have dreamed possible before. For example, at age sixty-two I obtained a BA degree, with honours. I taught ESL in Japan and volunteered at a school in Kathmandu. I trekked the Annapurna Circuit. At age seventy I completed a full marathon in Penticton. Last month, at age seventy-three, I cycled the 300 kilometres from Vancouver to Seattle, and fundraised for the British Columbia Ride to Conquer Cancer." She smiled shyly but proudly. "At seventy-three I'm teaching English and yoga, and volunteering with landed immigrant groups. I truly feel we all are challenged, at different times in our lives, by our marathons and triathlons, whatever they are," she said with conviction.

Dyane's words, example and courage inspired me. While our family issues — my own form of a marathon — were being resolved, I used Dyane's example. I looked deep within and found energy and strength I didn't know I had.

~Elizabeth Smayda
Burnaby, British Columbia

72

The Waterspout at White Otter Castle

Leave the beaten track occasionally and dive into the woods. Every time you do so you will be certain to find something that you have never seen before.
~Alexander Graham Bell

A
s a young filmmaker I was intrigued when I learned about the legend of White Otter Castle. Standing on the shore of a wilderness lake west of Thunder Bay, it was built single-handedly by Jimmy McOuat in the early 1900s. Legend has it that Jimmy, a Scottish immigrant, built his castle for a woman, a bride or a lost love. It remained standing long after he was gone, but by 1980 the large red pine logs that formed the foundation were rotting, the four-story tower was coming loose, and the roof was badly leaking. Remnants of fire pits and hundreds of carved signatures lined the interior of the unoccupied building. It was only a matter of time before the castle burned down or collapsed, disappearing altogether.

I quickly became hooked on the legend and embarked on an adventure to make a documentary film about it. First I met with Elinor Barr, the castle's historian. Apparently, as a young man, Jimmy ventured west from Quebec and started a farm near Fort Frances, Ontario. In 1887 he sent for a mail order bride, but he backed out and sold his farm to go prospecting for gold. In 1903 he became a trapper near

White Otter Lake, and there he began building his castle.

Needing to see it myself, I learned the only way to get there was by floatplane, boat or snowmobile. So on a gloomy day in mid-March I travelled north by train and rented a snowmobile. After an hour of travelling past frozen wilderness shores, I arrived at McOuat Bay at the north end of White Otter Lake. I could pick out the lonely grey castle in the distance, its fading red roof peeking out between the trees.

Climbing off my sled on the frozen beach, I stopped and simply stared at the building in reverence. The surrounding red pines lorded over a silence broken only by ravens squawking in the distance. Just below the tower I found an old wooden cross, surrounded by a small weatherworn picket fence. As I gazed at Jimmy's snow-covered grave my mission suddenly became clear: to bring this man and his lonely wilderness castle to life, perhaps even help preserve it. I managed to take a few shots with my old Bolex film camera, but I had to head back before dark.

***

"First we take the train across the top of Lake Superior to a railway town called Ignace," I explain. "Then, it's a thirty-six mile canoe trip [fifty-eight kilometres] with eighteen rough portages — with all the film gear. What do you think?" With a grin, and a high-five, my wife Cathy says, "I'm in."

The spring flowers are blooming when we board the train in Toronto. But the next day when we arrive at Ignace the ice has only just melted off the lakes; the air still has a chill to it. We rent a well-worn aluminum canoe and begin paddling south until we find a campsite. The next morning our tent is sagging from the weight of snow on it. Peering out the tent flap I see an entire landscape covered in three inches of snow.

As the day progresses the sun appears and melts everything. It also warms our souls as our wilderness confidence returns. After two more days of canoeing and portaging we arrive at the castle and set up our camp on the sandy beach. The evenings are cool enough to prevent mosquitoes and black flies from making a meal of us. Serenaded by loon calls, we watch spectacular sunsets.

In 1914, Jimmy was visited by a journalist. When asked why he built his castle, Jimmy responded, "When I was a boy out with my chums, one of them threw an ear of corn at a man and hit him in the ear."

Blaming Jimmy, the man cursed him: "Jimmy McOuat! Ye'll never do no good! Ye'll die in a shack!"

"I never forgot it," explained Jimmy. "Ye can't call this a shack, can ye?"

I film the massive red pine logs that Jimmy cut and set into position. Jimmy had used a hand driven winch to haul the logs out of the bush before squaring and dovetailing them. He then raised them into place using pulleys, poles and trays of rocks. A practical man, Jimmy created his own burial tomb in a small cave across the bay, with bags of cement and tools inside so

Photo taken by Dennis Smyk 1999

he could seal himself in when his time was near. But in 1918 Jimmy disappeared. The following spring two rangers found his decomposed body with a button caught in his fishing net. It is commonly believed he drowned while setting his nets.

With Jimmy's story in mind, I begin filming as many shots as I can. Cathy and I discuss paddling across the bay to see if we can find Jimmy's legendary cave, but decide against it in case a strong wind should come up and swamp our canoe. We would not last long if tossed into the frigid waters.

Just then, as if on cue, a powerful wind whips the branches of the tall pines surrounding the castle. Then a small twister appears in front of me on the beach. It whips up sand and debris and blows the clothes off our camp clothesline. After rattling our tent, the twister slowly spins around a large chunk of charred wood.

Our empty canoe sits on the beach, half in the water. Worried that it might blow away and strand us, I begin running toward it. But right before my eyes, the wind picks up the canoe on its stern, walks it over on its end, then gently places it face down on a log in the middle of our campsite.

If that isn't baffling enough, a large circular rapid suddenly appears in the small bay. It's so noisy we have to shout to hear each other. I run for my camera, and Cathy shouts, "Look Pete! A waterspout!"

It is unbelievable. A six-foot tall waterspout is now whipping and dancing in the middle of the circular rapid. I try to mount my camera on the tripod but my hands are shaking too much. Slowly the waterspout subsides and the circular rapid disappears. I manage to capture the tail end of it on film.

What a sensual experience! I feel the magical world in every ripple, every wave and every rustle of a leaf. Cathy and I look at each other wide-eyed and agree, "That was Jimmy McOuat. He just wanted to say hello."

***

The trip back to Ignace was uneventful. Back in Toronto I finished my film, hopeful that not only had I captured the physical remains of the castle, but something of the magical spirit of the place, and the legend. It was shown on television networks, in libraries, government offices, classrooms and a film festival. White Otter Castle became known.

Years later I was pleased to learn the castle had been restored, and apparently my film had played a big role in that happening. It turned out that not only did Jimmy not die in a shack, but his castle became his legacy and a testimony to his creativity and hard work. Maybe that magical waterspout was actually Jimmy saying thanks in advance!

~Peter G. Elliott
Mount Pearl, Newfoundland and Labrador

73

Temporary Town

> *Every new friend is a new adventure…*
> *the start of more memories.*
> ~Patrick Lindsay

I packed up my car and headed north — alone on the open road. I was both terrified and excited about leaving the safety of the familiar to explore a new region of Canada. Two hours into the drive I realized I'd neglected to pack a map. But it seemed simple enough: go north until you hit the Trans-Canada Highway and then turn west; enter Northern Ontario and enjoy new adventures.

I drove into the small town nestled on the shore of Lake Huron, and decided this was as a good a place as any to start. I would stay for maybe six months, and then move on. I rented one of the few brick houses in town, a rambling two-and-a-half story building on Main Street. The house was huge. It had no shower — just an old claw-foot tub — no TV, a rustic kitchen, and ancient wiring. But I thought it was beautiful.

I explored my temporary surroundings. A river divided the town in two, the few shops were closed by 5:30 p.m., and the closest movie theatre was an hour away. Children roamed the street and played outside.

Searching on the Internet for things to do was fruitless. I learned to read the local paper to find out what was going on. The community events section acted as a built-in social calendar. The locals were busy with a litany of things — wing nights, fish fry nights, concerts, book clubs, hunting, ATV rides, and everything else under the sun. But I needed to talk to people to become involved — word of mouth ruled the streets.

The first month was humbling. Everyone knew everyone else. And it seemed like everyone knew me. Strangers would start conversations. "Oh, you're the new girl working at the library," or "You're the one who runs, right?" Some days it seemed like everyone in town knew more about me than I knew about myself.

Yet this place was oddly endearing. There was a sense of community I had never experienced. When summer arrived and my grass grew long, there were offers of help to mow the lawn, offers of trips to nearby lakes, advice on where the best fishing could be found. Even mail hand-delivered to my workplace although the package only listed my home address. Moments of small-town kindness and enthusiasm. A small-town adventure.

I learned how to curl at the curling club on Main Street. I "hurried hard," played in bonspiels, and shared many a laugh after slipping on the ice. It became a winter home. A cozy place to share and to build memories. I discovered and learned to play the dulcimer in that town. A local woman volunteered her time to teach me and lent me her instrument. No questions asked. No money wanted. Just the pleasure of sharing a passion with a like-minded friend.

I gained a new appreciation of the word "camp." Growing up it had always meant summer camp. No longer. Now it means: a place in the woods or a place on a lake, all for enjoying the outdoors. "Camp" became hours near the water taking in the splendour of the Canadian wilderness. Watching kids learn to fish and catch a giant bass right off the dock. Laughter, bonfires, and starry nights. "Camp" is the North. Friendly, full of nature and amazing.

This small town nestled on the shore of Lake Huron surprised me. I expected to be here for six months. It was supposed to be one of many Canadian towns I passed through. A blip on a bigger journey.

But years later I'm still here. That temporary town became my adopted community and… my home. That small, seemingly insignificant town stole my heart.

~Krista McCracken
Thessalon, Ontario

The Spirit of Canada

Our Canadian Heroes

A hero is an ordinary individual who finds the strength to persevere and endure in spite of overwhelming obstacles.
~Christopher Reeve

74

Terry's Legacy

It was a journey that defied all logic, a three-thousand-
mile journey run by a boy who had lost one leg to
cancer. In the end, it was a journey that carried
Terry Fox into the hearts of an entire nation.
~Leslie Scrivener, Terry Fox: His Story

I was still in high school when Terry Fox began his Marathon of Hope to raise both awareness and funding for cancer research. I remember watching the progress of his cross-Canada run on the TV news: a small figure in athletic shorts and T-shirt, jogging slowly and seemingly painfully along the highway with his prosthetic leg, grim determination on his face. With his curly brown hair, youth and athletic build, Terry could have been the boy next door. It made him and his campaign feel more real and poignant than the usual news. Even in the early days of his run, he seemed like a real-life hero.

I didn't realize at the time the significance his heroism would have for my family. Although he was a stranger to us, the more we watched and learned about Terry, the more we felt we knew him. As a teenager, Terry loved sports — especially basketball. He wasn't the greatest player, but what he lacked in natural skill he made up with hard work. He eventually made his high school basketball team and even his university team. He never gave up.

But at age eighteen Terry was diagnosed with bone cancer and forced to have his right leg amputated fifteen centimetres above the

knee. That was 1977. Moved by the other cancer patients he met in the hospital, Terry was inspired to do something to raise money for cancer research. He decided that with his one good leg and one prosthetic leg, he would run across Canada. The next year he began training and making other preparations, applying his trademark dedication and determination.

On April 12, 1980, after eighteen months of training, which included running over 5,000 kilometres, Terry began his run in St. John's, Newfoundland with little fanfare. As his run progressed, the attention and donations grew. Through the Maritime Provinces, Quebec and Ontario, he ran close to forty-two kilometres a day. He went from being a lonely figure on an often-empty highway, sometimes running in cold, rain and darkness, to being cheered on by enthusiastic roadside crowds. By the summer of 1980 the whole country was watching and rooting for Terry.

But despite Terry's commitment and determination, after 143 days and 5,373 kilometres, he was forced to stop running on September 1st outside Thunder Bay, Ontario. Cancer had appeared in his lungs. As my family and I watched the news on TV, we could see the pain in Terry's face and we were deeply saddened. The following summer, on

June 28, 1981, Terry Fox died at the age of twenty-two.

Although the Marathon of Hope and Terry's life were both cut short, his inspiration continued. In the thirty-six years since Terry began his run, over $650 million has been raised for cancer research in Terry's name through the annual Terry Fox Run, held across Canada and around the world.

Terry's run gained a special meaning for my family when, less than two years later, my seventeen-year-old brother was diagnosed with stage III Hodgkin's disease — a particularly aggressive form of cancer. Doctors removed a grapefruit-sized malignant growth from his chest, and also removed his spleen before beginning chemotherapy. They told him that if the treatment didn't work, he would be dead within the year. His odds were 50/50.

Back at school, my brother had difficulty concentrating. He walked home, thinking about the doctor's words and flipping a coin back and forth in his fingers. Heads or tails. Live or die. My brother's diagnosis was devastating to my parents, and they perhaps carried more of its weight than even my brother did. He was a teenage boy, after all, and didn't really believe he could die. Without the awareness raised by Terry's run, the cancer and its treatment would have been even more frightening and isolating than it was for my brother and the rest of our family.

Before the Marathon of Hope, cancer wasn't talked about. It was a word that tended to be whispered behind closed doors. No one knew much about it, except that it killed people. Terry's campaign lifted the stigma and superstition associated with cancer. We could talk about what was happening, and other people wouldn't shy away as if they were afraid to catch it.

Terry also taught us about fighting cancer. And despite the tragic end to Terry's own life, Terry gave us hope. After gruelling weeks of chemotherapy, sickness, weakness and many missed days of school, my brother attended his high school graduation ceremony and walked up to receive his diploma to a standing ovation. Despite everything, he had finished. And he was cancer-free. Two years later, the cancer had not returned.

My brother and I took a month off from work and university, bought VIA Rail youth passes and rode the train across Canada. When we reached Thunder Bay, we got off the train, and friends drove us out to the spot where Terry Fox was forced to end his run. There, on the edge of the highway, overlooking Lake Superior, stands a bronze statue of Terry, caught mid-run, the expression of determination and perseverance still on his face, forever heading west toward his goal. We stood silently gazing at the statue of this real-life Canadian hero who had inspired and touched our lives, and the lives of so many others around the world. Terry, we will never forget you.

~Jacqueline Pearce
Vancouver, British Columbia

Our P.E.T.

We have been touched by greatness. Today we say
au revoir to Pierre and we bury the body.
But the vision continues. The vision lives.
~Roy Heenan, at the
State Funeral of Pierre Elliott Trudeau

I t was August 1968. My mother had made me an offer. "You can have a month at camp or spend a week with me at Stratford." For me this was a no-brainer. I was twelve years old and obsessed with the theatre. I hated camp.

We lived in Montreal, and this would be my first trip outside Quebec. My mother and I travelled to Stratford by train and spent the week attending Stratford Festival productions. We took a side trip to Niagara Falls, and then returned to Toronto to visit family friends. Now it was Friday, the end of our precious time together, and we were returning by train to Stratford for the evening performance of *The Seagull*, presented at the Avon Theatre.

Mum and I disembarked to find a crowd lining the depot of Stratford's tiny train station. We knew they weren't waiting for us, and actors in Stratford are as ubiquitous as squirrels in the park. "Maybe the Prime Minister is coming!" Mum jested. But even Mum was startled when she turned out to be right.

That summer was the height of "Trudeaumania," though not so much in Stratford, Ontario, which was conservative country. When we entered the Avon Theatre we saw Trudeau, Marchand and Pelletier, recently dubbed "The Three Wise Men," sitting in the centre of the ground floor flanked by plainclothes RCMP officers.

"Look at this!" Mum marvelled. "He isn't sitting in the front row, and he isn't sitting in a private box! Anyone could take a pot shot at him! He's a sitting duck for any crazy person. From where we are, I could shoot him right now! But here nobody does! Oh, I'm so grateful the Americans didn't want me! What a wonderful country this is!"

My beautiful young mother, brimming with *joie de vivre*, was a Holocaust survivor. She adored her adopted country, which had opened its gates to refugees from war-torn Europe in 1948. She knew none of the words to "O Canada" except for the first two, and thought the lyrics, our "native land" referred to the Indians. But Mum would tear up whenever she saw the Canadian flag. No matter how tough her lot she would tell my dad, "Here in Canada, nobody's trying to kill us, we have the children, and we have each other." Particularly in 1968, after the assassinations of Martin Luther King, Jr. and Robert Kennedy south of the border, Mum was grateful to have been transplanted to Canada.

At intermission, pen and theatre program in hand, Mum marched up as close as she could to the Prime Minister of Canada. Pierre Trudeau's political seat was in our Montreal riding, and Mum had proudly voted for him. A bodyguard stopped her. "I want to get his autograph!" Mum explained, stating her rights as a citizen. She was allowed to pass.

"Oh, Mr. Trudeau! I live in your riding, in Montreal! I voted for you!" Flashing his famous grin, the Prime Minister graciously signed Mum's program.

"Oh, Sharon," she cried, "you should see! I got so close I could see his pockmarks!" Like Richard Burton, acne scars did nothing to diminish Trudeau's appeal.

I was mildly interested in the Prime Minister's presence, but as a twelve-year-old I was more fascinated by a short and round young man I spied standing alone at the far end of the lobby. "Mummy, look! It's Charlie Brown!" Only two months before, Mum and I had seen a Canadian touring production of *You're a Good Man, Charlie Brown*. The young man who played the lead was now in the lobby of the Avon Theatre, just a few feet away. "So it is!" Mum confirmed. "You wanna get his autograph?"

"Sure!"

Mum marched up to Charlie Brown while I tagged shyly behind. The young actor was surprised and delighted to be recognized. He was also mystified. "But Trudeau is here!" he said. "Why would you be interested in me?"

For me, however, any actor was a demi-god. Knowing this, Mum took charge and soon she had Charlie Brown under her wing, as well as me. So it came to pass that Mum, Charlie Brown and I kept company in the lobby of the Avon Theatre on a sweet summer evening when our new Prime Minister came to town to see a play.

* * *

Pierre Elliott Trudeau died on September 28, 2000 and from then until the day of his funeral, Canadian society skidded to a halt. For five days, tributes and reminiscences poured into radio stations across the country. There were broadcasts of Trudeau's speeches. During that five-day period I finally heard and saw a bit of what my mother had experienced over thirty years before. Now I was hearing them for what felt like the first time.

Breaking away from the broadcasts, I stepped into the streets. Teenage boys were razzing each other in English and French, switching languages so swiftly and deftly that one couldn't tell what their mother tongues were. There it was. Trudeau's legacy in action: bilingualism had become so firmly entrenched it wasn't even an issue anymore.

On the streets I noticed predominately black, brown and yellow faces, and heard the sounds of Spanish. This, I recognized, was the legacy of the open-door immigration policy initiated by Trudeau in the early 1970s. The acceptance of official bilingualism had paved the way for an acceptance of multiculturalism.

In Parliament, a political opponent laid a rose beneath Trudeau's portrait. In Montreal, at the entrance to Trudeau's mansion on Pine Avenue, political opponents as well as supporters laid roses at the foot of his door.

The train tracks along the Montreal-Ottawa route were lined with crowds of Canadians paying homage to their former and fallen leader. In Ottawa, Trudeau's body was taken to Parliament where he lay in state before being returned to Montreal. It would be his last journey home.

In the wee hours of the morning Canadians stood by the railroad tracks, weeping. When the car bearing Trudeau's sons Justin and Sacha came into view, people spontaneously burst into cries of loving support, as well as applause.

In Montreal, the day of Trudeau's funeral was marked by the colour red: the red of the Canadian flag draped over his coffin, the red of the RCMP officers' jackets, the red of autumn leaves at their peak, and most of all, the velvety red of the roses being sold by street vendors and in florists' shops, and affixed to citizens' lapels. Trudeau was known for the red roses he routinely sported in the lapels of his dapper suits. On the day of his funeral, in early October, Montreal bloomed into a rose garden in honour and in memory of its beloved and lost P.E.T. — Pierre Elliot Trudeau.

~S. Nadja Zajdman
Montreal, Quebec

76

Sid, Please Sign My Jersey

They say the game has changed. But it's still four
corners, three zones, two legs, and a puck.
~Ron MacLean

I was forty years old when I played my first game of ice hockey. I had been inspired by three people, two of whom I had never met — Wayne Gretzky and Sidney Crosby. The third was my good friend Andy Vautour. Andy and I would often talk about hockey and our hockey heroes, Sid and Wayne. Sidney was still in his junior career with Rimouski Océanic of the QMJHL. We were so excited for Sid to break into the NHL, to see what amazing things he would do with the best hockey players in the world. I had always admired him for his ability to play a game that I loved, but could never play since I had never learned to skate.

With a lot of encouragement from Andy I thought, *why not just get out there and do it?* What a mess! I could barely stand up, and I couldn't stop properly. But I was hooked. I loved every minute of it. As time passed I eventually learned how to skate, stop and shoot a puck (none of it very well) but I could do it. No wonder I admired the guys who made it seem so simple, who were not only good at it, but excelled.

In 2009 when Sidney won his first Stanley Cup while Captain of the Pittsburgh Penguins, I was beyond happy for him. I also knew he'd be bringing the cup back to his hometown of Cole Harbour, Nova

Scotia, not far from where I lived. I looked forward to cheering him on during his parade, with all the thousands of other fans, excited to share in this celebration of our "Sid the Kid."

The day was perfect — sunny and warm — a great day to have a parade with the Stanley Cup. To top it off, it was Sid's birthday. I will never forget how it felt seeing him in person with hockey's "holy grail," the Stanley Cup. I had admired this gifted hockey player for so many years and now he was here — the youngest captain in hockey history to win the Stanley Cup. It was truly a WOW experience!

Fast-forward to 2016. My family and I were watching in excitement as Sid the Kid did it again — won another Stanley Cup — and

in the process got himself voted "Playoff MVP." I was so happy for him! Then I started thinking seriously about an idea I'd been playing with. I wanted to make a sign asking Sidney Crosby to sign my jersey. Why not? Neighbours reported that Sid would sometimes travel the area during the summer while at home in Cole Harbour.

So I got creative, and with the help of my wife Trish, my daughter Breanna, and her friend Morgan, I painted a big sign on a 4x8 sheet of plywood. In big gold letters on a white background the sign read simply, "SID, PLEASE SIGN MY JERSEY." In the top right corner we added what was probably the worst picture of a Stanley Cup ever drawn! Then I hung my game-worn Pittsburgh Penguins #87 jersey in the lower left corner, with a pen, in case he drove past while I was at work. At night I'd bring it in and hang it in the living room window with a light on, so he could see it from the road.

At first I had high expectations. You hear all the time about what a great guy Sidney Crosby is, and how he's always signing items for his fans. You read how he has showed up at the homes of Pittsburgh Penguins fans and personally delivered their season tickets. But as the days passed

I started to think that well, maybe he hadn't seen it yet, or maybe he was just too busy. After all, not only is he the world's best player, but he's also the only player in the history of the game to win a Stanley Cup, an Olympic gold medal and a World Hockey Championship — while

Captain of each team! I can only imagine how many people want a piece of him, and how many different directions he must be pulled in. After a week had passed I had to take the sign down — I needed the plywood for a project that had to get done. I figured it was a nice try. Still, I hung the jersey in my living room window, leaving the light on day and night so it could be seen from the road.

After a couple of weeks I let go of the idea that Sid might stop by to sign my jersey. Then, one Friday morning I was at work checking my e-mails when a message from my wife arrived. Her e-mails always catch my eye, but I was particularly intrigued by the subject line; "Check this out. An old friend dropped by."

When I opened the message, there was a picture attached. When I opened the picture I saw two people, one of whom was my daughter Madisyn, but then I looked at the other person. *Who's that guy standing there next to my daughter?* I wondered. *It looks like Sidney Crosby.* I looked closer. *It is Sidney Crosby! Where did Madisyn get a picture with Sidney Crosby?* Then I noticed the pictures on the walls in the background, and then I remembered the subject line, "Check this out. An old friend dropped by." And that's when I got it.

Suddenly I started yelling out loud, "HE'S IN MY HOUSE, HE'S IN MY HOUSE!" Naturally my co-workers came over to see what was going on, asking, "Who? Who's in your house?"

"Sidney Crosby!" I bellowed. "Look, look at the picture, he's in *my* house!" I was filled with awe, excitement and disbelief all at the same time. Because sure enough, Sidney Crosby had stopped by *my* home. He'd remembered the house with the sign and the jersey, and stopped. He'd parked his SUV in my driveway, walked up the walkway, rang the bell and when my wife answered he said, "Hi, I'm here to sign a jersey." It was unbelievable! Sidney came to *my* house!

While he was there that day, Sidney signed three hockey jerseys, a T-shirt and a picture of my daughter from when she played minor hockey with the Tasa Ducks. When I got home from work that day and looked at all the Sidney Crosby-signed memorabilia, I was simply amazed at how incredible this was. Sidney Crosby had been here, in my house and had signed my jerseys!

Even after several months had passed since Sidney Crosby had taken time out of his day to drop into my house to sign my jersey, I was still shocked. This was not a publicity stunt. There was no cameraman, reporter or team representative with him. This was just Sidney Crosby, world's best hockey player, making a fan's dream come true!

~Darryl Pottie
Enfield, Nova Scotia

77

Joni and Me

*Keep a good heart. That's the most important thing in
life. It's not how much money you make or what you
can acquire. The art of it is to keep a good heart.*
~Joni Mitchell

oni Mitchell is my Canadian talisman. She has provided the
soundtrack for my life. I remember hearing her sweet voice on
the radio when I was in the backseat of my mom's Pinto, and
how it made me feel safe and happy. When I was madly in love,
it was Joni who played on the CD player while we drove to my boyfriend's cottage, the landscape of the Canadian Shield becoming more
rocky and rugged as we blew smoke rings out the window. Her songs
were the perfect backdrop for sparkling lakes and feeling wild and
free. Her voice mingled with the smell of pine trees, and the magical
sight of the northern lights crossing over each other like glowing
sheets on a celestial clothesline.

Joni had the voice of the sweetest songbird and the soul of a poet.
She spoke to me when she was an outsider at other people's parties,
and when she felt like a gypsy with jangling silver bracelets on her arm.
Later, when that boyfriend broke my heart, it was Joni who patched it
back together. Somehow Joni could sing about heartbreak but remain
wry and sane. I'd listen to her sing, "dreaming of the pleasure I'm gonna
have/watching your hairline recede my vain darling," and marvel that
she could still sound affectionate in her lyrics. Her optimism managed

to steer me away from bitterness. For a while I toyed with the idea that I was Joni's long lost daughter whom she sings about in "Little Green." After all, I was the right age, and my sister did always tell me I was adopted whenever we fought as children.

"Are you serious?" my mother scoffed when I presented my theory. "You and your sister both have my feet. Sorry to break it to you sweetheart, but you're my daughter through and through." It was true. My sister, mother and I do have identical feet — strange, solid potato-farmer paws. Perhaps my bulky feet explain why I hate skating. I find ice skates incredibly uncomfortable and the whole ordeal to be treacherous. I'm sure Joni has delicate fairy-like feet that slip easily into ice skates. There is a photograph of Joni on her *Hejira* album, where she is skating like an exotic bird on a frozen pond, a cape of feathers spread out behind her. She looks like she could stay on the ice forever, untouched by the cold, impervious to tumbles and broken limbs.

Not long after Joni nursed me back from my broken heart, I was working on call as a massage therapist for a big Toronto hotel. But it was not the glamorous gig I had envisioned. In fact, I hated the creepy guests and the last-minute appointments. Usually I'd get a call in the evenings when I was already in my pyjamas and safely ensconced behind a TV tray of supper. Although I needed the money, I would often turn the work down. One night, when I was in my bathrobe with a bowl of ice cream, the hotel called. I was already saying that I was busy when the manager said the guest requesting a massage was Joni Mitchell. I was in a cab within minutes.

As I rushed to the hotel I worried that my icon would disappoint me, be dismissive, or rude or self-important. I was also afraid that I'd disappoint *her*, that my touch would feel hesitant or pokey, that she'd be alarmed by the nervous tremble in my hands and it would set her on edge.

When Joni opened her hotel room door she was on the phone talking in a low voice. She was lovely. I saw her guitar case leaning against the wall and squealed inwardly. I pretended to be a professional while I set up my table, but on the inside I was trying not to pass out.

We didn't talk beyond which muscles needed extra attention, and somehow I miraculously kept my cool.

At the end of her treatment she thanked me and said it was "delish."

Joni thought my hands were delish. I almost did back flips. When I was at the door I managed to squeak that it was an honour to meet her. I didn't try to keep the receipt she signed or palm a small item from her room as a souvenir. I don't remember if she tipped me, and I didn't try to shake her hand. I was almost cross-eyed with giddiness.

It's amazing that meeting Joni Mitchell in a hotel room was a pivotal moment in my life, while I was merely a blip in her evening. I tap-danced the entire way home while she probably smoked a cigarette, fell asleep and forgot all about me.

It's okay to meet your heroes when your hero is Joni Mitchell. She remains a legend and someone I would like to emulate. She is an embodiment of Canada: lonely and wild, harsh and poetic. Unapologetic and fierce. You can't put her in a box, say she is just a folky-hippy or a jazz artist or a painter or a poet. Likewise, you can't say Canada is just snow and ice and big trees.

Recently, at age seventy-one, Joni became the new face for Saint Laurent, leading the wave of older, strong women who are being featured in fashion campaigns. The photo shoot features Joni in a long white dress with flowing sleeves, those cheekbones as fierce as ever, and when she swoops her arms it reminds me again of the *Hejira* image of her skating across the ice. When talking about the campaign in *New York Magazine* she reminisced about how Warren Beatty once admonished her for carrying a Chanel bag when she should have been representing hippy/artist ideals. She scoffed and asked why she had to give up her individuality to belong to the club. She could have a wild heart and also love high fashion.

No one can pigeonhole Joni. She will never be tamed. Neither will Canada. The landscape will always be wild, the climate can be brutal, but overall it is awe-inspiring. The rest of us can just stand back and admire, and be grateful we are a part of it. I'll never like the cold and embrace winter. I'll never skate on a frozen pond like a mythical bird.

I may not be Joni Mitchell's long lost daughter, but I basked in her presence for a moment, and she thought my hands were delicious.

~Kristine Groskaufmanis
Toronto, Ontario

78

Never Give Up on Your Dreams

I honestly believe that my best work is in front, not
behind me. I am driven by a deep passion and need to
make a difference and leave this world a little better
than when I arrived. That's what keeps me going.
~Rick Hansen

In 1985, like most Canadians at the time, I watched in awe the heroic efforts of Rick Hansen as he set out on his Man in Motion World Tour to raise awareness for spinal cord research. For the next twenty-six months I checked the news daily for updates as Hansen made his way around the globe, wheeling the equivalent of two marathons every day through thirty-four countries on four continents. We all watched in amazement as he pushed himself in his wheelchair through the most dismal of weather conditions, up and down mountains that would reduce the sturdiest and most able-bodied among us to quivering masses of jelly. He hauled himself up the Great Wall of China, over deserts and rocky terrain, enduring blizzards, freezing rain, and scorching heat as the seasons unleashed their harshest, most dramatic conditions.

Most days there was film footage of Rick Hansen on the news, his massive biceps working at a level of strength most of us can only imagine as he moved with grace and total concentration. I was particularly struck by the sight of his index finger poking through torn gloves, swollen and bandaged, bloodied from wear and tear after thousands of hours spent pushing his wheelchair.

Early in 1987, Hansen and his team were nearing the end of his Man in Motion World Tour, making their way through Ontario. On a chilly March day I joined a cheering crowd of thousands gathered along Princess Street in Kingston, Ontario to catch a glimpse of the tour. The wind off the lake sent stinging hits of icy snow in our faces, which nobody seemed to notice. I found a telephone pole to lean on while I waited; at the time I was eight months pregnant with my first child and grateful for something to lean against.

There was a celebratory air as we waited to see our national hero. And then, all of a sudden, there he was. Rick Hansen sped past us, smiling as we cheered and waved, his arms pumping their familiar rhythm as he pushed his chair through the whipping snow. I had a very real sense of being in the presence of greatness. And I vividly remember wrapping my arm around the telephone pole and crying, overcome by the enormity of the moment.

***

Ten years later I was living in Halifax, Nova Scotia, raising a young family and working full-time as a musician. Rick Hansen was due to make a stop at the Metro Centre in Halifax to celebrate the tenth anniversary of the Man in Motion World Tour. He'd be available for a meet-and-greet with the public. My admiration and hero-worship of Hansen hadn't lessened since my sighting of him in Kingston, so on the day of his appearance I slipped out on my lunch break and made my way down to the Metro Centre at top speed.

I arrived too late to hear him speak, so I satisfied myself by standing at the back of the crowd peering over heads, absorbing the excitement in the room while officials and civilians took to the stage alongside Rick Hansen. People spoke from their hearts with gratitude for all he had done — his strength and perseverance in the face of adversity. The speeches were brief, some presentations were made, and then it was announced that Rick had a half hour to spend with the crowd. I rummaged in my purse for a pen, and clutching my Man in Motion Tenth Anniversary Tour brochure, I joined the waiting crowd.

As he made his way down the ramp from the stage I was so unnerved, I considered leaving. At that moment Rick Hansen smiled and extended his hand to a young man in a wheelchair and I watched, fascinated, as the two men began to talk. Rick's focus was so complete, his interest so genuine, it was as though they were the only people in the room.

I managed to pull myself together, and reminded myself that here was a person who had pushed himself around the world in a wheelchair to further a cause he believed in. The least I could do was to gather my courage and thank him for doing so!

Along with everyone else in the room I fell under Rick Hansen's spell, his ability to put people at ease, and his genuine interest in their stories. One woman wept as she spoke to him; he held her hand and smiled his encouragement, not once breaking eye contact with her as she struggled to find the words. A tall, strapping man warmly shook Rick's hand and thanked him. He had broken his back in an industrial accident a decade earlier. "I'm one of the lucky ones," he said before shaking Rick's hand and walking away. Rick nodded and smiled and gave him a thumbs-up.

And then Rick Hansen turned and looked directly at me. He held out his hand — the very hand that had pushed him in his wheelchair up the Great Wall of China and around the world. I looked at that well-muscled hand, the index finger bearing scars from his journey, scars I had seen as open wounds on news clips ten years earlier. He smiled as I took his hand and shook it.

To my complete surprise, I was calm and articulate. Like the others before me I spoke from my heart. I told him that in March of 1987 I had stood on Princess Street in Kingston, Ontario, vast with child, weeping as he wheeled by with his entourage. I added that some magic dust must have flown up from his wheels and landed on us, because there we were, ten years later, my daughter — that very same daughter — recently diagnosed with juvenile diabetes and taking the changes in her life in stride, making the best of a lousy situation.

I thanked Rick for his example, and told him that our whole family had taken inspiration from him, a man who had become a paraplegic at age fifteen in an accident.

At which point Rick Hansen smiled and thanked me — *me!* — and asked me to wish my daughter all the best. Then he signed my brochure for my two children: *To Tamsyn and Avery* — *Never give up on your dreams!*

I'm pleased to say that they haven't.

~Binnie Brennan
Halifax, Nova Scotia

79

Keep Moving

*True heroism is remarkably sober, very undramatic. It
is not the urge to surpass all others at whatever cost,
but the urge to serve others, at whatever the cost.*
~Arthur Ashe

The arid landscape is hot and dry. Our heavily laden steps kick up swirls of fine dust that mark the patrol's serpentine movement through the grape rows and mud walls of Kandahar.

Everything feels routine. My only concern is my struggle with the eighty or so pounds of weapons, armour and assorted kit on my body — actually a light load for this day — and where my rifle is pointing as I stomp the trail behind the soldier ahead of me. My mind loves to drift at times like this. It shies away from discomfort quicker than I can shackle it to the here and now. I try to focus. Left foot forward. My mind drifts. Right foot forward.

I ponder the ridiculousness of where I am. I'm the first born of a first-born child, and the first Canadian-born of a family line. I am an heir to Canada and a son of the Philippines. My destiny is to be short, well fed, momma-loved, and working in something technical and safe. I'm supposed to be married to a short, well fed, papa-loved Filipina beauty who does teeth for a living or some such noble way of life.

I'm not supposed to be who I am, but fate didn't bring me here. I'm a volunteer, like every other soldier in this patrol, and I'm on my second tour in Canada's latest war. My entire life at this point is devoted to this duty, and I've never been happier. I'm the first of my line to serve our new country. I'm a son of immigrants, just like most of my fellows were in the big wars decades ago.

The column suddenly stops and the dust settles. My mind quickly returns to the here and now. I'm aware of the heavy weight of the kit pulling down on me. The man ahead sets his rifle on a mound of dirt toward the right. I do the same toward the left. I don't quite know what's going on, but something is definitely up. Others closer to the front are making gestures about something in the distance. The normally idle chatter of the radio is now an unending ramble of grids and descriptions, "…to our direct front… likely enemy… imminent contact…"

Our interpreter scrambles into a depression in the earth, his young face covered by a handkerchief under an old green helmet. He's a native of Kandahar, and interpreters always know the ebb and flow of their homeland. If he's taking cover then so should we. I crouch a little lower behind my mound of dirt.

"Two Section! Prepare to move to the wadi," yells the Sergeant behind me. Pause…. two… three… "Move!"

"Moving!" The last half of our serpentine column disappears into a ditch. "Here it comes!" Yells someone from up front.

My eyes can't scan everything fast enough. "Where are they? Where are they?" I say.

Snap-snap! Snap-snap-snap! Tat-tat! Tat-tat-tat!

The opening fusillade of incoming bullets is fierce. Hot lead is splitting the air like gusts of wind above our heads. The noise echoes against the surrounding mud walls.

"Over there! Over there!" I hear someone yell, but without a point of reference, "there" could be anywhere. Where are they? Where are they? I can't tell if I'm speaking out loud or if this nagging question is trapped in my mind.

"Left flank! Left flank! Twenty metres!" Someone finally gives an actual indication, and it's close!

Doof! Grenades are being thrown. The unmistakable thrust of pressure hits my chest. Doof!

I see dust clouds to our left. I don't want to remain underemployed.

It's time to help the patrol with my rifle. My rifle spears out at nothing in particular. The view in my scope shows gaps in a wall with those dust clouds dancing in them. Anything that's not us and not a bush or a wall might be a lurking insurgent.

Pak-pak! Pak-pak-pak! I'm pulling the trigger as fast as I can without losing control of the rifle. Pak-pak! Pak-pak-pak!

I don't feel safe where I am. The enemy likes to pop out at us from all directions. My back feels eerily exposed. I decide to drop down in order to pop up somewhere else. I begin my descent from the mound....

The mound above my head becomes three little explosions of dirt. I don't hear it, I just see it a few inches above, and I'm aghast.

Some unseen enemy on the right flank has the back of my head in his sights and my only saving grace is less than a second of time and a fraction of a degree of deviation. I've never met this someone. I've done nothing to him so far as I know, but it's painfully clear he's trying to end me.

I sink out of sight to the earth. My soul is crushed. My being is emotionally defeated. This isn't a harsh breakup with a girl. This isn't the disappointment of a lost game. I am being hunted by another human. I'm no longer looking for work. I'm no longer firing my rifle. I'm no longer functioning like I'm supposed to. Someone wants to end me. My mind is adrift again.

A sergeant tries to monkey-walk by my quivering self, but stops to look at me. He sees what's happening. He knows I'm going through a close call. He puts a meaty hand on my shoulder. "Hey," he says, "as long as you're breathing, keep moving."

As long as I'm breathing, keep moving, I tell myself. That line becomes my new mantra. I lift my body up and heft my rifle and continue to fire back, pulling the trigger as fast as I can while staying under control.

Our patrol withdraws under sporadic, half-hearted fire. We all look exhausted. Our heads are hanging. Our rifles are swinging from our spent arms. Our boots shuffle through the dirt. We are intact, but spent.

This isn't our first battle, nor will it be our last. But it stands out to me, because it's the one where a human being saw me and tried to end me. I don't know his name. I don't know if he's Afghan or Pakistani. He may be Pashtun or Arab. He may be dead now. I don't know.

What I do know is that a fellow soldier has given me words I will use forever — "as long as you're breathing, keep moving." And I stupidly forgot to ask his name.

The desert remains and I'm left to walk across it. I'm not meant to be here, but here I am, and I don't want to be anywhere else. I'm the first born of a first-born child, and the first Canadian-born of my family line. I am an heir to Canada, a son of the Philippines, and I am a proud Canadian soldier.

~James Barrera
Etobicoke, Ontario

The Album

For the dead and the living, we must bear witness. For not only are we responsible for the memories of the dead, we are also responsible for what we are doing with those memories.

~Elie Wiesel

Had I not burst into the front parlour one day like the young whirlwind I was, I would never have known of the photo album. My father was sitting at his old oak desk flipping through pages covered in black and white pictures.

"What's that?" I asked without hesitation.

He didn't get the chance to stuff it back into its niche as I stared curiously over his shoulder. I somehow knew he didn't want to talk about it, but I was young, and discernment comes slowly to youth. After a pause, his quiet voice pushed out the words. "You're old enough. You should know."

Shifting aside enough for me to see the album clearly, he turned back to the first page. Glossy scenes lined up in neat rows and I could almost hear the soldiers singing and laughing as they enjoyed their downtime in barracks.

"This is me." He pointed to a slim, dark-haired soldier holding a guitar, the smile wide as he sang but the eyes somehow sad. His hand stroked the page for a brief moment as though there were things he wanted to say and couldn't.

The page turned.

"We were in Germany. This is Bergen-Belsen."

I stared at the tidy camp stamped on the paper in shades of white, grey and black. Pristine buildings squatted behind strands of barbed wire and I could almost hear the shouts of soldiers saluting their leader. Dad's voice softened more as the pages quietly turned. I didn't know much about this concentration camp where Jews had been imprisoned. Pointing to a broad paved road he told a story I would never forget.

"This was called 'The Avenue.' The camp was empty when we arrived. All the prisoners that were left had already been moved. See the line down the centre of the Avenue?" I nodded. "If the regular German soldiers crossed this line, they were shot by the Black Shirts," he explained, using the slang term for the SS soldiers.

Shock rippled through me. "They shot their own soldiers?" Surely he couldn't have meant that. My dad nodded, yes.

"And this is the acid pit." He pointed to another photograph. Tears filled my eyes as he explained the use of the pit that now sat empty. "And here's the monument to remember the 20,000 Russian Jews who were marched into the woods. They never came back."

My father looked at me then, as though weighing the burden he was sharing with me. Could a young teen carry such a weight? "You will remember them, won't you?" He whispered it, more as though talking to himself than to me. I nodded and turned my gaze back to the catalogue of empty buildings — all that was left of a group of people who had once celebrated life, laughed and cried together — and died together.

The final page of the album was blank — black archive paper with small brackets to hold pictures that had been removed.

"I took these out," Dad explained. "They were pictures of the building where some of the scientific experiments took place. I just couldn't leave those pictures there." He said no more. He couldn't. How could one put words to the things done to people in the name of science? My father then returned the album to its place, and closed the desk.

The days passed and the pictures faded from my teenage mind

until November 11th of the following year. My father came home from work and gestured for me to follow him to his desk. Again the album came out, and again we went through the pictures. He told the story again, a little easier with it now as though the first telling had offered some small healing. I was a year older and I remembered more this time.

Each year after that, Remembrance Day became a living thing for me. I grew to know the faces of those laughing soldiers. I pondered the nameless dead buried beneath that monument. I shuddered at humanity's potential for horror.

I grew up and got married and the tradition continued. My children were born and when they were old enough to understand, I invited my father to come and teach them how to remember. I still see him in my mind's eye, standing in our doorway in full dress uniform, photo album tucked under his arm. My children sat in sober silence as he shared the story with them. I watched another generation take hold of the responsibility that comes with remembering. And I saw that it changed how we viewed ourselves as Canadians — as people.

We now all stand just a bit straighter when we hear the national anthem. We all feel the tears in our eyes at the Canada Day celebrations because we know what being Canadian means. We have been taught that our freedom to celebrate our nation came at a very steep price — the price of our soldiers' hearts and minds as well as their bodies. When I see the flag lifted on the currents of a summer breeze I am reminded that there are good men and women who will face the horrors of war on my behalf. My mind skips back to the black and white photos tucked away in a khaki-covered album — photos that speak of tyranny, and the loss of freedom.

My children are grown and raising children of their own. My father has passed on but the album remains. It sits hidden in a cupboard waiting for that time of year when I will open it and remember the victims of hate. Then I will hear my father's voice again asking me, "You will remember them, won't you?"

The day will come when my grandchildren are old enough to carry the torch for their generation. I will bring the photo album and a picture of my father to their door on a frosty November day and I will tell them the story that should never be forgotten. I will teach them what it means to be Canadian.

~Donna Fawcett
St. Mary's, Ontario

81

Chicken Soup for the Soul

Backyard Memories

The game is bigger now, but it will never
be bigger than a small boy's dreams.
~Bobby Hull

It was bitterly cold and 2013 wasn't even a week old in our quaint little town of Queensville, Ontario. Outside it was bright despite the lack of sunshine, the deep white snow covering the ground.

School would be resuming soon and our three boys, along with a couple of their friends, had decided to take advantage of what was left of their Christmas break. They went out back to do what they did every chance they could. They laced up their skates and got ready to battle big with their taped up sticks and little black puck, making sure their sharp hot blades were ready to cut up the ice.

They had been out there for some time when I glanced out the window and saw someone I didn't recognize standing there behind the weathered fence watching them play.

Judging by the way he was dressed from head to toe, the vast field behind him must have been the playground that he and his snowmobile had used, his machine now parked a few feet away. But what he'd seen taking place, happening in our back yard, was definitely enough to make him stop.

Maybe it was the deke or dangle. Or better yet, the take-away before the goal. Or maybe quite simply, it was the heart-warming sight of a bunch of young kids having so much fun playing a great game.

I realized then this guy was Colorado Avalanche's Steve Downie, and figured he must've been visiting his mom who lived nearby. I also knew that because of the NHL strike at the time, he hadn't played a game yet that season.

There he stood, his arms crossed. Behind the back fence, watching a bunch of boys play what he got paid millions to do and no doubt missed doing that winter. Before long he and the young athletes had engaged in small talk. And then, without warning, he asked if they had a stick he could use. Of course they did.

And so, for a short while, on a homemade backyard rink, one NHL player and five young NHL wannabes played what we Canadians are known for.

There were no owners present. There were no contracts drawn up and definitely no money was exchanged. It was just six boys aged seven to twenty-five. Happy as they could be, playing the game they love to play. Simply because they wanted to.

And for me, standing there in the comfort of my kitchen, a feeling of warmth flowed into every crevice of my heart. It didn't matter that there weren't any cameras rolling back there that day. Instead, we had a real life memory in the making that was worth far more — just ask any one of the boys, they'll tell you.

It was priceless.

~Melanie Naundorf
Queensville, Ontario

82

Terry Fox — Our Greatest Hero

I loved it… People thought I was going through hell…
maybe I was, partly, but still I was doing what I
wanted… There was not another thing in the
world I would rather have been doing.
~Terry Fox

I have always been interested in the idea of heroes. As a boy growing up in the 1950s, many of my heroes played for the Montreal Canadiens, such as "Rocket" Richard, "Boom Boom" Geoffrion, and Jean Béliveau. In 1982 I read a magazine article that claimed John Wayne was the last American hero "and we are living in a time when there are no heroes." I thought, "How awful!" Then I asked myself, "Can this be true?" I was working as a free-lance writer at the time so I gave myself an assignment: Find out if Canadian children have heroes, and if so, who do they regard as their greatest role model?

Over the next few months, I surveyed hundreds of children across Canada and asked them to name their number one hero and give a reason for their choice. I received 564 replies from students aged seven to thirteen, in eight provinces. To my great relief, I learned that healthy hero worship was alive and well in the hearts and minds of Canadian children. The letters I received listed a wide variety of personal heroes, including, Wayne Gretzky, Jesus Christ, Jules Verne, Helen Keller, the men and women of World Wars I and II, Bugs Bunny, the kids' parents, the police, Mickey Mouse, the kids' grandparents, Robin Hood, a violin teacher… and many, many more. But out of all the answers I received, the overwhelming choice for children all across Canada was Terry Fox, the twenty-two-year-old from Port Coquitlam, British Columbia, who in 1977 had his right leg amputated due to cancer. As every Canadian knows, he later inspired all Canadians by attempting to run across Canada with one artificial leg to raise awareness and money for a cure for cancer.

Terry began his Marathon of Hope on April 12, 1980 in St. John's, Newfoundland. By the time he reached Toronto, he had become a national hero. I was assigned by a magazine to run alongside Terry on July 11, 1980 — Day 90 of his run, as the tanned, 150-pound youth ran on one good leg, and his plastic and aluminum right leg, along Queen Street toward City Hall. There, 10,000 people were waiting to welcome Canada's newest hero. As I jogged alongside him snapping pictures, I shouted, "Good luck, Terry! I hope you make it!" He glanced my way, waved his right hand, smiled and said, "Thanks!"

I saw him again the next day as he ran north along Yonge Street, also known as the world's longest street, through my hometown of Richmond Hill, a suburb of Toronto, as he headed to Northern Ontario and then west.

Everyone was so sad to learn that on September 1, 1980, Day 143, after running 5,373 kilometres, Terry had to end his amazing journey just south of Thunder Bay, Ontario. Cancer had spread to his lungs and he simply could go no further. He returned home to Vancouver for treatment, and to the great sadness of an entire nation, died on June 28, 1981.

In the years since the passing of this great Canadian hero, more than $700 million has been raised worldwide for cancer research through the annual Terry Fox Runs in 9,000 communities and through the work of the Terry Fox Foundation. Every year, international runs take place that help solidify the good name and generous spirit Canada has always had with people around the world.

Terry Fox often said it was the youth who would carry forth his efforts and work toward a world without cancer. One of the largest fundraising events takes place every year when millions of students across Canada take part in the Terry Fox School Run.

Thirty-five years after Terry dipped his artificial leg into the Atlantic Ocean to begin his odyssey, my wife Kris and I were pleased to learn that six of our grandnieces and grandnephews took part in the 2015 Terry Fox School Run for cancer research. Earlier that year Kris and I had both been diagnosed with cancer, so the six youngsters — Lucas, Matthew, Jacob, Mackenzie, Scott, and Sarah — "ran for Dennis and Kris because they have cancer."

The children had been learning about Terry Fox at school and they had lots of questions for their mothers (my nieces) when they got home. Six-year-old Jacob asked, "Did Uncle Dennis have his leg cut off like Terry Fox?" As Lisa assured her son that, no, Dennis did not have a leg amputated, her four-year-old daughter, Mackenzie, asked how Auntie Kris was "fighting" cancer. She was reassured that it was not in a ring with boxing gloves!

The questions continued among the youngsters. When Mackenzie learned in school that Terry had run through Richmond Hill, she asked her brother: "Do you think Uncle Dennis met Terry Fox?" Jacob answered, "No! That was a long, long time ago! Dennis wasn't even born then!"

When I had heard of these innocent observations I smiled. Then I retrieved from my Terry Fox file the magazine article I wrote in 1980 that includes a full-page photo I had taken of Terry, running with his famous uneven gait. The file also contains a newspaper clipping from a local newspaper that reported my observations of the unforgettable event. I had written at the time: *Children, especially, are attracted to the story of Terry Fox because it carries with it such an innocence and pure determination of the crusading, human spirit in the face of great obstacles.*

The children took my article and photo of Terry to their classrooms to proudly share with their teachers and fellow students. At a large family gathering that year, on Christmas Eve, I told my young relatives about a park in Richmond Hill, just a few kilometres from my home, that is dedicated to the memory of Terry Fox. The park features a life-size, bronze statue of Terry that captures the strength in his leg and the humility in his face.

"One summer," I promised the youngsters, "we are all going to gather at the park and have a picnic." The children were wide-eyed with excitement! They clapped their hands in glee at the thought of having "lunch with Terry Fox." On that Christmas Eve, six children were focused on a twenty-two-year-old man who gave the greatest gift of all—himself—in a valiant attempt to make a better world for youngsters like them, who would carry forth his efforts and work toward a world without cancer.

~Dennis McCloskey
Richmond Hill, Ontario

The Spirit of Canada

Grateful to Be Canadian

I am a Canadian, free to speak without fear, free to worship in my own way, free to stand for what I think right, free to oppose what I believe wrong, or free to choose those who shall govern my country. This heritage of freedom I pledge to uphold for myself and all mankind.
~Former Prime Minister John G. Diefenbaker

83

The Belated Canadian

*Canada is like an expanding flower — wherever you
look you see some fresh petal unrolling.*
~Sir Arthur Conan Doyle

"And where have you immigrated from?" the smiling
white-haired judge asked as he shook my hand and
handed me my Canadian citizenship certificate.

"Washington," I replied.

He frowned. "Washington, D.C.?"

"No, Washington State."

He frowned again. "That wasn't far." His perplexed expression
made me smile. He was clearly accustomed to passing out certificates
to immigrants from such faraway places as Asia, Africa and the Middle
East. The border I crossed when I first came to Canada was only a half
hour's drive from where we now stood! I was glad the judge didn't ask
how long it had taken me to become a citizen after I'd immigrated. I
was embarrassed by the answer — forty-three years! I suspected most
of the would-be-Canadians present had lived in Canada no more than
five years, all with intriguing and dramatic narratives as to why they
left their homelands. My story would pale next to theirs. But it was
still an important story to me — and to my children.

I grew up in a picturesque area of Washington. My two sisters
and I enjoyed a classic, idyllic outdoor childhood, roaming freely
without supervision or fear. Our parents instilled in us a love for God
and country. We were taught that the United States of America was

the best place on earth. We pledged allegiance to the American flag with hands on our hearts and sang "The Star Spangled Banner" with gusto. I never dreamed of leaving the "land of the free and the home of the brave"—until the summer our family went camping in Banff National Park, in Alberta. I was awe-struck by the Canadian Rockies and the blue-green alpine lakes. Wilderness and waterfalls and wildlife abounded. I thought I had died and gone straight to heaven!

"I want to live in Canada," I informed my sister Carolyn one day in our travels. "Well, you'll have to learn French," she replied. "They speak French in Canada, you know." But I was glad she didn't make fun of my dream. In fact, we both took French in high school. We even discussed the possibility of someday attending a Canadian college. At the time, it seemed like an adventure. I wanted to become either an English teacher or a missionary. So when I met a boy who was attending a Canadian Bible college, I asked him to send me information about the school. I had my sights set on a theological school in Seattle, but the Canadian one was less expensive. And wouldn't living in Canada be a dream come true? I didn't realize then that Canada was not all mountainous, and only a small part of the population spoke French!

The 500-mile drive from my home to Vancouver seemed like a trek across the world to my eighteen-year-old mind. And in many ways it was a different world. The small campus was old and crowded. I shared a room with five other girls: three Canadians and two Americans. I was startled by how "normal" my new Canadian friends seemed. But I wasn't prepared to be teased because I didn't speak "proper English!" My roommates laughed when I pronounced creek as "crik" and roof as "ruf !"

"Cathy, just look how it's spelled!" they chided. And they really guffawed when I said I was from "Warshington." Being a sensitive, people-pleaser person and wanting to fit in, I decided to learn how to speak like a Canadian. At least it was a lot easier than French!

I attended this college for three years, but while home one summer I met a military guy stationed at Fairchild Air Force Base in Spokane. Two years later, after my graduation and his stint in the Vietnam War, we were married. After a brief time in Spokane, we moved to his home state of Louisiana for work. Before long, however, we were talking about moving back north — to Canada. Like me, my young husband had adventure in his blood. He wanted to live in a place where there was good fishing and hunting — and mountains! I felt lucky to have married a man who was on the same page — or map — as me!

In February 1972 we emigrated to Canada with a baby in our arms and another on the way. My husband's job took us to Port Hardy, a wisp of a town on the northern tip of Vancouver Island. Here we learned to love the aboriginals and adapt to the Canadian way of life. We eventually lived in too-rainy Prince Rupert — where our daughter was born, too-freezing Yukon, too-hot Armstrong, and finally just-right Comox. British Columbia's coastal mountains were the closest we got to the Rockies — except for our camping trips.

From time to time we considered becoming Canadian citizens. But the thought of giving up our U.S. citizenship seemed like an act of treason. Wasn't Benedict Arnold considered a traitor because he sided with the British? And wouldn't remaining American allow our children the choice to work in either country when they grew up? At the time, we weren't aware of the possibility of dual citizenship.

In 1990 we divorced, and a few years later I was remarried — to a Canadian from Vancouver. I loved our old home in the suburbs, which faced a park and distant snow-capped mountains. And over twenty years later, I still love it.

My children were in their forties when my sons and I decided we were way overdue to become Canadian citizens. They both had been offered lucrative jobs in the United States, but planned to raise their own children as Canadians. As much as I appreciated my American roots, Canada now had a greater place in my heart. It made sense to become a citizen. I spoke like a Canadian, I thought like a Canadian, and I watched hockey like a Canadian!

It didn't work out for us all to be sworn in together, so in 2015 we all attended three citizenship ceremonies. For the first time, we voted in a Canadian election. And as dual citizens, we agreed we had the best of both countries — freedom to live and think as we choose. The United States is my country by birth, and Canada is my country by adoption. I feel honoured (or honored!) to belong to both. I'm happy to be a Canadian — even if I'm a belated one!

~Cathy Mogus
Richmond, British Columbia

84

The Humbling

Gratitude bestows reverence, allowing us to encounter
everyday epiphanies, those transcendent moments
of awe that change forever how we
experience life and the world.
~John Milton

I am the only member of my family born on Canadian soil. My parents fled from Germany to Belgium shortly after World War II, then came here with my three brothers. They settled in Montreal. I was born two years later, automatically becoming a Canadian citizen before they all did. I grew up hearing stories of the "old country" — ad nauseum — and the difficulties and dangers my parents escaped. Eventually, those dark tales neither fascinated nor repulsed me. I simply considered them ramblings about ancient memories and times. And, after hearing the same stories over and over, I became desensitized to their impact.

Similarly, when they launched into accolades about how great this new land was, I felt no gratitude for the so-called advantages they claimed Canada offered. Compared to most, we were dirt poor. Why would I feel privileged when I was forced to eat lard sandwiches with watered-down soup for the fourth day in a row? I hated the baggy homemade clothes Mama sewed that I could "grow into," the long monkey-sleeved sweaters knitted from wool scraps, and the shoes crushed down in back that Papa could only afford to buy once a year. I resented being the brunt of classmates' jokes, especially when Papa sent food, clothing and medicine "back home," spending what little money we had on someone else. My complaints were quickly stifled with the terse reminder that I lived in a land of freedom and plenty, a privilege denied to many. "Not everyone is so lucky," Papa would repeat.

It wasn't until I'd been married for almost a decade that I became truly aware of what Canada had to offer. Never having known anything else, I took for granted my peaceful life of freedom and democracy, with its unlimited resources. Religious, racial and gender equality were my birthright, along with freedom of speech. I stated my views openly, with no fear of reprisal, unlike my parents who still spoke in hushed whispers if something displeased them. Politics bored me. I usually voted for the same party as my husband, who explained the current candidates' platforms to me in a condensed version that didn't make me sleepy. I truly didn't care who ran the country as long as my taxes remained reasonable and none of my civil liberties were revoked.

However, my apathy and careless viewpoints changed drastically the year Papa, now finally financially comfortable, sponsored a four-month visit from his stepsister, Hela, who lived in Communist Poland.

Hela was a sweet, stout woman in her sixties. I liked her from the moment she enfolded me in her doughy embrace, seconds after stepping off the passenger ship that brought her here. Everything she looked at made her eyes light up with wonder, including my simple denim jeans. As she knelt to finger their texture, I noticed how worn and frayed her own clothes were. Her once-red sweater was a muddy pink from countless washings; her skirt was cleverly mended, but threadbare. A pathetically small, tattered cardboard suitcase held all her other belongings for her extended stay.

On the way home we stopped for a few groceries. Upon entering the supermarket, my aunt gasped, fell to her knees, and began sobbing. I looked around in embarrassment as Papa gently urged her to stand, cooing to her softly in Polish. Swiping at her tears, she apologized, explaining that she couldn't believe the amount of food and merchandise available to us. For the next two hours we patiently followed Hela as she wandered up and down the aisles staring incredulously at the abundance. She gingerly caressed cans, jars and boxes as if afraid they would disappear if she tried to actually pick them up. She pointed to unfamiliar products, listening intently while Mama and Papa described their function.

I looked at my husband in confusion. "Don't they have this stuff in Poland?" I inquired.

"Not really," he replied. "Because of sanctions and shortages, even basic staples could cost a fortune." He then explained that although some goods were available, most could only be bought on the black market for ridiculously high prices.

"But my father's been sending her packages for years!" I protested, remembering the generous boxes he'd prepared.

"Many probably never even reached her," he whispered. "Mail is intercepted and stolen all the time — especially something from North America." Stunned, I continued to watch my aunt cry as Papa placed what she considered to be delicacies, even luxuries, into the cart; a pineapple, coffee, teabags — all groceries I took for granted.

Hela stayed that entire summer. Papa bought her a large steamer trunk so she could fill it with articles to take home. I added something with every visit, including gifts for her daughters — clothes, slippers, pantyhose, undergarments — things I now knew she couldn't get in Poland. She accepted everything with weeping gratitude. Mama and I had to regularly check the contents Hela had packed after discovering she was hoarding perishables she believed could be reused. We removed bruised fruit, stale dinner rolls, small bags of coffee grounds and used tea bags, gently pointing out they would not survive the journey without going mouldy. Unaccustomed to this kind of abundance, Hela was used to consuming all leftovers, no matter how old they were.

Unlike the stories my parents recounted to me as a child, my aunt's both fascinated and moved me. She spoke of standing in long lines for hours to buy severely rationed food, sometimes leaving with only vinegar or mustard. Theft was rampant, causing her or her husband to stay up nights to guard what little they had. Medications were almost impossible to get. She whispered those stories to me, her eyes darting around nervously as if terrified she might be overheard or arrested — much like my parents still sometimes did. Listening to her,

I developed a new appreciation for my life. I asked why she didn't try to stay in Canada. "My family is in Poland. If I don't return, they will pay a price," she replied sadly. I didn't ask what the price was. The terror in her eyes convinced me it was an ugly one.

When we returned Hela to the harbour in September, her luggage bulged with new clothes and non-perishable food items. As we hugged her goodbye, we all cried. I knew I'd probably never see her again, and I wondered if exposing her to our abundant Canadian life had actually been a cruel torture rather than a blessing. Though she dreaded returning to the hardship and political repression of her homeland, her love of family was stronger than her longing to live in freedom. I admired her courage and wished her the best. I watched her ship as it disappeared over the horizon, then turned to go back to a life I would never again take for granted. Just as Hela had dropped to her knees that day in the grocery store, I wanted to drop to mine in gratitude for the advantages I had never truly recognized or appreciated before. I finally understood what "Canada, land of plenty and home of the free" truly meant.

~Marya Morin
St. Lin des Laurentides, Quebec

85

My Home, Sweet Home

*Throw your dreams into space like a kite, and you do
not know what it will bring back, a new life, a new
friend, a new love, a new country.*
~Anaïs Nin

I didn't know what to expect when I stepped from the familiar shores of Great Britain and onto the gaping deck of the RMS Empress of England. It was April 1967, and I was filled with a mixture of excitement and dread. Dad had already flown to Canada three months earlier in order to find work and a home for us.

That left our brave mum with the entire responsibility of getting four young children, our Collie, umpteen suitcases and many crates full of furniture and personal belongings on board the grand oceanliner headed for Canada. Somehow we all made it to our cabins with our suitcases and Lassie was safely stowed in her roomy dog crate on the top deck.

I thoroughly enjoyed the five and six courses at every meal, and when the chef made me a birthday cake partway through our journey, I was thrilled. Turning eleven years old in the middle of the ocean was certainly a highlight for me. Mum told me I was one of the lucky ones because I never got seasick. One of my sisters and my younger brother, on the other hand, were constantly seasick. Poor Mum. I am sure she could hardly wait to set foot on solid ground.

One night Mum told us we were nearing the Canadian shore. She tucked us in early so we would be well rested for our arrival. Then it happened. A loud bang woke us with a start.

With visions of the Titanic in her mind, I'm sure, Mum was convinced we had hit an iceberg. She shot out of bed and grabbed all our life jackets. As we struggled to put them on, Mum was lining us up and waiting for the signal from the crew. Nobody seemed overly panicked though, and the crewmembers were excellent at getting everyone moving in an orderly fashion. Passengers poured out of their cabins and on to the top deck, close to the lifeboats, awaiting direction.

Nothing happened, and soon the "all-clear" was sounded. Hundreds of relieved passengers made their way back to their cabins. As we headed back to ours, some Canadian passengers broke out in a rousing rendition of "O Canada" because while on deck we had spotted land! Apparently, we had just entered the waters off Newfoundland and, because it was April, there was a lot of floating ice. It turned out our ship actually had struck a particularly big chunk, which was why we had all felt that big bang.

Some time later, as we neared the dock in Montreal, I stood on deck, mesmerized. Enormous, spectacular buildings and pavilion-type structures dotted the harbour. I wondered if this would be typical architecture for our new home in Canada. Later, I discovered we had seen the opening of Expo 67 — the World's Fair, and a huge celebration of the 100th anniversary of Canada's confederation.

How blessed we were that day when our family stepped onto Canadian soil. Our lives were about to change in a big way, but we were ready. We had adjustments to make and plenty to learn about in our new country. I often wonder what it might have been like if Mum and Dad hadn't taken that giant step of faith to immigrate to Canada. Then I think about all the opportunities I have enjoyed over the years and I am so very grateful they did.

In 1990, when I received my official citizenship papers, a reporter at the ceremony interviewed me and asked why I came to Canada. I hardly knew what to say, but then I remembered Newfoundland, the life jackets, the magnificent buildings at Expo 67, and Mum working so hard to get us to Canada in one piece. I thought of Dad on his own in a new country for almost four months. I recalled the love and the sacrifices my parents made because they knew we would have a better life in Canada. "Canada might not be my native land, but it is my home," I told the reporter that day. "We came to Canada because this is a great country, and my parents knew in their hearts that it would be the best place to call home, sweet home."

~Glynis M. Belec
Drayton, Ontario

Our Yard, a Canadian Tale

*For to be free is not merely to cast off one's chains,
but to live in a way that respects and
enhances the freedom of others.*
~Nelson Mandela

A few years back I was visiting my parents at their home in Vancouver, seated at the kitchen table drinking Ovaltine and reading the newspaper. Dad was retired and I remember thinking that life couldn't get much more mundane than this. Then it occurred to me that I knew very little about his early life as the son of a Chinese immigrant in rural Saskatchewan.

My brother, sister, and I, as well as all of my cousins, were born in Canada. We were city kids, and knew we lived in one of the best countries in the world; we just didn't know why. All those times that Dad had said: "You never know where life is going to take you," I wasn't sure exactly what he meant. So that day I asked him about his past. My sudden interest sparked something in him I'd never seen before. He immediately rushed upstairs and dug out some newspaper clippings and mementos from his youth. As he laid the stained, yellowed clippings on the table in front of me, his eyes shone bright with excitement and his voice became animated.

"I was born in Canada," he began, "but when I was five years old your grandfather took the family back to China. We lived near Canton for nine years so I could learn the language, culture and traditions of the old country. But political unrest was brewing and the country became unstable because of war between China and Japan. Your grandfather was a smart man; he sensed that China was on the eve of revolution, and men like him with personal wealth and property would soon be unwelcome. There was talk that if the communists came to power, all personal assets of property owners would be confiscated.

"So your grandfather packed us up just before the attack on Pearl Harbor — your grandma and your four aunts and me — and we boarded a ship back to Canada. But first my mom and my sisters buried all of their jewellery in the riverbank. I don't know what happened to it, probably washed away or maybe it is still buried there!"

Dad paused to collect his thoughts, and I could see in his expression the images of his past returning to his memory. "When we returned to Canada I was fourteen," he said, "but I could no longer speak English so the Regina school officials put me in grade one." I widened my eyes in amusement and almost giggled before a pang of guilt silenced me. After all, Dad had worked his whole life to put the three of us through university.

He told me then what it felt like to be a teenage boy, so much taller and experienced than the six-year-olds with whom he was forced to attend class, and how he quickly learned to read and write, and speak English.

The following year he was admitted into ninth grade, only one year behind the kids his own age. By now he was a practicing artist, and still not quite fifteen. "You see," he explained, "in Canada, you can do whatever you want. If you want to paint pictures, you can paint pictures. And no one will tell you what the subject of your painting has to be."

He entered local art contests and won awards. He was mentioned in the *Regina Leader-Post* for being one of eleven artists chosen out of seventy-eight to have his work exhibited in a provincial show. His painting was a watercolour called "Our Yard," described by the newspaper as "the only winter scene… with bare-limbed trees and drifts of snow contrasting with the oblique lines of broken fence boards and angles of power lines and sheds." Oh so Canadian!

In grade ten Dad's artwork again made headlines; I read another brown-edged news clipping entitled: "Young Chinese Artist Star of Art Exhibit." My father did not need to explain to me how special this was for the child of an immigrant.

During his last year of high school a missionary came to speak about the plight of children in China — the hardships caused by the war. So my dad designed a poster that helped the school raise $1,000 — a fortune back then — to help feed these children and save them from the "black fever" that was ravaging the towns and villages. I found a newspaper interview where he was quoted as saying: *I was glad to draw the poster because as a Canadian I feel I should do what I can for the Chinese people... Several of my relatives suffered from starvation during the war... We have good food and clothing, while over there, there are a lot of people who are cold and hungry.*

When the Governor General, the Right Honourable The Earl of Athlone, made his final visit to Saskatchewan, my father was asked to design and paint the illuminated address that was presented to him in a formal public ceremony. In the last clipping my dad showed me, I read how this illuminated address was presented to His Excellency by the Acting Premier on behalf of the people of Saskatchewan. The fine workmanship, done in colour, won praise from all who examined it. The reporter wrote: *The artist who executed the work was a young Chinese lad of Regina, Danny Yee Clun, a student at Balfour Technical School.*

You never know where life is going to take you. I know that parents feel pride in the accomplishments of their children. But when I read this old newspaper clipping, so brittle and yellowed from being treasured all these years, I felt a tremendous pride that I was his daughter, and that he had saved these clippings so that sixty years later I could see them. The opportunities we take for granted living as Canadians come and go every day, and often we don't even recognize them.

Sadly, my dad has now passed away, but not without leaving us kids a valuable legacy. He never told us in so many words that you *can* do whatever you want, become *whoever* you want to become — *because* you live in Canada. But that afternoon I recognized the culmination of all the years of his *not* telling, but instead *showing* by example, what *was* and *is* possible. Never before have those words from our national anthem rung so clear: "the True North strong and free." Freedom is something I have taken for granted my entire life — the freedom to pursue whatever I wanted. We Canadians don't have to look far; the opportunities are right here — in our yard.

~Deborah Cannon
Hamilton, Ontario

Remembrance Tears

There is nothing in the world so
much like prayer as music is.
~William Shakespeare

Tears well up in his eyes as, hand over heart, Dad sits in his borrowed wheelchair paying homage to Canada. Canada, our home since we escaped war-torn Lebanon in the mid-1970s. Trumpets sound as the story of our journey to Canada flashes before Dad's eyes: taking a taxi ride in a cousin's car from Beirut to Damascus to escape gunfire, living in Athens for a month with two small children while waiting for paperwork, and finally boarding a British Airways flight for Toronto. With God's help, a new life begins. A life of taking the bus to work in the freezing cold, sticking out like a sore thumb on the subway, passing his driver's test, and going to school for his refrigeration license.

As the quintessential King of Quips, Dad would share sound bites of his witticisms at work with us while at the dinner table. Dad never returned to Lebanon. Canada was his home, hockey was his new favourite sport, and when the Toronto Blue Jays won the World Series, so was baseball. I've caught him watching basketball, too. It was a far cry from the all-soccer-all-the-time focus he had back in Lebanon.

Now, with glistening eyes and his hand resting proudly atop the letter "A" of his Team Canada Olympic hoodie, Dad's face was shining as the ensemble of veterans played "O Canada" on Remembrance Day. The hoodie he was wearing was not his usual attire. "Can you get me a jacket like yours?" Dad had asked one day. Over the course of a few months he uncharacteristically requested it as a gift, in his usual persistent manner, until I finally caved.

Dad never said no to the favours I asked of him: fix this, drive me here, help me with that. He had done more for me than most parents would do. Who says an eighty-year-old shouldn't wear a hoodie? It has, after all, C-A-N-A-D-A stitched on the front.

Two days after obtaining his prized hoodie, Dad was admitted to Toronto's Sunnybrook Hospital. "Sir," the doctors asked him, on the day they confirmed his terminal diagnosis, "do you know why you are in the hospital?"

"They say I have the cancer," Dad replied, "but it is not 100% sure."

Satisfied that Dad knew what was going on, the doctors left it to me to explain why he could not come home until his strength returned. Wanting to prove he was strong and still capable, Dad would often say to the hospital staff, "I used to swim the Mediterranean, diving forty metres deep until my ears bled. And I was a bodybuilder back home. I tried many different jobs before I decided to become an expert at refrigeration repair. You know those commercial fridges in the supermarket, the ones where there is ice cream? I build those. You know how much ice cream I have eaten?"

Within weeks my "He-Can-Do-Anything-And-Really-Is-Stronger-Than-Superman" Dad was confined to a wheelchair, speaking less each day. Being practical, Dad realized this contraption that restricted his mobility was also his best option for leaving his room as often as possible. He loved leaving his room, curiously looking left and right — like he was watching tennis. When he pointed at the Pepsi machine, I knew he wanted another bottle even though he had not yet finished the one in his hand. His eyebrows would arch in front of the Christmas tree taking centre stage beneath the hospital wing's high ceiling and brick fireplace-adorned lobby. One afternoon, we were surprised to see a vintage barbershop pole accompanied by fire-engine red vinyl chairs situated across from the gift shop. Then a poster for the Remembrance Day concert captured my attention. *Dad will like this music*, I thought. *He is such a strong tenor.*

When I rolled him out of the room the day of the concert, it was a temporary victory of sorts for us both. The hall was packed with veterans, other elderly patients, and their families. The louder the trumpets played, the more I couldn't take my eyes off Dad. As he clenched his fist during our last "O Canada" together, my admiration for him grew. Here he was in palliative care paying homage to Canada. He was so full of respect and love for Canada, even when his strength was fading.

I miss my friend — an eighty-year-old, silver-haired friend who is now in Heaven. I am so thankful he will always be my dad.

~A. A. Adourian
Toronto, Ontario

The Last Night of the Proms

*Music cleanses the understanding; inspires it,
and lifts it into a realm which it would
not reach if it were left to itself.*
~Henry Ward Beecher

lthough I have lived in Canada for sixty-three years, like most immigrants, I still feel a deep affinity for my native land. I was a child in England during World War II. I grew up listening to Winston Churchill telling us that this was our "finest hour" as our men came back, battered and bloodied from Dunkirk, and our pilots fought the Battle of Britain. Those were stirring times; times that infused a child with a lifelong love of country.

When I came to Canada in 1952 from London, England, and settled in Edmonton, I was homesick for my family and my native land. I missed so much about my life in London. For instance, the regular trips on the Underground to the Royal Albert Hall for a lively, stirring Promenade Concert. I felt a real longing for a good symphony, performed in a grand concert hall. In those days, in Edmonton, with a population of around 50,000 people, it was not to be. Once, the Minneapolis Symphony Orchestra came to Edmonton to perform under the baton of Antal Dorati. I was thrilled and quickly bought tickets. There being no concert hall in Edmonton at that time, the venue was the main barn of Exhibition Grounds, with the odd strand of hay still clinging to the walls. Not the ideal setting, but that was not enough to deter me. The music was magnificent.

Some time ago, I went to see the Vancouver Symphony and the Bach Choir perform at a performance of "The Last Night of the Proms," always a wonderful over-abundance of British patriotism. Union Jack flags were everywhere—even in the Bach Choir. I looked forward to the program of traditional favourites, including the obligatory sing-along of "Land of Hope and Glory," "Rule Britannia," and that stirring British hymn, "Jerusalem." And while the Orpheum is a grand old building, it is not quite as grand or as old as the Royal Albert Hall.

I took along a good supply of tissues in preparation for the tears I knew would come bubbling over when I joined in the sing-along. I've been to these "Last Night" concerts before; they are a staple of symphony orchestras wherever there are a bunch of ex-Brits. I went to one in Kingston, Ontario, when my daughter lived there, and discovered then that I couldn't make it to the end of "Land of Hope and Glory" without blubbering.

But this time, it was different. I sang right through to the end, with nary a tear. *Wait till we sing "Rule Britannia,"* I thought. *That's bound to get me.* Well, we sang "Rule Britannia," and I was still dry-eyed. *"Jerusalem,"* I thought. *That'll do it. I can never get all the way through "Jerusalem."* I sang it—all the way through. Never stopped for a sob. Never even caught my breath.

I must be getting hardhearted in my old age, I thought. Just one more item on the program. The "Bach Children's Choir" came on and performed the song, written for Expo '86, about Canada —"This Is My Home." That did it! Without warning, the tears came rolling down my cheeks and wouldn't stop. What was going on? And then it came to me. At long last, I'm finally a Canadian in my heart as well as on paper. I thought it was ironic that something as British as "The Last

Night of the Proms" would make me realize just how much Canada means to me.

~Pamela Kent
Aldergrove, British Columbia

89

Finding Canada

All my intensities are defined by my roots, and
my roots are entirely Canadian. I'm as
Canadian as you'll ever find.
~Donald Sutherland

A few years ago, my sister Kate and I flew to Winnipeg, Manitoba for a conference on immigrant settlement. I had never been this far east before. In fact, I had seldom been off Vancouver Island. The west coast, where I have lived all my life, is one kind of Canada — fresh, brash, more in tune with California and the whole Pacific Rim. The Rocky Mountains are a big divide from the other provinces — our history is new. I had never given much thought to the rest of Canada.

Kate and I were both members of the Cowichan Valley Intercultural and Immigrant Aid Society on Vancouver Island. Our Cowichan organization had grown from the early days of welcoming the families of the Vietnamese "boat people," to supporting and providing services for a broad group of ethnic people who now made their homes in our community. At the conference in Winnipeg we, as long-term board members in Cowichan, were asked to share our successes and learn what we could from others.

During the conference we had a block of free time so I contacted some Winnipeg friends who took us to "The Forks," where the Red River and the Assiniboine River meet. A park and meeting place were in the process of being developed and my friends, who were on the

Heritage Advisory Committee, were involved. They spoke passionately about the role the two rivers played in the survival of early Canadian settlers, and the urgent need to preserve this important cultural site.

School history books sprang to life in my memory: stories about the colourful fur trade and the settlement of the Red River Valley. According to my friend Ross, this land was the traditional gathering place of the Assiniboine, the Cree, the Ojibwa and the Dakotas. I learned that right here archaeologists had discovered evidence of aboriginal life going back 6,000 years!

Standing at the convergence of the two rivers it became impossible to not feel the power of place and history. As conversation around me faded away, I soaked in the atmosphere, and a strong feeling of déjà vu washed over me. I had been here before. I hadn't physically been here before of course, but the feeling persisted. I had a sense of rootedness here, a feeling of belonging. And then I remembered.

This is the Winnipeg my Irish and Scottish grandparents immigrated to in 1912 when it was advertised as the "Gateway to the Canadian West." This is where my mother was born. My DNA was here. Somehow this place suddenly felt like the real Canada for me, in a way Vancouver Island had never done.

For the three days of the conference I spent time with new Canadians who loved what Canada offered. They weren't shy about discussing what they had lost in emigrating from their countries. But equally, they expressed their strong feelings about how they felt safe here, which was new for them.

On the last night we gathered in the meeting hall for a potluck feast hosted by Winnipeg's Immigrant Women's Association. Trestle tables were laden with exotic foods from many countries. The tastes and aromas were amazing, and we stuffed ourselves. The conference wrapped up with speeches. But these were not the usual boring kind, but emotional, straight-from-the-heart sharing. No one had a dry eye as an Asian man talked of brutality, torture and persecution in his home country. "How do you heal those scars?" he asked. Then there was Mario, a handsome older man from Chile, who spoke with obvious pride. "My oldest son is Chilean but my youngest boy is Canadian." Marge, an East Indian woman from South Africa showed me her Canadian flag lapel pin. "I tell everyone I am proud to be Canadian." That truly struck home.

With a shock I realized that I too was proud of being Canadian. This country had welcomed my ancestors many years before. It was time I stopped being the typical self-effacing Canadian and let myself boast about our great country. The people I met this weekend, the refugees and the immigrants, all cared for my country in a way I had never considered before. As the evening ended someone began singing "O Canada." Soon everyone joined in and the voices swelled, the varied accents blending to a rich whole as the room filled with joy, and every face was wet with tears. I thought my heart would burst. Winnipeg and these newcomers had helped me find my Canada. I felt her in my deepest being and proudly took her home with me to the west coast.

~Liz Maxwell Forbes
Crofton, British Columbia

90

One Essential Ingredient

*We're very politically correct at times and I always
think, well, isn't politically correct just being
considerate and nice for the most part?*
~Mike Myers

I love travelling by rail across our vast land. I love looking out
at the mountains and prairies, the rivers and lakes and oceans,
and, of course, the opportunity to make new friends. On my
last trip, from Vancouver to Toronto, one of my table companions was a gregarious Irishman. We enjoyed our dinner and each
other's company and agreed to meet later that evening in the lounge
area. He was travelling alone and I was with a good friend, my sister
and her partner. A glass of wine in the lounge was our evening ritual.

"Pleased to meet you all," said my new friend, Waylon, as I scooted
down the bench to make room for him. "I'm not interrupting, am I?"

"Of course not," we said in unison. We were just discussing the
incredible countryside we'd been through—which parts we liked
best and why.

"Crazy as it seems," said my sister, "I love slowly pulling out of
Vancouver—seeing it from a totally different perspective—under
bridges and practically on top of the Fraser River and all that heavy
industry…" She was a town planner.

"I can't decide," added my brother-in-law. "I guess for me it's
the Rockies; but there is so much else that is absolutely startling—it
makes you suck in your breath."

"So," said Waylon, "if I were to ask each of you what you are most proud of—what is most Canadian for you, what would your answers be?"

My sister answered first. "Our cities and towns," she declared. "They are such a multiplicity, so multi-cultural and so cosmopolitan, and yet they're not cold. You know, they don't seem to have outgrown themselves—to have become impersonal."

We nodded our heads in agreement.

My brother-in-law was next to speak. "The countryside itself," he stated. "What we've just passed through and what we're passing through right now—mountains and prairies, glaciers and deserts. Where else on earth would you find such breathtaking diversity?"

I was fascinated by the Irishman's question, and was not about to give an answer without at least some deliberation. "For me?" I began, "it's our flag—one single red maple leaf. It's recognizable all over the world, and it usually says good things."

"Good things indeed," agreed the friend with whom I was travelling. "It's the help that we give other less fortunate countries—the recognizable flag and the help it brings." She paused. "Maybe I'm being a bit brash," she nodded to Waylon, "but you asked."

"Yes, I did," he nodded with a smile, "but you all missed it."

"Sorry?" I said.

"And again, you're proving my point. I say something that is not at all understandable, and you take responsibility. You are sorry for my mistake. In fact," Waylon continued, "I'm told that 'sorry' is the most used word in the Canadian vocabulary. Yours is one of the most multicultural countries in the world—two official languages. You welcomed and included me tonight, as you welcome and include people from all across the world. And yes, I agree with all of you—all of the choices you listed—all of the things for which your one red maple leaf stands," and he smiled at my apologetic friend. "But the one essential ingredient which you all missed—is yourselves. *You* are the welcoming committee, the aide givers, and most importantly, the voice of reason accepting responsibility for what is not your error and so creating peace. On all of these accounts, the people of Canada are peacemakers—to each other, and peacemakers to the world. *You* are your own greatest asset.

My eyes filled, and my throat suddenly had a lump in it. I truly believe that never in my entire life have I ever felt so proud—for all of us.

~Robyn Gerland
Chemainus, British Columbia

A Canadian Epiphany

*We can best serve the cause of Canadian unity and
understanding by living first in and through and
then beyond our own immediate traditions.*
~Former Governor General Vincent Massey

I became a Canadian in March of 1994. Actually, I was born in
Burnaby, British Columbia in 1975 but I didn't realize how
much this country really meant to me until I was eighteen years
old, and in grade twelve.

I was given the opportunity to travel to Ottawa to participate in
the "Forum for Young Canadians." At first I wasn't too keen on the
idea, but then I thought, it would give me a week off school, so why
not? So I packed my bags and left for Ottawa for seven days to study
the government, meet new people and see some new places.

There were six of us from British Columbia, and when we reached
Ottawa in the early evening we were immediately thrown into a whirlwind
of activity and excited chatter. There I was, standing in a room with 125
other participants from every Canadian province and territory. There
were different languages being spoken, and many cultural differences.
Ideas and opinions were all over the map, and we all carried with us
many preconceptions and stereotypes about each other.

The consensus seemed to be that those from the Maritimes were
all just fishermen; those from Quebec just wanted to separate, and
anyway, it's a province where you can't turn right on a red light! People
from Ontario were perceived as thinking they were the centre of all

worthwhile activity and the only real province. It was thought that those who lived on the Prairies were all unsophisticated farmers, and folks from British Columbia were seen as wandering about in a laid-back dream world. And the North, well, only saints or martyrs would live in one of the territories.

I was very dismayed by this, and began to wonder how this country ever came to be. Did we have nothing in common other than the fact that most of our families had immigrated here, and that we were trying to differentiate ourselves from our neighbours to the south? But then something happened that started to break down the barriers and bring this group together — a small and simple thing really, but oh so powerful.

It was the third day, and the group was tired from a long day on Parliament Hill. I remember clearly someone saying, "Are we not here to have the full Canadian Experience? We haven't even sung 'O Canada' yet!" We looked around at each other, and then as a group we all suddenly stood up and began singing our national anthem and, for the first time, I actually listened to the words.

I looked around the room and saw that everybody was singing. Everyone there came from a different part of the country and believed their part was the best, and I suddenly realized that all those best places together made up the best country in the world. As we sang our anthem, this group began to see just how wonderful our differences actually are.

The looks on the faces around me reflected my own feelings: the tears of pride in realization of our unity in diversity. I felt chills run up and down my spine as our voices reached a crescendo in this joyous and passionate hymn to our nation. As it came to an end, I felt the tears rolling down my cheeks, and realized, fully realized for the first time, how lucky I was to live in such a great and awesome country. I saw clearly that our diverse geographic areas and political and cultural uniqueness shape what is truly the Canadian Experience.

~Shawn O'Brien
Calgary, Alberta

92

I Was a Teenaged Separatist

Traveling — it leaves you speechless,
then turns you into a storyteller.
~Ibn Battuta

When I was in grade ten I took a basic Canadian geography test — and failed. The teacher handed out a map of Canada and asked us to identify the locations of the ten provinces, the territories, the major cities and the largest bodies of water. The test was out of forty, and I scored a whopping seven. I managed to correctly identify my home province of British Columbia, as well as Alberta, Prince Edward Island (easy because it was small), the cities of Vancouver and Victoria — and two oceans.

At age sixteen, as far as I was concerned, that was all I needed to know. So what if I didn't know Nova Scotia from Newfoundland, where Hudson's Bay was, or which lakes were supposed to be "Great" and which lakes were just above average?

At that time, Quebec was talking about separating, and I was failing French class. I was hoping they'd leave before the end of the term so I wouldn't have to take my final exam. I figured if Quebec could separate, then British Columbia could too — which wasn't an unpopular sentiment at the time. I wasn't sure what the rest of Canada had to offer, other than the CBC and the Toronto Maple Leafs.

That separatist-summer my best friend Bob and I bought VIA Rail passes to see Canada — although truthfully our plan was more about riding the train across the country than stopping at any particular destination. Bob was worldly. Not only was he almost eighteen, he'd lived in Quebec and Boston. I'd barely ever left British Columbia other than for a few family vacations to Hawaii, and that just involved flying across an ocean, not seeing anything along the way.

After many days on the train we arrived in Newfoundland, which I only knew as the home of "the barbarians who clubbed baby seals." During our first night in St. John's the locals at the hostel quizzed me about Vancouver, which they knew only as "the home of the people at Greenpeace" — who they didn't like much. Despite being outnumbered a half dozen to one, I held my ground and spoke or at least squeaked up for Greenpeace.

"You don't even eat the seals," I said. So they talked about poverty and eating whatever they could get, and then they offered me a slice of flipper pie. I declined. The next day the guy who ran the hostel handed me a badge that read, "Save our seals — eat flipper pie."

In Prince Edward Island public transit was almost non-existent, so in Charlottetown we hitchhiked to see the legislature where Canada was born and the Anne of Green Gables cottage. While we were there, two women sitting next to us at the *Anne of Green Gables* musical offered to show us Saskatoon on our way home. This was amazing to me. I was sixteen and looked it and they were adults with real jobs, and this really was just an offer to show us Saskatoon. From then on, everywhere we went — on the train or in the hostels — we made new friends who took us around and showed us the local sites.

We arrived in Quebec and I was completely smitten by the walled city. Unlike Bob, I'd also never been anywhere where people spoke a different language. I found it thrilling, and suddenly, learning French didn't seem stupid. I wished that I remembered more words than *bibliothèque*. The longer we spent wandering the fascinating streets of old Quebec, the more I wanted to learn French — and every other language — and travel to other places to try them out. Realizing this city was actually part of Canada made Canada suddenly seem a whole lot cooler than it had two weeks earlier.

When we got off the train in Toronto I was completely overwhelmed. Toronto was the biggest city I'd ever seen and I absolutely loved it.

In Winnipeg we wandered through "The Forks," dodging mosquitoes and eating at The Old Spaghetti Factory, which felt like home — and also very grown-up because I'd never eaten there before without my parents.

When we arrived in Saskatoon, Saskatchewan we toured the city and climbed "a mountain" made of trash and, being sixteen, after climbing it I asked where the mountain was. For some reason the folks in Saskatoon didn't find this half as hilarious as I did.

As we crossed the country, I was continuously impressed by the differences between each province and each community. As the days passed, I found myself beginning to believe that I really did live in the Canada we were learning about in school — the mosaic. I began to see Canada as a place with dozens of diverse cultures blending together and living in something resembling harmony. (Other than the occasional hockey fight, of course.)

The next year I took a French language class during my summer vacation — not for grades, but because I wanted to learn my country's other language.

Decades later I still can't spot New Hampshire on a map of North America, and I find it tough to believe that New England isn't actually a state — even though they have a football team. But if I took that Canadian geography test again, I'm sure I'd score at least thirty out of forty. I'm still not great with lakes. And I've still got my pin from St. John's that reads, "Save Our Seals — Eat Flipper Pie."

~Mark Leiren-Young
Victoria, British Columbia

93

A Special Retirement

There are two ways of spreading light — to be
the candle or the mirror that reflects it.
~Edith Wharton, Vesalius in Zant

"Come," my friend Sherrill said to me on the phone. "I'm not sure exactly what to expect, but I think you should come." So I drove the four hours to Jasper, Alberta to Sherrill's retirement celebration.

We knew to dress warmly because we would either be sitting outside, or in a tepee with little heating. Because of the wind, the tepee was chosen. A few of us worked to cover the cold floor with blankets, and one or two people brought in wood and started the little fire circle, just inside the door.

The invitations to attend had been personal but casual, so the final number had not been determined beforehand. As we entered we were gently guided to our seating areas: the men on one side and the women on the other. The three Elders, and three other men from the Stoney Nation who had travelled from the South, were seated in an oval shape between the men and women.

Two small drums, a rattle, colourful fabric, blueberries, pipes, tobacco and a few other items were placed in the centre of their formation. The men sat cross-legged. One Elder told us that women kneel rather than sit cross-legged, so we did. There were eighteen of us in total.

As we settled in, the fire began to crackle and burn. The man at the end of the line added wood periodically. Dallas, one of the younger

Stoney men, with long black braids, offered the "smudge" to everyone. From a dark container that looked like a shell, each of us gathered the smoke in cupped hands to spread over our heads, bodies and hearts. Those of us unfamiliar with this tradition learned from watching and listening. Charlie opened the ceremony with a brief explanation of Stoney beliefs, and followed by a prayer to our Creator, welcoming good guides and spirits. We all remained seated, and the Stoney sang to the steady heartbeat of their drum.

Then Charlie explained further that the reason for the gathering was to honour Sherrill and her work. He thanked us all for coming to share this celebration. We introduced ourselves around the tepee and explained our connection to Sherrill. She had worked for forty years as a Heritage Officer for Parks Canada, and since 1998 as Aboriginal Liaison.

The sounds of the sacred old traditions of the Stoney continued. Two long pipes were passed in traditional ways from one person to the other, with help from a Stoney man. The Stoney invited Sherrill to sit closer to them. Barry, one of them, said "you think you have done little, but to us you have done a lot to put us in the right direction with our ways and traditions. It is like a hunter finding the right path. We would like to give you this." He handed her an eagle feather with a short, pink, beaded and leather strap. Another Stoney, John, added, "We would like to give you a new name, *Anukatha G-A-O-E W-iye*, which means Soaring Eagle Woman."

Then they explained how the name came to them. "When we think of you, we think of a great soaring bald eagle, carefully scouting below, then tipping its wing in order to spot ones below who need help and support. We appreciate it."

Then it was quiet. They knew only too well the milestones they had accomplished with Sherrill through her dedicated work.

"We give you this certificate that adopts you into our Stoney Nation, and we welcome you any time. We would also like to give you these earrings."

After Sherrill received the beautiful beaded turquoise earrings, Barry joked quietly to her, "When you come to visit, you will have to paint this hat white and wear these gloves as claws." But Sherrill knew the twinkle in his eye and laughter in his heart all too well.

John added, "There is no word or meaning in our culture for 'retirement.'"

Mike, Sherrill's close friend offered, "It just means you put new treads on your truck and you are ready to go."

More traditional singing, drumming and chanting followed. The blueberries, a sacred food, were passed and shared by all. Charlie ended with a prayer of gratitude and thankfulness to the universe, releasing the good spirits that had been present. As we shared steaming tea, Sherrill thanked her guests and the Stoney for this honour. The Stoney thanked all of us again for sharing this special time for Sherrill.

Everyone said personal goodbyes to each other. We extinguished the last of the burning coals, and gathered the blankets and cups. One by one we left the tepee. As we got to the road, we took a last look at the white tepee standing against the mountain backdrop, and drove away knowing we had shared a uniquely Canadian experience.

~Glenice Wilson
Barrhead, Alberta

The Spirit of Canada

Chapter 11

How the World Views Canada

When I'm in Canada, I feel this is what the world should be like.
~Jane Fonda

94

A Trip to Remember

Gratitude makes sense of our past, brings peace for
today, and creates a vision for tomorrow.
~Melody Beattie

B
ack in 1981, when my now husband and I were dating, we
lived in Germany, where I'm originally from. I met John
when he was posted there with the Canadian Air Force.
We were part of a motorcycle club called the "Lost Angels."
Most of the members were Canadian soldiers. The club took every
opportunity to explore Europe, as most destinations were reachable
on their motorcycles. Many of them proudly drove Harley Davidsons
they had brought with them, machines not commonly seen back
then in Europe.

The camaraderie of our club members was astonishing; it felt
like we were a big family that always stuck together. Whenever a long
weekend came up we were off to visit places we'd never been before.
We drove to France, the Netherlands, Austria, Belgium, Luxembourg,
St. Tropez and Bavaria, just to mention a few. On Easter weekend of
1981 we decided to take a trip to northern Italy. We drove through
Switzerland, and had to ride up one side of the Alps and then down
the other into Italy. To our surprise, the top of the Alps was still in
a deep winter and we were poorly prepared for the snow and the
extreme cold. So we rode without stopping to get out of the cold as
quickly as possible.

Once we got down the Alps and into the province of Milan it

warmed up a bit, but driving south through these mountains was a sad experience. The hills were bare, and there was hardly any vegetation anywhere. We wondered what had caused this. We stopped in the first little village we came to for a bathroom break and to find a restaurant for a hot lunch. The village had neither, and looked to be very poor, with old grey houses and cobblestone streets.

We were in the centre of this little town, stretching our legs — with the bikes lined up in a row — when we were approached by a local. He spoke no English and none of us spoke Italian. But we understood him because he kept repeating over and over, "Canada, Canadian?" The man had noticed our Canadian license plates and flags sewn onto the jackets and become very excited. When we answered, "Yes, we are Canadian," people began approaching us. They started shaking our hands smiling at us and saying, "*Grazie, Grazie.*"

We had no idea why they were thanking us, until one man began speaking to us in heavily accented English. He explained that back in the 1970s this region was hit by an enormous earthquake that left many people missing and trapped by debris from the mountainside. Their town had been partially swallowed up by the rubble. He went on to tell us about the devastation and how they had no water or supplies to dig for those who were lost. They had no choice then but to wait for help.

"The first to arrive were the Canadian Military," he said. They came with helicopters from their base in Germany. They showed up with supplies and manpower and ready to help. The Canadians got there even faster than their own countrymen, and helped for as long as they were needed.

He then explained that the local people never really got a chance to thank the Canadians, and so would we please accept their hospitality now? "Please," he said, "let us thank you our way."

Within minutes, tables were brought out and filled with bread, all types of meats, cheeses, beer and wine. They brought us into their homes to use the bathrooms, and took pictures of our group with the bikes. Even after we told them that none of the Canadian soldiers with us today were part of that aid mission in the 1970s, they fed us and kept thanking us. They did not care; we were the first Canadians they had seen since the earthquake and they were not going to miss this opportunity.

We spent a couple of hours with these wonderful, grateful people — eating, drinking and laughing. Some of them were older, grandparents with white hair and beards, enjoying the company of a few Canadian motorcyclists. I thought how odd this would appear to someone if they were to see a group of bikers dining like this with the locals. Eventually we told them we had to get back on the road in order to make it to a campground outside of Savona before dark.

But leaving that little town proved to be an even bigger challenge then crossing the Alps had been that day; they kept hugging us and asking us to stay the night with them in their village. We finally got back on the road, but only after we took a picture with the whole town.

We made it to the campground before dark, and the conversation around the campfire that night was all about this amazing experience. We also realized this was only possible due to the enormous generosity of Canada and Canadians — always there to lend a hand when people around the world are in these dire situations. I will always remember this day — more so than the rest of the trip. The generosity of the people in that little village — sharing whatever food and wine they had — was their way of expressing their gratitude to Canada. And we were the lucky recipients.

~Isolde Ryan
Tottenham, Ontario

My Australian Introduction to Team Canada

*Hockey is Canada's game. Nothing
else is: nothing else will be.*
~Ken Dryden and Roy MacGregor

I was genuinely happy for my son, Ryan, when his work relocated him from Toronto, Ontario to Melbourne, Australia. At the same time I was upset there would be such an enormous distance between us. Secretly I hoped he wouldn't like living there and would return to Canada within a year or two, but that was not the case. In fact, Ryan thrived in Melbourne and chose to make it his permanent home.

During the summer of 2009 I met a man named John who specialized in booking flights for tour groups to Australia. I mentioned that Ryan lived in Melbourne and that at some point I had to get there to spend some time with him. To my surprise, that December John called and said he could fit me in with a tour group leaving in mid-February for a month in Australia. I didn't have the money in the bank, but it was a great package. After giving it some thought I realized the years were slipping by as I waited for the "right" time to make this trip. So I phoned John and said, "I'm in." Then I e-mailed Ryan to let him know I was finally coming for a visit.

My flight, with stopovers, took thirty-six hours, but it was all worth it when I got off the plane in Melbourne and saw Ryan waiting for me. After our reunion, we made a couple of stops on our way to the condo he rented. I was intrigued as I heard him seamlessly switch between an Australian accent when he was talking with locals, and his Canadian accent while he was talking just with me. He explained that it just made life easier not having to answer questions about being Canadian all the time.

A few days later I experienced my own introduction to the locals when I had a chance to get out and explore Melbourne on my own. The weather was as warm as the people I met, and I was truly surprised by the number of people who guessed I was Canadian as soon as I spoke. However the first time someone said, "You must be so proud of Team Canada," I found myself at a loss for words. Our little family had never really followed sports, so while I was aware that the 2010 Winter Olympics were being held in Vancouver, Canada, they had not really been on my radar. By the time the fifth or sixth person had excitedly mentioned Team Canada, I was feeling decidedly unpatriotic at my utter lack of knowledge of this major event currently taking place in my own beloved country. I couldn't have named even one hockey player on Team Canada but, according to the Australians I spoke with, they were doing really well.

Back at Ryan's place I pulled out my laptop and looked up Team Canada. Of the twenty-three players on the roster Sidney Crosby was the only name familiar to me. It would have been hard not to know who he was as the media was in love with this young, good-looking, talented player. I sent an e-mail to my friend Larry (an ardent hockey fan) and asked him to provide me with his insights on the Olympic hockey games. When my son got home I happily told him about my day, including the fascination many people had with Team Canada.

"Australians love sports," Ryan explained with a laugh. Apparently he'd been making a point of watching the daily recap of the Olympics prior to my arrival. That evening we watched the day's Olympic results together. While Ryan's interest in hockey was still minimal, we did make a point of watching the last period in which Team Canada was playing. I actually started to look forward to the games, and even had favourite players. In support, Larry continued sending e-mails full of his opinions and observations about the teams and players he thought I should know about.

One afternoon I went for a long walk and got a bit muddled about where north, south, east and west were. A young man about Ryan's age stopped and asked if I was lost. When I told him which street I was looking for, he immediately burst into a giant smile, touched my arm and said, "Wow, isn't Team Canada doing awesome at the Olympics?"

I grinned back and said, "Yes, we're doing an amazing job!" I used the royal "we" as if I personally had something to do with them continuing to win games!

Ryan and I watched the entire medal deciding game between Canada and the USA, and when Sidney Crosby scored the winning goal in overtime for the gold, we were truly elated. It had taken me a journey to the other side of the globe to finally appreciate my own country's national sport. That evening, as I heard our national anthem on TV and watched the players of Team Canada receiving their gold medals, I can honestly say I felt my Canadian blood pulsing proudly through my veins!

On my flight home I found myself grateful on so many levels. I was pleased to have experienced Melbourne, and felt a new level of comfort that Ryan had chosen this wonderful city to be his new home. I had the validation in my heart that, although distanced by a world of miles, my connection to my son was as strong as ever and it will always be that way.

And, while I reflected on my visit, I couldn't help but appreciate what I'd heard from so many Australians — that Canadians were their favourite people, and Team Canada was their favourite team. But what I was most grateful for on that flight home was the passport I carried in my purse that proves I am a Canadian citizen. And, in my own mind, that I *am* part of Team Canada.

~Laura Snell
Wasaga Beach, Ontario

96

A Father's Stories Come to Life

*It's the possibility of having a dream come
true that makes life interesting.*
~Paulo Coelho

"I think I'll stay here," Marianne told her three companions. "I have no desire to tramp through the forest and possibly come face-to-face with a wild animal," she finished with a shudder.

So the three men headed out without her. Soon they were brushing their way through debris and thick underbrush to get to the ridge. "A moose must have slept here recently," the guide pointed out when they came to a freshly trampled spot. "We must have startled it."

Lutz looked around nervously, recalling the postcard of a moose his dad had sent from Canada back in 1945. The moose was chasing a man with a camera dangling from his neck, and had been sketched by a German prisoner of war (POW) to commemorate a comrade's birthday. Although loving his Canadian adventure, Lutz was nervous at the idea of this bit of history repeating itself.

With their father on their minds, Lutz, his son Marcel, and his sister Marianne were touring the Riding Mountain National Park in Manitoba with their guide Michael. Nostalgia was setting in for them as they remembered their father's stories. For along with 35,000 other German soldiers captured on the battlefields of World War II, a teenaged Richard Beranek had been sent to Canada as a prisoner of war. Assigned to Camp Mafeking in Manitoba, he spent his time working in a Canadian lumber camp.

Years of listening to their father's stories about Canada's wildlife, beautiful forests, prairies and friendly people had left Lutz and Marianne with a deep fascination for this country. They longed to follow in their father's footsteps and share his experience. Perhaps they might even get a glimpse of the animals he had seen. Oh, except for the small black and white one Dad had tried to catch and take back to camp as a pet. Not long after Richard's arrival, two of his comrades had suggested he catch the skunk. Never having heard of this animal before, he knew nothing about the little fellow's potent defence mechanism! "*Willkommen im Lager!*" his fellow prisoners had laughed, thrilled with their welcome-to-camp trick.

According to the Geneva Convention, prisoners could not be forced to work. However, when given the option, many decided it would be better than being bored behind barbed wire in one of the twenty-five camps they were held in. They ended up working in parks, lumber camps and on farms during the summer, and were paid fifty cents a day. And many of them fell in love with Canada.

Richard told his young children that he had loved nothing better than exploring the woods around his camp. "Do you know what the guards told us?" he said with a laugh. "If you try to escape, there are wild animals waiting for you! But we were treated so well, I can't remember anyone wanting to take off while I was there."

I've always been intrigued with this time in my community's history: when pacifist Hutterites hosted some of these German POW soldiers in our own community. Through my research I learned there had been a shortage of labourers in Manitoba, so five hundred German prisoners were employed to help with the sugar beet and grain harvests. Satellite work camps were set up in farming communities, with German prisoners supervised by the Veterans Guard. During the summers it was common to see men clad in dark blue uniforms with a large red circle on the back — "easy targets," the prisoners joked. Curtis Camp, located in an abandoned creamery a mile east of my own Hutterite colony, housed seventy-five prisoners. Over noodle soup, roast duck and sauerkraut served at the communal kitchen, some German prisoners became good friends with the Hutterites.

One day, during my research, I received an intriguing e-mail in a roundabout way. Written in broken English, a German guy named Lutz Beranek was seeking information on his father, Richard Beranek, who had been a POW in Canada. So I put him in touch with an acquaintance, Michael, who was studying POW history. Since Michael spoke no German and Lutz no English, I translated for them. In this way, Michael was able to answer Lutz's questions and provide him with documents relating to his dad. Lutz and I stayed in touch, and he often told me, "I've been fascinated with Canada ever since I was a little boy."

Then, during a visit to Germany, I met Lutz and his wife Antje and spent a memorable weekend with them. That's when I started helping Lutz make travel plans. He and his sister, along with his son, decided to make this pilgrimage to Canada, and get to know their father's past.

Now I was watching them finally experience Manitoba, and I was touched as I saw how much the experience meant to them. "This place is so peaceful," Lutz said softly, as we walked around our colony. "Everyone we meet is so friendly and it's obvious they love this communal life. No wonder the prisoners enjoyed visiting here." With child-like fascination they climbed into semi-trucks and tractors. Proudly perched on a combine seat Lutz chuckled, "Our fields at home are too small for such big machines." He was gazing at the Canadian prairieland stretching around them for miles in all directions.

Then the day came when they were able to visit Camp Mafeking. "Standing in the ruins of this former POW camp building, I felt very close to my dad," Lutz shared. "It was like he was right there with me." Framed in time, Marcel captured Lutz with his camera, gazing through a window. "I wonder if my dad actually stood right here seventy years ago?" he reflected.

One day, when the men were traipsing through the forest, Marianne experienced a moment that none of her dad's stories had prepared her for. "You'll never guess what just happened!" she announced excitedly when the men returned a few minutes later. "As I was bent over taking pictures of wildflowers, I heard something behind me. Thinking it was you returning, I didn't look up right away. But when I turned around, there was a huge moose, and it just stood there watching me!"

"A moose! What did you do?" Lutz asked anxiously. "Where exactly was it?"

"It was so close, just over there," she replied, pointing to a spot about seven metres away. "I was frozen to the spot. After staring at me for a few minutes the moose turned and ambled off into the forest. I stumbled to the car only to find it locked. Next time you venture out on foot, you must leave me the keys!"

"Did you take a picture?" I asked her later.

"No, I couldn't move! I was too scared to even think!" she replied emphatically. "I only remembered the camera after the moose was gone. All I would have needed would have been for a bear to have come along then as well! And me locked out! We did see a bear later though," she laughed, "but from the safety of our car."

Richard Beranek died in 1988, but his children's dream of seeing the country he had fallen in love with remained alive. "My father always said he never felt like a prisoner in Canada, deeming his time here as the best years of his life," Lutz beamed. "Now I know why; I've enjoyed it as much as he did! I'll always be grateful for this visit to Canada; it's allowed my dad's stories to truly come to life!"

~Linda Maendel
Newton, Manitoba

97

My Big Country

My country is very fantastic. We are lucky to
be Canadian, to have such a big
and wonderful country.
~Marc Garneau

It is another beautiful hot, sunny day. My husband and I decided to leave our home in Ontario's cottage country and, through our church, travel and teach on this tiny Eastern Caribbean island called Bequia. Winter is a long way away.

The roads here are poor, not like the good roads and highways in Canada. The bus driver speeds along, negotiating the ancient potholes. He uses the weighty momentum of the dollar-bus to climb out and up onto the other side of the gap. I watch as our heads bob up and down in unison. The bus is similar to a long van and aptly named, since it costs one Eastern Caribbean dollar to ride anywhere.

This island is only one mile wide by three miles long. When the bus slows down I look up to see a familiar young man get on. *What's Jeff doing here?* I wonder. Normally, young people on this small island walk. Then I spy the reason he is riding today: three green plastic sacks by his bare brown feet containing fuzzy round fruit. It is harvest time for sapodilla, a fruit similar to our Canadian Spartan apples. Jeff hauls the bags down the aisle, motioning for people to shift so he can sit beside me.

"We is crowded today," he says loudly, speaking to the driver up at the front. He turns to me and in a whisper asks, "Whut you hear from my friend Sally?" Sally, a pretty Peace Corps worker, had befriended Jeff when she rented a room in our apartment before returning to her home in Whitehorse, Yukon.

"Sally's fine... her letter says to say hi to Jeff."

He beams. "You visit Sally, when you go home?"

"No... Jeff," I explain. "It's too far away. Sally lives in Whitehorse." He gives me a blank look. "We live close to Toronto... in Ontario, a province in Canada." Jeff still has a blank look. "Okay Jeff, wait." I shift on the seat so I can use my hands and say, "You know how far Bequia is from Canada?" I draw an imaginary arc in the air as though my right hand is a plane crossing an ocean expanse to Toronto. He nods. Then with my left arm, I make an equally large arc saying, "Sally lives as far away from our city to Whitehorse, as Bequia is from Canada."

He whistles air through the space in his front teeth. "You foolin' me. Canada be so big?" I nod. The bus chugs along, and in that moment I think how many times I have looked at a map of my country, but only now realize how big it actually is.

That evening my husband Brian and I invite our Bequia friends Velma and Picky over for a dinner that includes, for dessert, my attempt at sapodilla crisp. They enjoy it, but I miss the apples. The young couple explain that they want to leave Bequia. "We dream of going to Canada," they say.

We remind them about their lovely island, the abundance of fish, and fruit and vegetables when in season. I think about the food shelves in our stores carrying everything from lobsters and tuna from the east coast, to salmon and cherries from the west coast, maple syrup from Quebec, and southern Ontario peaches.

They talk about the pictures they have seen showing superstores overflowing with choice. Velma says, "You can buy anything, anytime." It's true. They talk about Canada's healthcare. "You have real medicine, skilled doctors and the latest technology," Velma says. Velma wants to be a nurse.

I reflect a moment on the basic health kit we needed to bring with us. Even pain reliever, like Tylenol is rare here. "You have jobs," Picky says, "and make money." He adds frowning, "We could buy our own house there instead of living with my parents." Velma nods. I try to cheer them up and talk about how fortunate they are to have family living close by and schools — one elementary and one high school — although Brian adds, "They could both use a coat of paint." Paint is also hard to come by here.

I share a look with Brian across the table. Neither of us mentions this will be our last year here. Our son starts kindergarten next year and without question we want him to be educated in Canada. Velma has heard about our four seasons and asks, "What is winter like?" Brian and I both laugh. They stare at us. Then Brian gets up, walks over to the fridge, another luxury on the island, and opens the freezer door. He sticks his head in and calls out, "This is it." I laugh again but turn to see the puzzled looks on our guests' faces. "That is what it's like all winter long," Brian sits down chuckling.

"Lakes freeze," I say. "Imagine the sea, if it is hard like ice and you can walk on it?" Their eyes grow wide.

We're not sure if they understand exactly, but when we both giggle again, the laughter is contagious. I pump water by hand from the cistern that collects rainfall, and put the kettle on the gas stove. I think about the abundance of fresh water in Canada. As night falls we light a candle and get out the cards.

It is hard for me to concentrate on the game since in the back of my mind I am now thinking about the winter challenge. I remember a time when it snowed two feet overnight. We both started shovelling as though dealing with the snow and not letting it overcome us was our Canadian duty. We showed the world that winter does not get the better of us.

Later we got the car stuck in our driveway. But we did not let it get our spirits down. Instead we used the trick everyone learns in Canada. We put an old piece of carpet under the tire. I rocked the car back, then forward and then, Brian said, "On the count of three go for it." I gunned the engine and he pushed from the back, and we got out. "Hooray," we shouted, beaming with pride.

Will we once again embrace Canada's cold? I think about the snowsuits, boots and hats we will have to buy. But bundled up, we *will* be warm. It's not so bad. I look forward to building the first snowman with my son. I wonder about driving on icy roads, but know that I will drive more slowly in the winter and with caution. I look forward to ice-skating and ice fishing. Maybe our son will want to play hockey.

I'm sure we are up to the task. We've been taught from an early age to live through a Canadian winter, and appreciate the beauty and fun of it as well. I imagine my big country and feel like I want to put my arms around it. Suddenly I am excited. We are lucky to be going home soon.

~Kathy Ashby
Bracebridge, Ontario

98

Sorry, Not Sorry

We're known for being polite…
but we can be proud too.
~Heather Reisman

W hen Canadians enter into conversations, we are usually considered to be very friendly and polite. More specifically we are known for our use of the word "Sorry." Well, sorry, we can't help it! It just comes out without even really thinking about it, or at least it does for me.

I was born and raised in Nova Scotia, and, growing up I was always very concerned for the wellbeing of others. So naturally, like those around me, I adopted this common word for everyday use. Whether it was bumping into a stranger on the sidewalk or asking a question, "sorry" always weaseled its way in. It wasn't until university that my so-called "Canadian habits" would be put to the test.

I had been accepted to study abroad for six months in Sweden as part of the Saint Mary's University exchange program. By January 2014, I was on my way to Jönköping, Sweden, a town about the size of Fredericton, New Brunswick. I would be living with other international students and I would take four classes. I had been to Europe before on vacation, but never to actually live and study, so I was thrilled to have the experience.

Once I was unpacked in my room, I introduced myself to everyone in my path. I seemed to be well received by my peers and soon had a great circle of friends. Naturally, every so often I would utter the word "sorry," but unlike at home in Canada, I would get chastised by the other students. "Stop apologizing! You did nothing wrong," they would say. They soon began to tease me and placed a "sorry" jar in our kitchen. I had to put a Swedish krona in the jar every time I spoke the word. "I'm just trying to be nice!" I would explain. "Sorry, not sorry."

In March I went on a trip to Amsterdam with my Australian friend to visit a few of her friends who were living there. We enjoyed our time immensely, and her friends showed us around beautiful Amsterdam. "Sorry" came up a few times, of course, which made the Aussies burst into laughter because, not only did I say it frequently, they found my Canadian accent to be an additional source for laughter. "Sorrrrreeeeeeeee" they would say, to imitate me, as they thought the correct way to pronounce it was "Saw-ry." After a few days of the teasing I stood firm, and mentioned that when kids in Canada have speech impediments they sound Australian, and it's considered an improper way of talking. At this they laughed even harder and said "touché." Sorry, not sorry.

Not only was my sorry-saying apparent, but my friendliness as well as my outgoing personality identified me as an "extreme Canadian." In April I went on a school-organized trip to Prague. I had always wanted to go, and though none of my friends were going I was happy to meet other students. There were many international students on the trip as well as Swedish students. One night we ate at a tavern where we got a taste of traditional Czech food. I was alone, so I sat down at the first table where there was a free seat. As it turned out the people sitting with me at that table were all Swedes. I introduced myself and started chatting away, asking them where they were from, what program they were studying, etc. They answered very quickly and did not ask much in return, but as I knew no one, and we had two hours to kill, what else was I going to do?

After a few minutes, one of the guys said, "You ask a lot of questions. It's very hard for us Swedes to answer and ask questions like you Canadians." I was taken aback by his comment, but I brushed it off, as I had found most Swedes tend to be shy and reserved compared to Canadians. However, I thought it was a bit rude. I was there on exchange, I knew no one, we went to an international school where half the population were on exchange from other countries... were we supposed to not talk to each other? Sorry, not sorry. Luckily, that was my only negative experience for being Canadian.

My sisters visited me in May and I showed them around Jönköping. One of my favourite places was an antique store where they had a barn filled with various trinkets and collectables. My sisters and I picked up a few keepsakes and went up front to pay for them. The owner asked where we were from.

"We're from Canada," answered my sister, "and I live in Toronto."

"Ah! Toronto!" the man exclaimed happily. "My sister lives there." He seemed so pleased to speak with us. And when we tried to pay, he wouldn't accept our Swedish kronor. "No, no, it's free for Canadians," he said. Very touched, we thanked him immensely, and then continued on our tour of Jönköping.

I guess it helps to be Canadian sometimes! But in reality there is so much more to being Canadian than our friendliness and good manners. Though I enjoyed my time in Sweden immensely, I was so happy to return home. I am so proud of my roots and I will never apologize for being Canadian. Sorry, not sorry!

~Megan Pothier
Fredericton, New Brunswick

99

With Glowing Hearts

The world needs more Canada!
~Former U.S. President Barack Obama

It was my birthday, and my son phoned to wish me a happy day and to suggest I turn on the TV. Not so much to watch, as to listen. Listen and sniffle. The Winter Olympics were on and a Canadian was about to receive a gold medal. That meant "O Canada" would be played, and he knew that hearing it would produce some deep emotion. There's nothing like a few happy tears on your birthday.

A typical Canadian, I usually hide my patriotism. I join with the multitudes that grumble about taxes, bureaucracies and government waste; I worry about unemployment, university fees and Medicare; I wonder about national unity, gas pipelines and the CBC. But beneath all that angst, I am thankful to be a Canadian, and nothing elicits that gratitude faster than the national anthem.

My attachment to "O Canada" goes back to my adolescence during the anti-everything era of the late 1960s. My high school music department arranged a student music exchange with a school from Portland, Oregon. That trip became the focal point of life for all of us for months. Heady daydreams were second only to scrimping, saving, fundraising—and maybe even practicing. We were going to the States! Real cool. The land of promise. The centre of the universe.

Our introduction to Americana, however, was not what we thought it would be. Our friends to the south were going through some very difficult times and it showed. Wandering the school halls, we were awed by the expense of the facility, and unnerved by the extent of the tension. Our American counterparts were a divided people in almost every way — blacks not hanging out with whites; students protesting the Vietnam War; cool kids not mixing with the un-cool ones. They congregated in their little groups, staring suspiciously at passers-by. We survived our five days by staying as inconspicuous as possible.

Concert night arrived and we were on edge with excitement and anxiety. Their band and choir were the biggest and the best. We were nobodies from Canada, hoping to make a good impression. We processed through the auditorium to the first two rows of seats, which had been reserved for us. There we sat: fifty Canadian teenagers and 500 American adults waiting for our national anthems to be played.

Suddenly the first chord of "O Canada" rang through the auditorium. Without discussion or planning, and without hesitation, we fifty leapt to our feet and began to sing. As the music ended we sat down, each of us surprised at the depth of our own emotion — and the way it was shared amongst our peers.

Seconds later we were startled by loud applause. Our American hosts gave us a standing ovation. Afterward, one stranger said, "Hearing you kids sing your national anthem gave me the shivers. I've never seen such patriotism. I wish Americans could be like that."

Our last hours in the United States were spent driving north on Interstate 5 in a cramped school bus. The exuberance of the southward journey was gone, and we were a subdued bunch, each of us absorbed in our own thoughts. When we finally crossed the border even the bus seemed to sigh with relief. Suddenly, a loud voice rang out, "We're home!" Whistles and whoops filled the air, along with an array of hats, shoes, books and souvenirs. Home had never felt so good.

Many years have passed since then, but whenever I hear "O Canada" I find myself back in an auditorium in Portland, Oregon, singing with conviction, love, and pride. Whatever its deficiencies may be at any given time, home still feels good. Pass the tissues, please.

~Lydia A. Calder
Edmonton, Alberta

The Woman on the Bus

Thank you is the best prayer that anyone could say.
I say that one a lot. Thank you expresses extreme
gratitude, humility, understanding.
~Alice Walker

There were fourteen of us in an old school bus loaded up with supplies. We were taking the supplies from Prince Edward Island all the way to a "street children's" educational program in Quetzaltenango, the second largest city in Guatemala. On our old bus, we travelled south through two Canadian provinces, fifteen American states, and Mexico, passing three border crossings in fourteen days. The Guatemalan civil war that ran from 1960 to 1996 had ended two weeks before we crossed the border into that war-torn country.

In remote areas of Mexico we were often stopped at checkpoints by members of the military. But our bus driver had come prepared. He gave each soldier a Canadian flag pin. The serious-looking soldiers would suddenly crack grins, and usually became friendlier as they examined the pins. They always asked the driver where we were going, why, and for how long. They checked our passports and then motioned the driver to go. I believe the gift of those Canadian flag pins was the reason we were never harassed or detained for very long.

Once we arrived at our destination in Guatemala I began my volunteer work. I lived with Mayan families, visited women's' organizations, and helped out at a refugee camp the size of a small city.

This was my first trip to Central America, and I was surprised to learn that the symbol of Canada, our beautiful flag, was so easily recognized there. On one particular day, I was travelling by bus through the rugged countryside of Guatemala, and I was the only foreigner. The banged-up bus was jam-packed with Guatemalans sitting four to a seat or standing in the aisle along with squawking roosters and hens in cages. The slow-moving bus crawled along dusty roads, dodging huge potholes, through villages surrounded by volcanoes and lush green mountainsides.

I had become so entrenched in this new world that I wasn't paying much attention to the woman who was now crushed against me in the seat. Overcome by the heat, the woman had fallen asleep, her head resting on my shoulder. She was short and middle-aged, with cropped black curly hair that framed her round face. Her hands lay at her sides as if they too were resting.

I had met enough women there to surmise that she had probably gotten up long before sunrise to prepare food for a family, perhaps caring for children, and doing necessary household chores before leaving the home of her employer.

I wanted to move, but did not dare rob her of her sleep. The bus eventually jolted to a stop, causing her to wake. Half asleep, she grinned at me, a toothless ear-to-ear smile. And I smiled back. I did not speak Spanish well enough to converse with her.

At the next stop, vendors of all ages flooded onto the bus, calling out, "Fruit, water, sweets for sale!" Now wide-awake, the woman pulled out a pouch tied around her neck and hidden in her bosom.

She carefully counted out a few coins and bought a piece of fruit. After the purchase, she tucked the pouch safely back in her bosom. Without any hesitation, and with a big smile on her weather-beaten face, she broke off a piece and offered it to me. Touched, I smiled back and graciously accepted it. I knew the poor of this country did not have the luxury of buying snack food. She must have been very hungry, and yet she generously shared with me.

I wanted to give her something in return, but my knapsack was stuffed with clothing and a few personal items. Eyeing the Canadian flag pin on my shirt she asked, "Canadiense?" In Spanish I replied, "Yes, I am Canadian," surprised that she had recognized the symbol because of the remoteness of the area I was travelling through.

I then took off my Canadian flag pin, and carefully pinned it on the collar of her shirt. The woman reverently touched the Canadian symbol with one finger, as if it were made of gold. She beamed with appreciation, and thanked me in Spanish. As the bus clunked along, she wore her Canadian flag pin with noticeable pride.

When the bus finally arrived at her destination, she placed the palm of her hand against the palm of my hand and smiled. I knew it was her way of saying goodbye and safe journey. I watched her get off the bus, and I continued to watch until she was out of sight. The memory of her simple kindness remains with me today.

~Stella Shepard
Morell, Prince Edward Island

A Lesson in Germany

*A hero is someone who has given his or her
life to something bigger than oneself.*
~John Campbell

After university I was given the opportunity to travel with a Christian theatre group. After two years travelling in the United States, the director asked me to go to Europe to continue the work and I happily accepted. My music and drama team covered a large territory: The British Isles, Ireland, the Netherlands, Belgium, Switzerland and France.

Europe was everything I had imagined — full of history, incredible architecture, art and intriguing foods. I looked forward to working on my French, which had never progressed beyond a rudimentary vocabulary, even after three years of high school French in Ontario. I had no fears, and everyone I met seemed genuinely friendly and receptive to visitors.

But I must admit there was this one time when, at the outset, I wasn't sure. We were staying in our German headquarters, in between tours, and I had discovered a long, isolated stretch of beautiful countryside to explore. I walked contently in silence, enjoying some rare "alone time." I wasn't paying much attention to the road ahead, and was not expecting to see anyone else and, as a result, I was quite startled to hear a voice.

I looked up to see a woman of about seventy apparently intent on communicating with me. My German was pitiful, and I knew she would not find it easy. She went on for a while, and then hesitated, likely sensing my lack of comprehension. Then she asked, "Canada? You Canada?"

"Yes," I nodded, wondering where this would take me. The woman then began to tell a story, I guessed, though I couldn't understand any of it. I smiled politely and pretended to listen. After several minutes, she pantomimed guns shooting, complete with some appropriate sound effects. Now I felt a bit worried. After all, I was in Germany. Canada had fought with the Allies against this land's population. I wondered if she might possibly be blaming me for her father's death or the destruction of her home. A knot began to form in my stomach. Then she threw her arms out to the sides and imitated the rolling motion of a plane flying. A good storyteller, her face mirrored the seriousness of war. But I couldn't tell whether the Canadians were the good guys or not. The knot in my stomach grew.

I have no idea how long we stood on the side of the road while she told her story, but it sure felt like forever. For an older lady, her stamina was impressive. I was exhausted just listening. It takes a lot of energy to try to decipher a language when you only know a few words. I was so intent on trying to understand her story that I was once again startled when a voice spoke to my left.

In a heavy accent, though clear enough for me to understand, a man's voice explained, "She is telling you how the Germans came to her village in the Netherlands. It was the Canadians who came to free her people. She thanks you for those soldiers from your country who came so generously to free their country from the Nazis."

Since I wasn't fluent in Dutch either, I wondered which language she had been speaking. I had only assumed it had been German. My translator was a German in his forties. He added no praise of his own—but then again he wasn't hostile either. Suddenly, the older woman began to smile broadly, her story over. She pumped my hand and said "*danke danke*" over and over again. Even I knew that word. I smiled back, and then she went on her way, still talking. I heard the word "Canada" once more before her voice faded in the slight afternoon breeze. I thanked the translator for his help. He nodded his head briskly and continued down the road.

I stood still for a bit, and thought about the young men and women who came to a strange land to fight an evil regime and risk their lives for people they didn't know. I knew about the war from books and a safe distance, yet this continent was still full of survivors who had experienced it first-hand. I didn't know it then, but in the months to come I would meet many of them: men and women in nursing homes who had experienced two occupations in France, a sweet man playing an accordion on a Belgian street corner wearing his World War II Army uniform, children of soldiers that proudly told of their relatives' involvement, and those who had experienced first-hand the terror of the fighting — of the war.

On our tours we passed and visited many cemeteries and memorials. The rock on the beach at Dieppe with the Maple Leaf, huge memorials in France commemorating specific battles, and the final resting places of soldiers from both sides. Seeing those huge fields with rows and rows of crosses touched me. The young men under those crosses were just as much victims, with grieving families at home, as the allies. Each cross bore a name and a tragic set of dates that showed the extreme youth of many of them, sometimes with a sibling or two beside them.

I felt many stirrings of national pride during my travel in Europe — though never more than after my encounter with that older woman in Germany. She proved her enduring gratitude to our country by insisting on telling her story to me, and thanking me as if I had been one of the liberating Canadian soldiers from the war. People everywhere still remembered and were grateful. What I hadn't realized is that I needed to "remember" too. Every Canadian should be proud of our country and its history. I know I am.

~Janice M. McDonald
Ingersoll, Ontario

Meet Our Contributors

A. A. Adourian is thankful, curious and loves to learn. She thanks God for each day, is curious to watch her faith grow, and loves to learn how the Holy Spirit changes hearts. She wants to inspire and encourage others through her writing, and makes her home in Toronto. Learn more at aaadourian.com.

Tanya Ambrose is the daughter of Russian parents displaced by World War II. The memories her parents shared shaped her appreciation of their losses and sacrifices. She wishes she had asked more questions when she was younger. Her parents' experiences are often the catalyst for her writing.

Kathy Ashby is the author of *Carol: A Woman's Way* published by DreamCatcher Publishing. As quoted on the back cover, Dr. Helen Caldicott says, "A very important fictional account of the activity of women to preserve the environment. Indeed most successful movements have been and are started by women." E-mail Kathy at ashbykathy@gmail.com.

Alma Barkman is the author of nine books and her writing has also appeared in numerous publications, both secular and Christian. She is the mother of four boys and grandmother of eleven. Her interests include photography, quilting and gardening.

James Barrera was a soldier in the Canadian Armed Forces from 1997 to 2014 with several deployments to Kandahar, Afghanistan. He plans to write a book about his experiences.

Patti Leo Bath is a registered nurse and writer. She loves to travel, and her favourite trips have been helping her grandmother complete her bucket list. They saw every province of Canada by train and ferry, and took a steamboat down the Mississippi River. She just completed her first novel and is hoping to publish it soon.

Glynis Belec is a former registered nurse and retired tutor who now works as a full-time freelance writer, inspirational speaker and award-winning children's author. She cannot imagine a world without little people to inspire her. Glynis loves capturing life in words and cannot wait for tomorrow so she can feel inspired all over again.

Rahaf Bi arrived in Canada in May of 2016. Since then, she has shared her incredible story with kids in schools throughout the Kelowna area and has helped many Syrian families settle in the Okanagan. She received her Bachelor of Science with a major in Chemistry at the University of Damascus.

Wayne Boldt is now a middle-aged man who no longer needs to borrow his sister's bicycle to have an adventure. A cowboy, husband, wilderness canoeist, father, ocean sailor and grandfather, Wayne is reflecting on his many experiences and is starting to write about them.

Barbara Bondy-Pare has four children from her first loving husband, Ronald M. Bondy. Since he passed away from lung cancer, she has married a high school classmate, Eddie Pare. Their twelve adorable grandchildren keep them young, active, and entertained. Barbara is all about love, family, and hugs.

Binnie Brennan is a musician and award-winning author of three books of fiction. She is a graduate of Queen's University and the Humber School for Writers. Since 1989 Binnie has lived in Halifax, where she plays the viola with Symphony Nova Scotia.

Liaison and spokesperson for Lewisporte Area Flight 15 Scholarship Fund, **Shirley Brooks-Jones** was born in Vinton County, Ohio, and is the eldest of nine children. She received a BA in English and was awarded Emeritus status, both from Ohio State University. She is a recipient of the Order of Newfoundland and Labrador.

Rose Burke and her husband live in Rusagonis, NB. After retirement, she began writing her mother's life story, which will be published later this year. She often blends prose with her other passion, photography. Her fiction and personal essays have been published in anthologies and in the *United Church Observer*.

Lydia Calder has published magazine articles and inspiration pieces, and writes two blogs. She has a busy life as a wife, mother, grandmother, pet owner and lay minister. In the quiet times she enjoys reading books, writing books and colouring books. Learn more at lydiaonajourney. blogspot.ca.

Deborah Cannon is a writer of fantasy, suspense and romance. Her interests are diverse and range from a Chinese epic fantasy, *The Pirate Empress*, to a series of Christmas romances for pet lovers under the pen name of Daphne Lynn Stewart. She trained at Toronto's Humber School for Writers and lives in Hamilton, ON.

Jennifer Caseley loves to collect letters to put behind her name. She has her BSc., M.Ed., and is a CPHR (Chartered Professional in Human Resources). She enjoys sewing, photography, quading and travelling. She has settled down in Northern Alberta.

Carla M. Crema was born and raised in Port Alberni, BC. She has been a Certified Dental Assistant for thirty-eight years and is currently a Certified Podologist with four years experience. She has a passion for children and spends her free time with elder people. She enjoys painting, knitting, gardening, and numerous outdoor activities.

Sherry Taylor Cummins, SHRM-SCP, CMP, CMM, earned a Bachelor of Arts in Human Resources in 1993. She has two published books and well over 200 contributions to books, articles and blogs. In southeast Michigan, she enjoys spending time with family, writing, speaking and travelling. E-mail Sherry at cummins.sherry@gmail.com.

Born in Ottawa, Ontario but living in Quebec, **Julie Hamel de Belle** has been writing in both official languages since her early teens. Julie de Belle is a retired ESL teacher, has taught in China and James Bay, and now works freelance from home, both writing and translating.

Michelle Dinnick, B.Sc., writes both nonfiction and fiction. She lives in Southern Ontario with her family, and has three young boys. A regular contributor to several local magazines, in April 2016 Michelle was shortlisted at the Ontario Writers' Conference Story Starters Contest. E-mail her at michelledtds@gmail.com.

Lynn Dove has been married to her best friend, Charles, for close to forty years and they are blessed with three wonderful adult children, and three precious grandbabies. She loves to connect with her readers through her award-winning blog, *Journey Thoughts*, or on Facebook and Twitter @LynnIDove and through her website lynndove.com.

Brooke and Keira Elliott are compassionate young women who want to make a difference in the world. When Brooke isn't deep in a book, or figuring out how to help others, she loves to play volleyball and soccer. Keira has the voice of an angel and sings her way through the day brightening the world for others with her kind, generous heart.

Peter G. Elliott is an independent filmmaker, video editor and writer with a strong passion for Canadian history and the outdoors. His first professional film, *The Castle of White Otter Lake*, ignited his career to share unique stories from Canada's backwoods. Peter now lives in St. John's, Newfoundland with his family. E-mail him at blacksprucetrees@gmail.com.

Jane Everett is an artist who lives and works in Kelowna, BC where marmots are, unfortunately, plentiful.

Donna Fawcett is a retired creative writing instructor for Fanshawe College in London, ON. She enjoys sharing her stories in *Chicken Soup for the Soul* books and has had the privilege of having received awards for her novels and song lyrics. Learn more at donnafawcett.com.

Liz Maxwell Forbes is published in three previous *Chicken Soup for the Soul* books as well as in other anthologies. Her latest book, *Growing Up Weird*, is her memoir of growing up with eccentric parents in Oak Bay (Victoria, BC) in the 1940s and 1950s. You can learn more at osbornebaybooks.com.

John Karl Forrest passed away July 20, 2016. He was a loving husband and devoted father. He was always proud to have his stories published in the *Chicken Soup for the Soul* series. He is greatly missed by his family, friends, and his many admirers at Chicken Soup for the Soul.

Robyn Gerland is the author of *All These Long Years Later* found in the Canadian library systems. She is a columnist for several magazines and newspapers including *Polar Expressions* and the Federation of British Columbia Writers *WordWorks*. She also teaches creative writing at Vancouver Island University.

Paula L. Gillis has a Bachelor of Arts and Education from St. Francis Xavier University. After living in Fort McMurray for twenty-two years she moved to Edmonton but still has friends in the community. Paula left the workplace a few years ago and began working on other projects and submitting to the *Chicken Soup for the Soul* series.

As a teenager growing up in the 1970s, **Lacy Gray** wrote for escape. "What inspires my poetry is life. Anything that touches the heart, good or bad," states the mother of two grown sons. Lacy enjoys travelling and spending time with loved ones. She plans to continue pursuing her dream of touching lives through her writing.

Kristine Groskaufmanis lives in Toronto with her adorable husband and equally adorable dog. When she's not eating carbs, she enjoys hiking, listening to Joni Mitchell and plotting how to stay in her pyjamas and get paid for doing so.

After co-authoring fifteen books for high school geography, **Rob Harshman** has begun writing nonfiction stories. Rob and his wife live in Mississauga where he loves to spend time with his three grandchildren. He also enjoys travel, photography and gardening. Rob plans to continue writing short stories.

Anthony Hoffman grew up in Fort McMurray and currently works as a firefighter/EMT for the municipality. His chronic curiosity has taken him around the world, and into the fields of film, radio, finance, flight and emergency services. He logs personal musings and observations at charactercrackers.com.

Durre N. Jabeen was born in Bangladesh and now lives in Canada. She is a civil engineer and loves to write and cook. She has published two collections of short stories: *My Jardin* and *Savage and Alluring*, and a cookbook: *Great Grandmother Grandmother Mother We: Bangladeshi Family Recipe*. E-mail her at djabeen2009@yahoo.com.

Mitchell Kastanek is a high school student living in Amery, WI. He enjoys playing football, tennis, reading, and playing drums in his high school's band. He plans on attending college to earn a bachelor's degree in business.

Pamela Kent received her Diploma in Creative Writing when she was sixty. Twenty-six years later she still writes every day. Her articles and stories have won awards and appeared in magazines, newspapers and online.

Liisa Kovala, a Finnish-Canadian teacher and writer, is inspired by life in Northern Ontario. Her fiction and nonfiction have appeared in a variety of publications. Her first book, *Surviving Stutthof: My Father's Memories Behind the Death Gate*, will be released in Fall 2017 by Latitude 46. Learn more at liisakovala.com.

Elizabeth Kranz always dreamed of living in the north. But life's complications moved her to many homes and adventures. Her five children and various jobs give her so much writing inspiration, especially the canoeing adventures that she drags her computer geek husband on in Algonquin Park's wilderness. E-mail her at lizkranz@gmail.com.

Bonnie Lavigne loves gardening, hiking, cooking, and nature. She lives on the shores of sunny Lake Ontario far, far from black fly country.

Sharon Lawrence is a retired educator, artisan, speaker and writer. She and her late husband established a private wildlife sanctuary in Ontario where they raised, rehabilitated and released injured and orphaned wildlife. Sharon is currently penning short stories about some of the unique animals housed at the sanctuary.

Deborah Lean is a mixed media artist and writer from Cobourg, ON.

Mark Leiren-Young's most recent book is *The Killer Whale Who Changed the World*. He's the host of the Skaana podcast and he won the Leacock Medal for Humour for his debut book, *Never Shoot a Stampede Queen*.

Leslie Lorette is passionate about travel, animals, nature, cooking, the arts, and culture. She believes travel is transformative and appreciates the people she has met and the opportunities she had to explore seven continents and close to sixty countries. She lives in Toronto and is grateful for her friends, family, and Lola.

Nancy Loucks-McSloy, a community service worker, is a published writer based in London, ON. Growing up in rural Southwestern Ontario in the 1950s and 1960s, Nancy enjoys reminiscing about the good times when life was much simpler. She is a wife, mother, and grandmother who is very much a community activist.

Julia Lucas is retired from a career in architectural drafting and construction estimating. She enjoys creating needlework designs in cross-stitch, Hardanger embroidery as well as knitting and crochet. She has been married for thirty-nine years, has two stepsons and two step-grandsons.

Zabe MacEachren holds a Ph.D. in Craftmaking as a Pedagogy in Environmental Education. She currently coordinates the Outdoor and Experiential Education program at Queen's University. She has been travelling by snowshoe and canoe for decades, and holds fond memories of her experiences teaching in the north.

Linda Maendel lives on a Hutterite colony in Manitoba, and works as an educational assistant. She blogs at hutt-writevoice.blogspot.ca. Besides freelancing, she's the author of two published books: a German children's book, *Lindas glücklicher Tag;* and *Hutterite Diaries*, a collection of Hutterite stories.

Lesley Marcovich, a life story coach, believes that "stories are the invisible strands that tie our DNA together." She runs biography workshops and an online memoir program. She lives in Newmarket with her husband and her ever-growing family, all great fodder for any life story. E-mail her at lmarcovich@biographytimeliner.com.

Nada Mazzei has a Bachelor of Arts in French and Italian and a Master of Theology from the University of Toronto. She received her Master of Arts in Theology from the University of St. Michael's College. Nada is currently a freelance writer in Toronto. She enjoys reading, music, and art.

Dennis McCloskey has a Journalism degree from Ryerson University in Toronto. He writes freelance articles from his home in Richmond Hill, ON, where he lives with his wife, Kris, a retired teacher. This is Dennis's fifth story published in the *Chicken Soup for the Soul* series. E-mail him at dmcclos@rogers.com.

Krista McCracken is a public historian and writer living in Northern Ontario. Her nonfiction work focuses on archives, residential schools, community, and outreach. When she's not writing she can be found drinking tea, watching *Doctor Who*, and editing Wikipedia. Learn more at kristamccracken.ca.

Though primarily a poet, **Janice M. McDonald** enjoys all kinds of writing. She also enjoys crafting, scrapbooking, gardening and many other creative endeavours. Janice dreams of more time to write but as a mother, wife, volunteer and employee it can be quite a challenge.

Frances McGuckin is author of the bestseller, *Business for Beginners,* and *Taking Your Business to the Next Level.* After a life-altering car accident in 2005 and serious brain injury, she recently resumed writing, focusing on life experiences. She loves horses, fitness, helping others and just being alive. E-mail her at franmcg@telus.net.

Erin McLeod is an adventurer at heart and loves to write, take photographs, knit, and volunteer when she is not working as a speech-language pathologist in Northern Ontario. A prior journalist and copy editor, she has published several poems in Canadian journals.

Linda Mehus-Barber has just retired from a successful teaching career of forty-two years. She is excited about this season in life as she will now have time to do more of the other things she loves — hiking, swimming, cycling, writing, reading, and walking her dogs with her husband.

Patricia Miller writes about the best emotion — love! She's a wife and mom of two, living in Bradford, ON. Patricia enjoys cottage life, pizza, and snowboarding. She studied creative writing at Durham College after earning her BA from University of Western Ontario. She plans to write children's books. Learn more at AuthorPatriciaMiller.com.

Cathy Mogus is a freelance writer, inspirational speaker, and author of *Dare to Dance Again: Steps from the Psalms When Life Trips You Up*. She has been published in the *Chicken Soup for the Soul* series, *Guideposts* and many other publications. She resides in Richmond, BC. E-mail her at acmogus@shaw.ca.

Marya Morin is a freelance writer. Her stories have appeared in publications such as *Woman's World* and Hallmark. Marya also penned a weekly humorous column for an online newsletter, and writes custom poetry on request. She lives in the country with her husband. E-mail her at Akushla514@hotmail.com.

Mary Lee Moynan is a Christian, passionate wife and compassionate mother and grandmother. Her inspirational book, *Get Off Your Knees*, is available through Amazon.com. She believes there's a time to pray. Then there's a time to get off your knees and change your life. E-mail her at moynan-marylee@hotmail.com.

Nicole L.V. Mullis is the author of the novel *A Teacher Named Faith*. Her work has appeared in newspapers, magazines and anthologies, including the *Chicken Soup for the Soul* series. Her plays have been produced in New York, California and Michigan. She lives in Michigan but called Kitchener, ON home for two years.

Melanie Naundorf is a stay-at-home mom who lives in a busy household with her best friend Doug (who also happens to be the same cute guy she married more than twenty years ago), their four great kids (Jamie, Luke, Anna and Matt), a crazy but fun dog named Baxter, Kada the curious cat, and Buddy, their blue budgie bird.

N. Newell worked for BC Tel/Telus for thirty-four years and won several service awards for his work. He is now retired and lives on Vancouver Island.

Gerri Nicholas lives in Sherwood Park, AB with her husband Don. They have three married children and six grandchildren. Gerri has contributed to seven books, and has had inspirational writing and children's material in a variety of publications. Her special interests include reading, travel and watching hockey — Canada's game!

Shawn O'Brien grew up in British Columbia's Fraser Valley and is now residing in Alberta. He has a major passion for aviation and is living his dream.

C.S. O'Cinneide had her first short story "Family Role Play" published in *Blended: Writers on the Stepfamily Experience* in 2015. She lives in Ontario with her husband and two youngest daughters. Only her husband will still go camping with her.

G. Norman Patterson was married to the love of his life, Eleanor Mae, for over fifty years. After the war, Norm became a CA and was proud of his thirty-three years with Simpson's Toronto credit department. He loved to golf, travel with Eleanor, and spend time with his daughters Janet and Ruth and grandsons Woody and Nick Rochlin.

Jacqueline Pearce is a children's book author and poet with degrees in English literature and environmental studies and a love for nature, history and travel. She currently lives on the west coast of Canada.

DG (Darlene) Peterson, born and raised in Vancouver, was a certified court reporter in the Supreme Court of British Columbia. After fifteen years and 1,500 trials, DG left to pursue a writing career. Published in many areas, crime fiction is her focus. Other interests are animal welfare, gardening and cycling.

Élise Phillippo is currently residing in Fort McMurray with her husband, Brandon. They have four fur children: Dodger the rabbit, Chloe the cat and Nova and Tig the dogs. They are very excited about their new family addition, a bouncing baby boy, named Kellan Xavier born on Feb. 23rd at 3:33 p.m.

Anne Phillips is a retired senior administrator with the Presbyterian Church in Canada. This is her first attempt at writing. Getting to know their Syrian family has been an amazing experience and they are proud to call them friends. Anne and her husband enjoy international travel and plan to do more.

Wendy Poole has always been a storyteller through telling or writing. She considers her greatest compliment to be when her grandchildren ask her to "tell another story." She is thrilled to have a third story published in the *Chicken Soup for the Soul* series.

Megan Pothier received her Bachelor of Arts in Psychology along with a certificate in Human Resources in 2014. She lives in Fredericton, NB. She and her soon-to-be husband Shane are getting married on Canada Day. Megan enjoys writing, travelling and spending time with friends, family and her dog, Winnie. She continues to write on a daily basis.

Darryl Pottie currently lives in Enfield, NS with his wife Trish. They were married in 1990 and have two daughters together: Breanna and Madisyn. They are all avid Team Canada and Sidney Crosby fans. Darryl dreams one day of playing in the NHL!

Anne Renaud lives in Westmount, QC. She writes picture books for very young readers, as well as Canadian historical nonfiction books for nine- to twelve-year-olds. She also regularly contributes to kids' magazines, such as *Highlights*, *Spider*, *Cricket*, and *Fun for Kidz*.

Kim Reynolds is teasingly called "Canada's spirit animal" by her two children because of her passion for all things Canadian. Her essays have appeared in newspapers, online and in two previous *Chicken Soup for the Soul* books. She lives and writes in the nation's capital. Visit her blog at kimreynolds.ca.

Lisa Reynolds is a teacher holding degrees from York University. Lisa enjoys writing short stories and poetry. She belongs to an online critique group and regularly attends workshops to improve her craft.

Chris Robertson is a bestselling author and award-winning professional speaker. Chris has previously been voted Best Keynote Speaker by his peers in the professional speaking industry. He is also the founder of the Canadian Speaking Hall of Fame. Contact Chris for your next meeting or event at chrisrobertson.ca.

Brad Rudner has degrees in philosophy and education. He was a wilderness guide for twelve years, a teacher, a clinical trainer on medical devices and currently runs a wellness business. He is working on his first nonfiction book and has published numerous articles in several publications. Learn more at bradrudner.com.

Isolde Ryan was born in Germany but Canada has been home since 1984. Isolde is a loving wife, mom to three, oma to two and working on her first novel. She is a member of a local writing group and creates landscape oil paintings, while operating her Doberman breeding business of thirty-plus years. Creativity is her way of life.

Walter Sawchuk came to Canada in 1956 with his Dutch wife and two daughters, and taught them to always be grateful for life in Canada. Although he spoke several languages, his English was not sufficient so family and friends met with him to help him write this story. He enjoyed hearing it read before his death in 2009.

John J. Seagrave was born in downtown Toronto but spent his adult life in the Canadian North as a fur trader. Later in life he settled in Yellowknife NWT where he married and adopted two daughters of Inuit heritage. He was a writer, husband and proud father until his untimely death at the age of forty-six. His stories live on.

Janet Seever and her family have lived in Alberta since 1993, where she writes for a mission organization. She also enjoys doing freelance work. She and her husband have two adult children, one of whom is married, and a grandchild.

Stella Shepard is an Indigenous/Acadian writer living on Prince Edward Island with her family. Her first novel, *Ashes of My Dreams*, was published in 2016 by the Acorn Press, Charlottetown. E-mail her at rphelan@pei.sympatico.ca.

John Silver is a retired school administrator. He is married with two daughters. One daughter is an accomplished skier and the other daughter is a white water canoeist. John is an avid skier who has spent long periods of time skiing the mountains of British Columbia. Canoeing for many years was a highlight of his family's summers.

Elizabeth Smayda has four stories published in the *Chicken Soup for the Soul* series. She works in the field of social services and has co-authored a study involving eating disorders that was published in 2005. Elizabeth loves to use her writing and art to make a positive difference. She is grateful for her lovely family.

Lorette Smith told her story to writer/inspirational storyteller, Darlene Lawson, who considers it an honor to write/share Lorette's story in this celebration of Canada. Living in Southeastern New Brunswick they share their love of the great outdoors. At eighty-two Lorette continues to skate, ski, snowshoe, and bicycle in the summer.

Laura Snell and her dog Gus Gusterson live in the resort town of Wasaga Beach, Ontario, where she operates a web development firm GBSelect.com. Her son Ryan lives in Melbourne, Australia. This is her seventh contribution to the *Chicken Soup for the Soul* series. E-mail her at laurau@rogers.com.

Lisa Timpf is a freelance writer who lives in Simcoe, ON. Her writing has appeared in a variety of venues, including *NewMyths*, *Third Flatiron*, *Third Wednesday*, and *Scifaikuest*. She has self-published a collection of creative nonfiction and poetry entitled *A Trail That Twines: Reflections on Life and Nature*.

Cheryl Uhrig was copywriter and creative director for many years at Toronto ad agencies and the CBC. She also taught at Seneca@York. Cheryl now works as an artist, illustrator, and cartoonist. Her art is in local galleries, published children's books and magazines. Cheryl lives in Newmarket ON, with her family.

Carla White is a transformational speaker and international best-selling author. She is on a mission to create healthy, inspired, resilient and engaged workplaces. Carla is living an adventurous life with her family in Northern Canada.

Glenice Wilson enjoys nature, walking, skiing, canoeing, humour, travel, writing, art and music, along with the people and surprises they all offer. She grew up on a farm on the Manitoba prairie but ventured off to live in Edmonton and Jasper. She now lives again in prairie country, but in Alberta.

S. Nadja Zajdman is an essayist and short story writer. She published the short story collection *Bent Branches* in 2013. Nadja has just completed a memoir of her mother, the prominent Holocaust educator and activist Renata Skotnicka-Zajdman, who passed away in 2013.

Meet Amy Newmark

Amy Newmark is the bestselling author, editor-in-chief, and publisher of the *Chicken Soup for the Soul* book series. Since 2008, she has published 140 new books, most of them national bestsellers in the U.S. and Canada, more than doubling the number of Chicken Soup for the Soul titles in print today. She is also the author of *Simply Happy*, a crash course in Chicken Soup for the Soul advice and wisdom that is filled with easy-to-implement, practical tips for having a better life.

Amy is credited with revitalizing the Chicken Soup for the Soul brand, which has been a publishing industry phenomenon since the first book came out in 1993. By compiling inspirational and aspirational true stories curated from ordinary people who have had extraordinary experiences, Amy has kept the twenty-four-year-old Chicken Soup for the Soul brand fresh and relevant.

Amy graduated *magna cum laude* from Harvard University where she majored in Portuguese and minored in French. She then embarked on a three-decade career as a Wall Street analyst, a hedge fund manager, and a corporate executive in the technology field. She is a Chartered Financial Analyst.

Her return to literary pursuits was inevitable, as her honours thesis in college involved travelling throughout Brazil's impoverished northeast region, collecting stories from regular people. She is delighted to have come full circle in her writing career — from collecting stories "from the people" in Brazil as a twenty-year-old to, three decades later, collecting stories "from the people" for Chicken Soup for the Soul.

When Amy and her husband Bill, the CEO of Chicken Soup for the Soul, are not working, they are visiting their four grown children.

Follow Amy on Twitter @amynewmark. Listen to her free daily podcast, The Chicken Soup for the Soul Podcast, at www.chickensoup. podbean.com, or find it on iTunes, the Podcasts app on iPhone, or on your favourite podcast app on other devices.

Meet Janet Matthews

Janet Matthews is a best-selling author, freelance editor and inspirational speaker. As co-author of the Canadian bestseller, *Chicken Soup for the Canadian Soul*, since 2002 she has been inspiring audiences across Canada with her heartfelt journey of creating this unique Canadian book. With her stories, anecdotes, and passionate delivery, Janet lights up a room. After spending the first twenty years of her professional life in Toronto's fast paced fashion-photography and advertising industry, in 1997 she became involved with producing *Chicken Soup for the Parent's Soul*. When Jack Canfield invited her to co-author *Chicken Soup for the Canadian Soul*, she jumped at the chance. When it was released in 2002 it shot to the top of bestseller lists all across Canada.

Since 2003 Janet has utilized her editorial expertise to help other authors bring their books of personal or spiritual growth to publication. Working with American co-author Daniel Keenan she completed a book-sized version of *The Navy's Baby*, an amazing story first appearing in *Chicken Soup for the Parent's Soul* and then in 2015, *Chicken Soup for the Soul: The Joy of Adoption*. She now has stories in eleven *Chicken Soup for the Soul* books and, with the release of *Chicken Soup for the Soul: O Canada The Wonders of Winter* (2013), *Chicken Soup for the Soul: Christmas in Canada* (2014) and now *Chicken Soup for the Soul: The Spirit of Canada*, Janet remains honoured and proud to be part of the Chicken Soup for the Soul family.

An eclectic individual with diverse interests and talents, Janet is a certified Love Yourself Heal Your Life workshop leader with training based on the philosophy of Louise Hay. She is a certified canoeing instructor, couturier seamstress, passionate roller skater and joyfully plays her violin in a community orchestra.

Now living in Aurora, Ontario, Janet has been a guest on countless television and radio talk shows across Canada, and gives a very dynamic interview. She is generally available for guest speaking spots and interviews, and you may contact her through janetmatthews.ca or canadiansoul.com.

Thank You

We are grateful to all our story contributors and fans, who shared thousands of stories about what Canada means to them. Janet was thrilled to have so many great choices, although it was a tough road narrowing the list down to only the 101 stories that are included in this collection. In addition to our writers, we have many talented people to thank. In Canada, Janet thanks Tracy Bailey for her ongoing website support and timely updates, and Glen Davis for his always reliable technical support.

Stateside, at Chicken Soup for the Soul, we thank Associate Publisher D'ette Corona for being our right-hand woman in creating the final manuscript and working with all our wonderful writers. Barbara LoMonaco and Kristiana Pastir, along with outside proofreader Elaine Kimbler, jumped in at the end to proof, proof, proof. And yes, there will always be typos anyway, so feel free to let us know about them at webmaster@chickensoupforthesoul.com and we will correct them in future printings.

The whole publishing team at Chicken Soup for the Soul deserves a hand, including Senior Director of Marketing Maureen Peltier, Senior Director of Production Victor Cataldo, and graphic designer Daniel Zaccari, who turned our manuscript into this beautiful book.

Changing the world one story at a time®
www.chickensoup.com